IN THE COVERS
The Best Cricket Writing of the Year

Also by David Rayvern Allen

A Song for Cricket
Sir Aubrey: A Biography of C. Aubrey Smith
A Word from Arlott
Arlott on Cricket
The *Punch* Book of Cricket
Another Word from Arlott
Cricket's Silver Lining
Peter Pan and Cricket
Cricket on the Air
More Cricket on the Air
Arlott on Wine
Cricket Extras
The Early Books on Cricket
The Essential Arlott
Cricket: An Illustrated History
The Field Book of Cricket
More Cricket Extras
Arlott: The Authorised Biography
The Cricketers' Quotation Book
More Than a Game
Last Over (*with E.W. Swanton*)

IN THE COVERS

The Best Cricket Writing of the Year

David Rayvern Allen

HEADLINE

To Zia, Rashid and Payina
who provided sufficient fodder
to finish the task

First published in 1996
by HEADLINE BOOK PUBLISHING

10 9 8 7 6 5 4 3 2 1

British Library Cataloguing in Publication Data

Allen, David Rayvern
In the covers
1.Cricket
I.Title
796.3'58

ISBN 0 7472 1790 4

Typeset by
Letterpart Limited, Reigate, Surrey

Printed and bound in Great Britain by
Mackays of Chatham PLC, Chatham, Kent

HEADLINE BOOK PUBLISHING
A division of Hodder Headline PLC
338 Euston Road
London NW1 3BH

Acknowledgements

A compilation such as this relies a great deal on goodwill and I owe a great debt to the many writers who have so readily agreed to place their work 'In the Covers'. This book is a reflection of their endeavours, not mine.

I am also extremely grateful to the various newspapers, magazines and publishers for permission to reproduce both extracts and complete articles.

A huge thank you too, to Andrew Rennard, for his unswerving dedication to the task of collecting the newspapers 'who were most likely to' throughout the year. The job would have been impossible without his help. I am indebted also to other friends who made suggestions – some of them decent – intermittently, particularly my literary agent John Pawsey and in editorial harness at Headline, Ian Marshall and Lindsay Symons.

Janet Reeve dazzled as always with her virtuoso keyboard skills on the word processor and if the Hoffnung Concerts were still in existence she would, I'm sure, by now have had a concerto specially written for her. Much gratitude.

My long suffering wife – well, at least she says she is – has been extremely resourceful in disarming visitors who queried somewhat aggressively whether I was intent on denuding the woods of the world still further. At these times they were generally gazing in amazement at the vast amount of newsprint covering every part of the carpet from view. And while we are dealing with sights at sockline, a pat on the head for my two daughters who, on the infrequent occasions when they were at home, remembered not to throw away the piles of papers to the mercy of the refuse-collectors.

On a more sober note, acknowledgements and thanks are due to the following for use of copyright material:

The *Daily Mail* (Solo Syndication); the *Daily Telegraph* and sports editor David Welch; the *Sunday Telegraph* and its sports editor Colin Bibson; the *Evening Standard*; the *Guardian*; the *Independent*; the *Observer*; *Times Newspapers Limited*, 1995/6; all for various articles: *Cricket World* and Thrasy Petropoulos for 'Sanath Jayasuriya'; *The Cricketer* and Richard Hutton for 'The Greatest Escape' and Geoffrey Dean for 'The Brown Bomber'; *Inside Edge* and Jim Melly for 'The Cat is Back'; *Wisden Cricket Monthly*, Tim de Lisle and Marcus Berkmann for 'Age of Despair'; *Cricket Lore*, Richard Hill and Fraser Simms for 'Cricketing Cliffhanger in St Helena'; *Country Life*, Sandy Mitchell and David Acfield for 'Reviving England's Doldrums'; *Country Living* and Frank Keating for 'Howzat!'; Dari Press and Roy Clements for the extract 'Stumped and Bowled in Tipperary' by Terence Prittie from *A Short History of Irish Cricket*; *Esquire* (National Magazine Company Limited) and Mike Marqusee for 'War Clouds Ahead'; *GQ* magazine (Condé Nast) and Tim de Lisle for 'Graham Thorpe'; Northamptonshire C.C. Handbook and Andrew Radd for 'Dennis Brookes at 80'; Robson Books and David Foot for an extract from *Wally Hammond: The Reasons Why*; the T.C.C.B. and John Stern of Hayters Sports Agency for 'My Memories: Tom Graveney'; *The Spectator* and Simon Barnes for 'Retired Hurt'; the *Watford Observer* and Andrew French for 'Beaten 'Bury Hold Their Heads High'; Hodder Headline and Ray Illingworth and Jack Bannister for an extract from *One-Man Committee*; Hodder & Stoughton and Richie Benaud for a piece from *The Appeal of Cricket*.

I would also like to acknowledge and thank most warmly the many other individual contributors:

Michael Atherton; Simon Barnes; Scyld Berry; Henry Blofeld; Mike Brearley; Pete Clark; Nick Coleman; Tony Cozier; Jon Culley; Peter Deeley; Matthew Engel; Pat Gibson; Suzanne Goldenburg;

Ian Hawkey; Michael Henderson; Simon Hughes; Martin Johnson; Frank Keating; Imran Khan; Miles Kington; Omar Kureishi; Alan Lee; Tony Lewis; John Major; Vic Marks; Robin Marlar; Christopher Martin-Jenkins; Allan Massie; Paul Newman; Mark Nicholas; Michael Parkinson; Sarah Potter; Derek Pringle; Tim Rice; Peter Roebuck; Mike Selvey; Rob Steen; E.W. 'Jim' Swanton; Adam Szreter; Ivo Tennant; Simon Wilde; Robert Winder; John Woodcock; Ian Wooldridge and Graeme Wright.

To end on a semi-formal note, both the publishers and compiler wish it to be understood that every effort has been made to trace copyright holders in order to obtain permission to include their work in this anthology. And, in matter of fact, contrary to what some might think, in putting all this together often the pleasantest moments were the conversations with writers while clearance was being sought. Even so, it is possible that omissions may have inadvertently occurred and we apologise if that has happened and for any errors that may have been made in the form of acknowledgement.

Contents

CHAPTER THREE

County Crusades

CHAPTER FOUR

An Early Indian Summer

CHAPTER FIVE

Late Pakistani Swing

CHAPTER SIX

Here's Looking At . . .

CHAPTER SEVEN

Issues Contentious and Polite

CHAPTER EIGHT

Odds and Ends

Introduction

Cricket has always been a game about which people wanted to write and there are no signs that it will ever be any different. It has also been a game about which people wanted to read and thank goodness, there are no signs that is about to change either. One begats the other and often in reverse order.

One reason why cricket has attracted so much writing is because there is never any shortage of subject matter. Apart from twenty-two individuals any or many of whom might do something out of the ordinary, there are the others who might do the ordinary very well . . . and those who don't do very well, at all. There are captains with their tactics; umpires with their decisions; groundsmen and their pitches; weather conditions; surroundings, form-guides, statistics and a host of peripheral this and thats upon which to dwell. The reporter has a wide-angle lens available above his word-processor.

Give or take a word or two that was the message a teacher was trying to put across to his moderately ruly pupils in the Compton Stand at Lord's earlier this season. One of them had asked a question about the men behind the glass-front in the Warner Stand opposite: 'Who are all those people, sir?' Big mistake. The answer seemed to go on forever.

Well, those magnificent men (and women!) with their sitting machines are, of course, some of the very same who fill these pages. The results of their labours arrive among the piles of print on any current day's doormat. A rummage soon reveals some startlingly good pieces. Nobody could guess the pressure and distractions under which they work, comparable and more often than not surpassing anything holding the dust in place at Colindale Newspaper library where the encomiums of a more leisured age find a permanent home. So to all that, good, because otherwise there would be no need for this book.

Looked at in its overall context, cricket never ceases to be in a transitional state, permanently unsettled. I suppose that is part of its appeal and yet as the latest eddy drifts uneasily across the boundary boards it does not always seem so: disputes and their aftermath; new legislation in attempts to eliminate infringements of the spirit of the game; searches for a structure to maximise its potential; seeking a balance in the registration of overseas players; and, on a parochial level, what sometimes seems a never-realisable aspiration to mould an all-conquering England team.

All this and much more made news in the last year. A World Cup clouded by controversy and the pressures of politics at the start, finished with a glorious affirmation of unshackled cricket as Sri Lanka, the one-time minnows, defied received conceptions, and became the triumphant victors. A further blow for the also-rans was struck when Kenya conquered the mighty West Indies. Who knows? In the new millennium and on an enlarged European stage, we could see Germany beating us at cricket as well as at football.

The South African tour was at times a mardy one, unless you were a supporter of the home team. Public admonishment of players by the England management was followed, rather predictably, six months later by public admonishment of the manager. Phrases like 'rights of reply' were bandied about, somewhat to lose their semi-legal potency in high summer when the Law Courts summoned the games' practitioners from their fields of play to play instead games of verbal riposte in Strand. Wig and gown could become acceptable clothing for any future timeless Tests.

The twin tourists India and Pakistan, each in their inimitable way, delighted cricket-watcher and writer alike with their deeds and a World Cup Final at Lord's in late summer between the two nations at under-15 level only emphasised the abundance of amazing talent on tap.

The County Championship too was full of exciting encounters throughout the season and with the outcome only decided at the last gasp, for once it attracted the hyperbole more often reserved for its one-day rivals.

In every season characters make their entrances and exits. Umpire 'Dickie' Bird, after a record 66 Tests, went to stay in gentler pastures for, at least, another season (see fellow Yorkshireman Michael Parkinson's marvellous study). And coming to the fore with galvanising performances for Surrey was Adam Hollioake, an all-rounder with Australian connections.

Unusually too, there was at least one re-emergence, witness Nasser Hussein, after the force had seemed to pass him by and a probable postponed retirement with Grand Master Gooch still able to outscore colleagues half his age.

As always the writer reflects the happening for the majority – the TV replay helps, of course, but there the choice is limited and not everybody is around to watch it. And the pictures on the page retain their own vivid image for much longer.

We have been remarkably well served by our cricket writers. The broadsheets, in the main, give them a spacious platform, or should it be a kitchen? – the *Daily Telegraph* most notably, with the *Guardian*, *Observer*, *The Times* and *Independent* not far behind.

The magazines too – *The Cricketer*, *Wisden Cricket Monthly*, *Cricket World*, *Cricket Lore*, and the self-labelled 'new voice of cricket' *Inside Edge* – continually stimulate ideas and encourage ephemeral elements that might otherwise remain obscured. And then there are quirky or differently slanted views from unexpected sources. Even health magazines have been known to recommend a course of press-ups at the back of the pavilion. For those who enjoy plunging away from the mainstream please turn to the 'odds and ends'.

Many lean towards a particular writer, often perhaps because he is within the daily newspaper of their choice. Awareness of another in another paper and their loyalties are divided. But perhaps the cricket writer for a fanatical follower defines the choice of newspaper in the first place.

For years I bought the *Guardian* just in order to be able to read Frank Keating. I then took the *Independent* to enjoy a laugh-a-line with Martin Johnson. But before this becomes too personal and invidious I should say that, at the same time, I had and have total admiration for many others on the campus.

To mention the reasoned, concise, beautifully constructed prose of Christopher Martin-Jenkins and the charged, stimulating essays of Robin Marlar (no prisoners taken) alongside the prognostications from on high by the ageless 'Jim' Swanton together with the knowledgeable offerings by the younger school, Peter Roebuck, Mark Nicholas and Derek Pringle, who have recently exchanged pitch proximity for a lap-top view, is not to decry or ignore the splendid scribing by so many others in these pages. There is such a thing, after all, as uniform excellence.

Not to be found in these pages is much that deserved inclusion as well. A weekly resumé of the season, though perhaps desirable, cannot be confined within the scope of an accessibly-sized and priced volume.

In this era of giant on-field replay screens, bowling-speed guns and the space age so-called 'skyline gherkin' soon to house the press at Lord's Nursery End, it is salutary to remember that the man who made cricket a national institution had his book collection auctioned a few months ago over 80 years after his death.

W.G. Grace's response, as his set of *Wisden's* went for practically six figures, would probably have been no different to what he said about the written word a century ago: 'All that reading spoils the eyesight. No good for your cricket.'

The South African Tour

Introduction

This was most definitely the winter of our discontent. For English cricket followers expectancy had been high. An historic return to South Africa, after their years in the wilderness, and a World Cup looming. The plan was straightforward, or so it seemed. First finding and then consolidating a Test Match winning formula, before building on our reputation in the one-dayers as a prelude to peaking in India and Pakistan. But we all know what happens to plans, even those not best-laid.

There were though, some moments to savour. The visit to Soweto under the presidential eye of Mandela; Atherton's epic innings at the Wanderers ground in Johannesburg; Russell's record breaking haul in the same match and Cork scampering terrier-like throughout the tour trying to retrieve lost situations. South Africa, however, were too strong. With Donald's tracer deliveries ably assisted at the other end by Pollock, McMillan's combative all-round skills, and inspired fielding by the whole side, they were a flexible, indeed formidable unit. There was threat too, from the unlikely contortionist bowling of Paul Adams, whose action was likened to 'a frog in a blender'! The home team could not be denied.

But before all that had happened, there was the past to write about.

Atherton's tourists in shop window as new nation expects

E W Swanton

A little over four years ago, in Johannesburg, I had the pleasure of being present at the dissolution of the old racial cricket authorities and the inaugural meeting of the United Cricket Board of South Africa. That same evening mine was the privilege of speaking words of welcome at a great dinner of celebration attended by 700 cricketers of every age and colour, including famous names from every Test-playing country. Major change was in the wind, though the miracle of Nelson Mandela's bloodless election victory had yet to happen.

Dr Ali Bacher and his colleagues had worked fast, and they continued to do so. Helped by the determined diplomacy of Sir Colin Cowdrey, chairman of the 1991 International Cricket Council, they achieved an immediate return to the body which their predecessors had formed, in company with England and Australia, 80-odd years before, and from which they had been excluded on the departure of South Africa from the Commonwealth in 1961.

Every overseas tour of an England Test team has an impact for better or for worse on hosts and visitors alike; but a special significance surely attaches to the one that is about to begin, the first by an official team from this country since M J K Smith's MCC side of 1964-65.

In those days, as from its beginnings, cricket was the game of the English-speaking South Africans, rugby football that of the Afrikaners. There were periods when, despite having to draw from such a restricted field, South Africa were a match for England and Australia

– and in the middle and late 1960s, immediately before the general antipathy to apartheid brought down the curtain on international sport against South Africa, more than a match.

Over the span of history, however, South Africa inevitably had the worst of it: England had won 46 Tests to their 18, Australia's margin was 29 to 11, seven of those 11 gained in the Republic in successive series between 1966 and 1970.

Today, the overall picture is much more favourable to South Africa in that many more Afrikaners now bring their aggressive philosophy to the game while the generation of black and coloured boys, introduced to cricket since apartheid ended, will surely soon be competing for places in the national team.

For these youthful cricketers the England tour, covering 14 different grounds from Johannesburg to Cape Town, will be the game's shop window, these next three months; that for Michael Atherton and his team is their challenge and their opportunity. To an extent which at moments may test their self-discipline, they will be on parade both on the field and off.

One's first tour naturally sticks in the memory, especially if it opens, as mine did, with Table Mountain rising out of the mist as the ship glides into harbour. A few days later, over Christmas 1938, I found myself perched in a little box on the old Wanderers' Ground at Johannesburg, giving the first BBC commentaries ever sent home from overseas.

During the last half-hour of the second day, play was exceedingly quiet and I was doing my best to keep English listeners awake: suddenly Tom Goddard, of Gloucestershire, bowling off-breaks, caught and bowled Dudley Nourse, South Africa's most dangerous bat. A tailender appeared whom Leslie Ames stumped first ball. Even a tyro like me at the microphone could make something of the prospect of a hat-trick: and, eureka, it happened. Goddard clean-bowled Billy Wade and so inscribed his name on an English Test hat-trick list which contains only two since, those of Peter Loader at Headingley in '57 and Dominic Cork at Old Trafford last July.

This firework apart, runs on soporific pitches were wondrously cheap in this series – Len Hutton was *sixth* in the Test averages with 44 – the climax coming in the final 'Timeless Test' by which the tour is remembered. It lasted 10 days and was left unfinished because the MCC team had to leave Durban by train (three nights, two days) in order to catch the *Athlone Castle* at the Cape.

The key to this travesty of a match was the regulation which enabled the groundsman to roll at his discretion after overnight rain. So two storms, two fresh, sun-baked 'cakes', each even easier than the one before, and England, at 654 for five, were 42 short of their target when more rain had the last word. Broadcasting unaided two hours a day, as a freelance being paid by the day, I was pleased thereby to show a modest profit. Both teams by the end were bored to death and after the War it was ordained (contrary to a custom in Australia) that every Test should be played to a time limit.

Considering that in seven years prior to 1938 South Africa had engaged in only one tour apiece, to Australia and England, and had not had the stimulus of a single Test series at home since 1930-31, they did well to restrict Walter Hammond's MCC team to a single Test victory.

After the War MCC sent three sides, F G Mann's in 1948-49, P B H May's in 1956-57 and Smith's in 1964-65. Much the best and most positive cricket came in the first of these, even though the attack was so lacking in speed (Bedser, Gladwin, Jenkins, Wright, Compton and Watkins) that, believe it or not, the wicketkeepers, Evans and Griffith, were never required to stand back.

England won this series 2-0, drew the second 2-2, and won the third, which I did not see, 1-0. Too often easy-paced pitches and the philosophy of opponents too mistrustful of their own ability were reflected in the English attitude. Enjoying Trevor Bailey's enlightened summaries over the air since his retirement, how I have wished that his conversion had preceded his 80 in 395 minutes at Durban in 1957 or that soul-destroying 68 in 458 minutes at Brisbane the following year.

The classic case of the over-modest mentality of the South Africans was pathetically exemplified at Durban in 1949-50 when, after bowling out Australia for 75 and leading by 236 runs, they refrained from enforcing the follow-on: whereupon Australia shooed them out for 99 and made 336 for five (Neil Harvey 151 not out) to win the match.

This is not to say the early post-War South African sides did not contain some admirable cricketers: for instance, Melville, Nourse, Mitchell, McGlew and McLean as batsmen; Waite, wicket-keeper-batsman; Goddard, all-rounder; Tayfield, off-spinner; Adcock and Heine, fast bowlers. The irony was that a new generation had shown a rare quality in the 1960s immediately before hostilities were suspended. Graeme Pollock and Barry Richards were batsmen of the highest class, Mike Procter and Eddie Barlow great all-rounders.

The sympathy felt in the world of cricket for their expulsion was heightened when at a trial match at the Cape the teams walked off the field in protest against their government's policies. When, after the long hiatus, normal relations were resumed four years ago, the new South Africa of Wessels and Cronje found their feet at Test level remarkably quickly. Much money and energy have recently gone into bringing the Test grounds and others up to fresh standards.

How different an atmosphere will the England party find compared with the preceding two tours. In 1948-49 the Nationalists had only just won power from the United Party and were just, as it were, testing the pace of the wicket. Eight years later the climate had grown ominous.

Today, the generation of the 1950s and 1960s, having 'seen it all', are busily pointing South African cricket towards the future; men such as president Krish Mackerdhuj, ex-Robben Island prisoner Steve Tshwete, minister of sport, and, of course, the managing director of the UCBSA and former captain, Bacher.

With the missionary aspect of the tour clearly in mind, the board have fixed a low Test admission charge of approximately £2.50 with a graduated system of payment, two-thirds from lunch onwards, one-third after tea. The five-Test series looks an even-money bet. The only blot on the horizon is the dreary saga of seven one-day internationals at the end as a protracted preparation for the World Cup. One hopes, naturally, for what would be the first series victory by England overseas since New Zealand were beaten in 1991-92. Before that it was Australia in 1986-87.

Much will rest on the establishment of a happy management-player relationship, a fusion of qualities as between two contrasting personalities, Messrs Illingworth and Barclay, with a strong-minded captain. What with these two off-spinners, and the coaches John Edrich and Peter Lever, who will be with the party for the early weeks of the tour, captain and team will not be short of technical advice. Nor when the Tests start in mid-November will they lack support from home.

In the heat, England will be found to have too little spin bowling, while seven one-day internationals on seven grounds within 13 days will be a mortification of body, mind and spirit. With these provisos the auspices are favourable for a congenial tour in a fascinating country.

Daily Telegraph, 17 October 1995

Cure sought for travel sickness

Michael Atherton

Our mauling at home by the Australians in 1993 is now a distant memory. Since that time England have defeated New Zealand and drawn against South Africa and West Indies. On foreign soil a different story emerges.

England are notoriously bad travellers, with rare away series wins in both the 1980s and 1990s. That is why this winter's sojourn to South Africa is of some significance: the progress maintained at home must be continued this winter.

My experience of South Africa is limited. Naturally so since this is a historic first tour since the D'Oliveira affair. Recuperating from a spinal operation in 1991, I later spent about a month in South Africa, at the time Graham Gooch's England squad were achieving near-glory in the last World Cup.

In Johannesburg at the time of the England-South Africa semi-final, a lone voice shouting for the 'Poms', I remember the fervour with which that game was watched and the disappointment that followed.

I have played at the first two Test venues, Centurion Park in Northern Transvaal and the Wanderers' in Johannesburg. I also witnessed some provincial cricket at Newlands in Cape Town. I know how dearly the South Africans hold sporting success. In fact, the tour could well be Australian in its atmosphere: highly hospitable, highly charged and ultra competitive.

We are, of course, acutely aware of the historical significance of this visit. While we will be judged solely in terms of the results, and for that reason the cricket must get absolute priority, we will naturally do all we can to promote cricket among the black population and within the townships. Sport has been a driving force in breaking down the barriers of apartheid and cricket has been at the vanguard of this through the work of Dr Ali Bacher. At present, the team are scheduled to attend functions in the Alexandra and Galesheve townships.

Both sides will draw upon the experience of the 1994 drawn series. South Africa will have fond memories of Lord's, where disciplined bowling and electric fielding won the day. We feel that we had the better of a draw at Headingley and, along with the stunning win at the Oval, that we were marginally ahead by the time the Texaco Trophy was claimed.

South Africa will feel that they are an improved side from that occasion: a side with greater experience and with Brett Schultz back.

I also believe that England have made strides since that Lord's occasion. Robin Smith has returned and will relish his dual with South Africa's quicker bowlers. Dominic Cork, of course, was the major find of the summer, adding bite to the bowling and sturdiness at the lower end of the batting. South Africa will find him a real handful, as they will Darren Gough when he rediscovers last winter's form.

I fervently hope that this can be a series where England can field a full-strength side with regularity. It has been an unprecedented series of injuries – a fact which we have tried not to remark on too often – but one which, nevertheless, is frustratingly disruptive.

My other hope is that we find our form early in the Test series, it being too much to ask a side to keep coming from behind. The first three Tests are on the likely result pitches, where the series will probably be decided.

Sunday Telegraph, 22 October 1995

Mzikizana stars on a day of toil

Robin Marlar

To promote the playing and watching of cricket by 38 million of the 43 million South Africans is the huge and complex task facing the United Cricket Board of South Africa. Playing a mould-breaking four-day match at Soweto is but a milestone on that long road. And it has to be travelled fast; barely 1,000 Sowetans, a fifth of Friday's crowd, were present yesterday when Ray Illingworth, the England manager, gave £50,000 from TCCB coffers to the local development fund.

Meanwhile, on the field, the Invitation XI had the throttle stuck first at slow ahead – and then reverse. They fell apart on the newly laid pitch, well-watered to hold it together. There were wickets galore but no English hat-trick to match Pringle's success on Friday. Cronje, the South Africa captain, was eventually bowled behind his legs for 56, but top wickets fell cheaply at the other end.

With the spinners, Illingworth and Watkinson, taking wickets regularly, the Invitation XI were facing the follow-on at 138 for eight. Then Mzikizana, the 22-year-old Xhosa wicketkeeper from Eastern Province, played the bravest of innings, putting on 69 with

Pringle, who hit three sixes. Rhodes, the world's greatest fieldsman, was among the failures. With only one half-century in his past 15 Test innings, his Test place is thought to be in jeopardy, although Peter Pollock, South Africa's chairman of selectors, still managed to refer to him as a big-occasion player.

For England, Stewart and Crawley put in useful, disciplined hours at the crease. As for the bowlers, they discovered – Ilott in particular – what so many of their predecessors learned 30 and more years ago, namely that leg before decisions are hard to win in South Africa.

Friday was a magical day. The appearance, at seven minutes' notice, of Nelson Mandela at the ground transformed an historic sporting scene into a spiritual one, blessing a doubly unique experience – England's reappearance in South African first class cricket, and in a black township.

The president has such an aura, a compelling smile never far from mouth and eyes. He is 77 years young, spare of frame, sloping of shoulder. He walks with the stiff hips of an old football player (misleadingly: 'At college, I was involved in athletics and a little boxing,' he told us).

He knows – even more so after South Africa's success, and his own, in rugby's World Cup – that 'sport reaches circles beyond the influence of politicians'. He paid real tribute to Ali Bacher and the others who had used cricket to help unify the country. His performance was deeply impressive, so natural, even if the man they call he-who-wears-colourful-shirts turned up in the same long grey job he had worn the day before when being stern with some who had stepped out of line and sought refuge in the delays of the judicial process. Everyone in South Africa, not least the cricketers, must wish him long life.

The ground was en fête with tents and umbrellas, the Canterbury of the veld. It would be easy to criticise the pitch. If the object of playing here was to promote the game to school-children, and even a few adults, then batsmen had to be able to play strokes. For that, pace and bounce were needed, not a pudding of a strip.

Then you ran into Basil Petersen, one of whose Danish ancestors jumped ship in Durban, and realised what a miracle has been achieved. Petersen and his three sons run a can-do company specialising in creating sports facilities. He worked at Lord's for a spell and has a strong link with Peter Dury, the Nottingham pioneer of artificial pitches, many now installed in South Africa.

These Soweto acres were once an ash tip. When Petersen first arrived on site 18 months ago he did so with a bodyguard, and a revolver strapped to his hip. It is still there.

His first task was to ring the site with razor wire. Then came convoys of lorries bringing in soil, a precious commodity in this land of continuous erosion. For the outfield came turf from previously agricultural land outside the city, and for the square they imported Bulli, which we would call clay, from a creek area of the Vaal river near Kimberley, a long haul. When Petersen built the Test ground at Verwoerdburg, now said to have the quickest pitches in South Africa, the thickness of topsoil laid was double that at Soweto. In groundsmanship, you get what you pay for.

Funds for township sports facilities are scarce. Money comes from Britain, among other sources, which explains why John Major was keen to open the new ground at the smaller – and possibly even more volatile – Alexandra township on his visit last year. Eleven new township stadiums are completed or planned. Each cost £50,000. The United Cricket Board spends even more than that every year on running costs in the township, providing kit, coaching and transportation for teams. Creating the Soweto Oval had its own hazards. Of the trees planted, 80% died. Parts of the outfield had to be seeded seven times. Two pick-up trucks went walkabout. Petersen was mugged and then had to talk the locals out of dispatching the villain on the spot.

As for the England party, Malcolm has been in the doghouse, which is sad. The problem is that he is not listening to the coaches. He believes that speed and wicket-taking is his sole concern, and the spells where batsmen hit him to all parts are an essential part of management's risk with him.

Possibly all this has been fed by his encounter with Mandela. 'Ah! You are the Destroyer,' said the president on meeting him, referring to his series-saving nine for 57 against South Africa at The Oval last year. The hero-worshipping Malcolm was visibly moved by Mandela's humility and humanity. 'He thanked me,' Malcolm said, hardly believing what he had heard.

Still, he turned in two relatively straight spells at threequarter pace yesterday, welcome not least because they showed that his right knee is sound. Just how far his experiences in South Africa will penetrate the Derbyshire bowler's psyche remains to be seen, but he still has work to do. Management must prevail, over Malcolm and anyone else with crazy ideas about their current performance.

To be a sustained threat on this tour, Malcolm has to be trained out of an attitude which could lead to a repetition of Headingley 1995, where he was unfit even to be trusted with the new ball.

Peter Lever, the bowling coach, has in Malcolm a sick patient. Lionisation by South Africans will not help the cure, and the first Test is less than three weeks distant.

Sunday Times, 29 October 1995

The greatest escape

Richard Hutton

Michael Atherton assured his place in the firmament of great English batsmen/captains at The Wanderers in Johannesburg. For almost 11 hours he stood alone, head and shoulders above England's mainstream batting in defying a South African side supremely confident of winning what had been a one-sided contest for much of its duration.

His monumental effort was a credit to his outstanding powers of concentration and endurance, to his resolution, to his devotion to duty and his courage in adversity. Throughout he remained undaunted as his partners at the other end failed to take similar root to him and in the face of some ferocious bowling which stretched to the full his technical efficiency as well as frequently threatening life and limb.

In the end equally responsible for saving the game for England was Jack Russell who crowned his personal triumph of breaking Bob Taylor's 15-year-old wicket-keeping record of 10 dismissals in a Test match with an occupation of four hours and 40 minutes. But what Atherton and Russell achieved would not have been possible had the pitch not held together so remarkably well. Other than the bowlers' follow-through marks, evidence of wear and tear was minimal and batting conditions at the end were as ideal, if not better, than on the first morning when under the manager's influence England decided to give South Africa first use.

As if this largesse was not enough England's batting then caved in to the innocuous, slow left-arm of Clive Eksteen, whose previous five Tests had yielded him five wickets for 359 runs (avge 71.80). His spell of seven overs for nine runs either side of tea on the second day appeared to have condemned England to inevitable defeat. Victory for South Africa, though, would have been as much England's making as the result of their own ardour and aggression, and a draw was a fair outcome.

It was all a great disappointment for South Africa, who were left to examine the wisdom of their going off for bad light on the third evening when in total command, and of not allowing themselves more than five sessions and 20 minutes to bowl out England. They could also point to some surprisingly indifferent fielding in the second innings. Atherton was dropped twice – at slip when 57 and at short square leg when 99, both off Donald – and Pringle missed a simple caught and bowled from Russell near the start of his marathon.

Nevertheless several personal milestones were reached by the South Africans. Gary Kirsten made his maiden Test century, Brian McMillan made his first on home soil in an overall performance of almost Bothamesque proportion, and Allan Donald whose sense of direction otherwise seems to be leaving him, took his 100th Test wicket.

After Cork had beaten Hudson's outside edge in the first over

England were discouraged by the absence of movement in the air or off the pitch. There was little movement off the bat either and 25 minutes had passed before the first run came from it. In the same over Hudson was given out caught in the gully when it looked as if the verdict should have been lbw, the first of several strange decisions by the host's umpire that had important consequences.

Some wayward bowling followed, particularly from Gough whose initial three overs went for 21 runs. This helped Kirsten and Cronje to raise 50 in the next hour from 82 balls.

Kirsten missed little off his legs and also reached the boundary with square cuts. Cronje, driving and pulling, took three fours in an over from Gough, but a switch of ends by Cork ended Cronje's forceful innings when he played indeterminately at one he could have left and Russell took the first of his 11 catches.

This was the second of several spells by Cork, without whom England's bowling might well have been taken to pieces, and in the course of his 26 overs in the day he retrieved England from several unpromising situations. Before then Cullinan was lucky to survive his first ball which pitched on off stump and missed everything. But his luck held throughout an innings containing several involuntary strokes. Two fours over the slips took him to 50 and he was then dropped by the 'keeper, all off the unfortunate Gough in his second spell.

In comparison Kirsten was typically impregnable and by tea, with his score at 76 and South Africa 185 for two from 58 overs, England's decision to insert their opponents required explanation. By then the four quick bowlers had needed the supplement of Hick. He accounted for Cullinan, playing for non-existent turn, and he was still on when Kirsten square-cut him for his 100 after being in for 20 minutes short of five hours.

In the meantime Jonty Rhodes did little to advance his claims to a place at number five, but McMillan continued to underline his stature as a genuine all-rounder. Anything short was despatched fiercely and assuredly, and with Kirsten still acutely judging the short single the match moved decidedly one way.

However, Cork's persistence and a reinvigorated Malcolm brought the day's proceedings to an unlikely 278 for 7. Armed with the second new ball, Malcolm removed Kirsten and Richardson within three balls of each other in the third over. Richardson paid the price for taking his eye off the ball, but soon after Pollock escaped when Smith, who otherwise had a very fair match, failed to hold a sharp prod from the last bat in the same position. In a dramatic last over McMillan struck a four, survived a convincing shout for a catch at the wicket from the next ball, and was lbw to the next.

During the remaining 70 minutes of the innings Shaun Pollock gave an able demonstration of his all-round prowess. With an exemplary high left elbow and showing the full face of the bat he drove strongly and it was due to him that South Africa added another 54 runs, which included a shot of the highest class, a pulled drive through mid-wicket off a good length ball from Fraser. He was eventually tempted by a short one from Malcolm which he hoiked into the hands of a strategically placed deep square leg.

When England batted it looked as if the match was being played on a different pitch. If Donald's direction had been the equal of his menace Eksteen would not have been required. In two spells either side of lunch he bowled little more than two straight balls. The first, received by Atherton, came back sharply to clip the outside of the off stump as the bewildered batsman aimed to leave it. The second was a half-volley, around which Ramprakash drove fatally having spent 33 balls getting off the mark.

At the other end an intriguing contest between Stewart and Pringle was waged. With his dangerous out-swing the bowler had Stewart fishing more than once outside his off stump, but anything of fuller length was classily driven for four. Pringle was unlucky not to have had Thorpe's wicket when straightening a ball to which the left-hander played no stroke, but Stewart having played several speculative pulls without moving his feet, lofted one off the top edge as far as mid-wicket where Pollock undid all his previous deeds by dropping a sitter.

Thorpe survived a strenuous appeal for a catch at the wicket when he was 23 but he was sawn off unjustly after the pair had added 50 by Eksteen's first ball, delivered from over the wicket into the left-hander's rough and turning enough to beat his forward stroke by a substantial margin but not the appeal by the surrounding close catchers as the ball travelled via the pad to short square leg.

Thorpe's disbelief was tantamount to dissent as he remained at the crease for several seconds before dragging himself away. Thereupon an even deeper malaise descended on the rest of England's batting. On the stroke of tea Stewart chipped McMillan into the hands of an unusually placed short mid-wicket and immediately afterwards Hick struck one that he should have been hitting over the top straight back to the bowler at knee height. When Russell hoisted another straightforward delivery to mid-wicket England were beyond salvage.

Fired up by such an unexpected swing in their favour South Africa's quick bowlers, particularly with the young Pollock eager to atone for his earlier boob, were more than a match for what was left with an excess of short stuff. For once Smith, who batted with customary courage, was unable to keep his lower-order intact and he was the last out, scooping a low full toss back to the bowler.

After the capture of Kirsten's wicket in the second over of the day and Hudson's after 45 minutes, South Africa took an unassailable control over proceedings. Cullinan played a starring role in an innings of a different class to his 69 on the first day. Amidst an array of cultured strokes, as he and Cronje asserted their authority, the only discordant note was the public address announcer's, informing a member of the crowd that his wife had gone into labour.

It was an even longer labour for England's bowlers. Frequent aberrations of line and length were met with classic drives and square cuts until Cullinan played his only false stroke, failing to get inside the line and mistiming a pull to mid-on.

Cronje replicated his dismissal of the first innings but any hope England had of making terminal inroads into South Africa's innings were dashed by Rhodes and McMillan in a fifth-wicket partnership of 99.

Initially Rhodes gave little sign that he was playing for his life, taking 11 from his first three balls. Thereafter he settled down and his quick footedness between the wickets allied to McMillan's muscular shot-making took the game well out of England's reach. After Rhodes had nudged Fraser to Russell, Richardson was given every opportunity to reveal his talents on the back foot until he deposited another short ball conveniently into the hands of deep square leg, by when South Africa had stretched their lead to 428 with McMillan on 76.

With uncharacteristic timidity he added only six more during the first half hour of the fourth day. After the desertion of the lower-order only the arrival of the last man galvanised him into action. A fiasco followed. When he had reached 99 Cork held one up enough for him to be given out lbw. At the next ball, an immaculate out-swinger, he played and missed narrowly and then pushed the next straight to short extra and ran, which would have left his partner stranded by half the length of the pitch had Ramprakash's underarm throw been on target.

McMillan's influence on the match did not end there. His removal of Stewart and Ramprakash in the same over wrecked a promising start to England's second innings. Having weathered some ferocious new-ball bowling the openers had pushed the score to 65 from 15 overs, Pollock being the chief sufferer in conceding 20 from three overs. But Stewart had already played some hair-raising strokes when he missed a straight ball without moving his feet. Again Ramprakash played round a half volley and sadly failed to rise to the challenge that his counterpart Rhodes had scaled earlier.

With Thorpe for company Atherton reduced the temperature for a time and it was not until after tea that Pringle, still getting the odd ball to swing, beat Thorpe's forward stroke with a ball that straightened. Four overs later Hick presented Donald with his 100th Test wicket, but Smith held firm for the day's remaining 15 overs, by when Atherton had been in occupation for 10 minutes short of five hours, including half an hour's overtime on account of South Africa's over-rate.

England embarked on the final day theoretically in search of 311 runs. If Smith had remained England might have carried off the most sensational robbery in Test history. The prospect was immediately unlikely because in the third over, having just square-cut Donald for four, he survived a mass appeal for caught behind. The score then advanced by 26 when the second new ball was taken only for Atherton to be put down. He then pulled the next ball for four to reach his six-hour century, and he had matched Smith in adding 65 runs in 80 minutes before Smith had the misfortune to be caught at third man from a top-edged square cut.

After that runs became academic as Russell and his captain withstood for 76 overs numerous bowling changes and tactical permutations. Eventually South Africa's sole hope was the two's weariness but after five overs with the third new ball they too had had enough and all were grateful to leave the field, bringing to an end some 10 minutes before the scheduled close a long, hot, hard struggle in which the two sides had fought themselves to a virtual standstill.

The Cricketer, January 1996

Action man embarks on new mission

Mark Nicholas

'He's quite a guy your Atherton,' said the panting doctor, 'unusual ability to concentrate . . . most impressive.'

It is six o'clock in the morning, the morning after the second Test match. The Johannesburg sky is a clear, pale blue and the air is warm and clean. The suburbs are peaceful though the barbed wire on the garden walls and the iron gates with their alarms betray the mood of an angry city. Dr Ali Bacher, managing director of the United Cricket Board of South Africa, is on his daily run.

'*One of the great innings . . . very good for cricket in this country long-term. We are re-educating after so many years on the one-day diet. Heroic performances will attract attention to the five-day game and, in this case, explain the merit of a draw,*' he added breathlessly, before jogging on at snail's pace. But he never misses a morning, not anywhere.

'*Love it, it gives me time to think, to plan my day. I decide on most of my moves here, as the sun rises, on the suburban streets that are my home.*'

Home is nothing flash, the doc is not a material man, but it is around the corner now and the Bacher beat increases with the anticipation of his working day. He lives for his work, which is the game of cricket, and for his family, who are precious.

Doctor Aron 'Ali' Bacher was born in Johannesburg in 1942. His parents left Lithuania in the mid-Thirties – '*In time to escape the Holocaust*' – and settled in the nerve centre of the most bewitching country in the world. Dad made money in the rag trade and bought a farm where young Ali ran free, mirroring the instincts of his uncle Aaron, a sports nut who had played cricket a couple of times for Transvaal in the Fifties. Mum doted on her boy – '*She used to underline keynotes in Sir Donald Bradman's book* The Art of Cricket: *y'know, high elbow, head still, that sort of thing, and leave the page open by my bed at night.*' But mum did not much get on with dad, so the home split, which hurt the emotional Ali and gave him a lesson in providing security and support.

He qualified in medicine in the late Sixties and went straight to work in the biggest black hospital in South Africa.

'*I went there for the experience, for the sheer volume of cases,*' he claimed as he sipped on hot coffee and popped pills: '*I have been taking tablets to keep the cholesterol down every day since 1965. I had a heart condition that was wrongly diagnosed and had a bypass in 1981. It was one-foot-in-the-grave stuff but nowadays the cardiogram is normal.*' Which is amazing considering the man's work rate.

He had been at his study desk long before I arrived, he starts at 4.30-ish, and sifted through the correspondence that drives him crazy. He has three secretaries and their pile is before them when they arrive at the office: '*I reply to every letter I receive, you must, but the girls are so good they virtually answer for me.*' His working life is his diary and his telephone; the office is for meetings and communication, not for paperwork. He is a thorough if unorthodox businessman who relies on instinct rather than organisation for his inspiration. He has been the first man in South Africa to put a sporting body on a sound professional basis. By all opinion, cricket in South Africa is superbly run.

7.20am: '*Cricket is about marketing. You must get the product right. The product is the players so we look after them. Sixteen are contracted to the Board and are well paid for their commitment. No, they are not pampered, they are disciplined and efficient. A back-up team of eight experts in fields ranging from physiotherapy to nutrition will accompany the 14 players to the World Cup. Why spare expense if the prize is the ultimate?*'

7.45am: Breakfast at the Wanderers with the whole South African team and Seiko, the watch people, who are sponsoring them. Bacher makes a short and telling speech.

'*In the dressing room last night our team looked down. They need not have, they played with all their heart and played proudly, as Hansie [Cronje] said so well on television this morning. They were defied by a great innings and credit to the England captain for that. Most of all, though, the match and its dramatic final twist gave our audience an idea of the culture of Test cricket. Make no mistake, Test cricket is a culture and the fantastic crowds, 90,000 over five days, proved we're getting the product right.*'

Applause. Cronje grinned broadly and stood to receive his timepiece. Beneath his veneer were frustration and disappointment; truth was, he had England by the proverbials and made a hash of it.

Back to the office among the leafy trees and the bowling greens of the Wanderers club. '*Imagine if we were to win the World Cup, which we could. Think how cricket awareness would soar. We have half a million blacks who either watch or play the game. Having won their World Cup, rugby have a unique opportunity to spread their gospel. I only hope they don't become too immersed in the satisfaction of international acceptance and waste it.*'

If half a million blacks are following cricket where were they at the Test match?

'Attendance is a problem because Soweto, where our development programme is most advanced, is a 25-minute drive out of town. Transport in the townships is negligible so live cricket is a problem. We bussed 600 kids into the Wanderers and provided them with food and drink. Many others watch on TV and listen to radio. In spite of the hurdles, a cricket culture is arriving. In Port Elizabeth and Cape Town 40 per cent of the crowd will be black or coloured.'

10am: Three executives from Coca-Cola arrive. Head office in Atlanta want a more conspicuous return for their investment into South African cricket. Bacher, who dominates the meeting with racy ideas, quickly fixes things. The executives leave happy – within 35 minutes they have become one of an elite group of 10 'official suppliers' to South African cricket.

During the morning people come and go. Bacher handles them all personally. A man comes to sell ties, another to deal in shirts. Cricket writing is faxed in from all over the world. Always the phone rings and always the mug is filled with coffee.

He began the development programmes in the townships in 1986. He remembers the day well.

'October 20th, I got lost in the middle of Soweto and the police said, you've driven in, pal, but you may not drive out! I hadn't even told Shira [his cricket crazy wife] that I was going. We had advertised on radio but had no idea what to expect and four or five of us were in there relying on blind instinct. We took Coke and biscuits with us and a thousand kids turned up. It was astonishing and more came each Saturday morning until after a month it dawned on me. Soccer is their game because they have it, cricket couldn't be because they were denied it.'

Nine years on, nearly 400 schools in Soweto alone play cricket in some form or another. All over South Africa the game is catching on with the young black children.

12.15pm: Khaya Majola arrives with a budget breakdown for the boss's appearance on the *Newsline* television programme later in the week. He tells Bacher that they have spent 11.5 million rand on multi-purpose sports facilities in the townships since 1986. Even Bacher is surprised.

Majola is from the hardline ANC area of the Eastern Cape. He was the best of the non-white cricketers who were outlawed by apartheid and he loathed all that Bacher stood for.

It is the absolute irony that Majola is now the director of national development and works alongside Bacher for the United Board. 'We moved in two different worlds, with two different cultures,' points out Majola. 'The "Doc" simply could not see that sport and politics had to mix. We [the non-white South African Board, as it was known] told him long before unification that his beloved cricket could never be international without us.

'Ali has his faults, of course, and sometimes he takes too much of the credit for the dramatic changes. But they could not have happened without him. He has a vision, to ensure that cricket is the No 1 sport in South Africa, played by all the people.'

The unification process was awkward, what with its inevitable in-fighting and the fact that it came hard on the heels of the disastrous 'Gatting rebels' tour.

1.15pm: Over a sandwich the doctor chatted on: '*White South Africans lived in a cocoon of nationalistic propaganda while Mandela was imprisoned. We had a false impression that there was no opposition to the rebel tours. Interest in domestic cricket had waned through our isolation so we worked harder to cope. Naively we thought the West Indian rebels would stimulate interest in the townships. Yet no-one spoke out against us because the laws prevented them.*

'*By the time of the Gatting tour [February 1990], F W de Klerk had allowed freedom of movement and expression; the demonstrations and the hostility nearly finished me as the conflict of interest became unbearable. I went against my mandate from the Board's executive to cancel the second leg of the tour but I knew that 30,000 demonstrators were waiting in Cape Town and that Mike and his players, who I shall not forget for their bravery, would be in serious danger. It was the first time I saw the rooted problem of apartheid from the side of the blacks and I knew the tour was doomed.*

'*My board lost faith in me; "F W" said I had capitulated, for the first time in my life I lost confidence in myself. Stress got the better of me and I hibernated for two months.*'

Stress has never sat well with Dr Bacher. He had finished as a GP in 1979, worn out by living the pain of his patients. He accepted a commercial post in the pharmaceutical industry, and within two years Bacher the businessman was running Transvaal cricket. By the mid-80s he was MD of the whole shooting match.

3.15pm: Iqbal Khan, cricket correspondent of the *Daily News* rings in. Bacher on his Cellphone congratulates Khan on the front page story: 'Durban Test Ticket Rush'.

In return Bacher had given Khan's evening newspaper the South African World Cup squad scoop first thing that morning. For once the evening papers were ahead of the game.

3.25pm: Some peace. '*Life is about perceptions and images. Integration was an embarrassingly slow progress but it was morally right, and it made cricket sense and business sense.*'

Unification became reality on June 29, 1991. Within weeks South African cricketers, as if by an act of God, were playing in Calcutta and shaking the hand of Mother Teresa. The constitutions had joined as one, with primary thanks to Steve Tshwete, who acted as the mediator between the 'white' Union and the non-white 'Board'.

'*Tshwete and President Mandela went public to support us as they saw the progress in cricket as the ideal way to begin redressing the balance. Their backing has been amazing ever since,*' said Bacher.

4.30pm: The letters that he began 12 hours ago return to be signed; a couple of Board members telephone wondering why their Test players, Shaun Pollock and Allan Donald, have been rested for the weekend's Castle Cup matches. '*Because we feel they need a break prior to the Durban Test and the South African team* must *take priority over provincial requirements,*' he said firmly, but with sympathy.

Ali Bacher captained South Africa in four Test matches and won them all. He led Transvaal to victory over the Australians in the November of 1966 scoring a mammoth 235 himself. He was a nudging and working sort of batsman who was good enough to keep Barry Richards out of Test cricket during that Australian tour. He thinks that Test cricket has changed beyond all recognition – '*It's so intense now, so confrontational, and it will only get better*' – and he is grateful that he has an efficient staff and an excellent executive board to help him through the modern demands of the international game. He is a likeable, articulate man, and the most innovative and stimulating sporting administrator I have met.

5.30pm: Home early, we are both tired after the sapping Test. Has he ambitions?

'*To be in the job when we host the World Cup in 2003 and to make it an extravaganza that shows the world how all South Africa are playing the game of cricket. Contrary to popular opinion I have no designs within the ICC or within national politics here, I love what I do at the moment too much. My as yet unfulfilled dream is that black and brown and white play cricket together for South Africa.*' And that, as one man's mission, is quite enough.

Daily Telegraph, 11 December 1995

Hamlet has need of the gravedigger

Matthew Engel

The beauty of a five-Test series is that it retains the structure of the Shakespearean drama. The weirdness of this series is that we reached Act Five and absolutely damn all had happened: Act Two was a bit spicy but Acts One and Three were intermissions and Act Four mostly *longueurs*.

Now, in the first two scenes of Act Five, we have had the lot. And, if this play has Mike Atherton in the role of the tragic prince, then yesterday afternoon – between 4.38 and 5.44 pm South African time – was when Hamlet was finally driven potty.

When Atherton trudged off into the twilight half an hour later, having got out to a shot of uncharacteristic indecisiveness, the denouement was approaching very rapidly indeed.

(Incidentally, 12 former England captains have been spotted in Cape Town this week. Any one of these might reasonably play old Hamlet's Ghost though Graham Taylor, who is also present, would be an alternative possibility.)

Nothing in cricket is so demoralising to a fielding side than a big last-wicket stand, most especially in a low-scoring game. One can bear being torn apart by a Richards or a Lara. But being turned into Charlies by a No. 11 is ghastly and England have been caught this way twice in the series.

Deeply flawed cricket teams are always vulnerable to this kind of thing. It is also characteristic of teams coached by Bob Woolmer that the second half of the order often bat better than the first half: Warwickshire are just the same.

The tragi-comic stand between Richardson and Adams defused one of the tensest passages of play witnessed in modern Test cricket. The low-scoring match combined with the state of the series meant that every run seemed to count not double but quadruple.

When Cork was responsible for four overthrows just after Adams came in, they were cheered as though they were 20. And he held up his hands in a gesture of contrition that would have sufficed for dropping Lara off a sitter on nought.

From then on England's cricket grew ragged, as it had been in the morning. And by the end, when Adams was square-driving Fraser as if he were Walter Hammond re-incarnated, the tension had vanished. One had to laugh, really. It was the only way to avoid bursting into tears.

Between lunch and tea England had got back in the game through doing all the little things so very well: Martin and Fraser strangling the innings, the fielders picking up everything. But there is no margin for error in English cricket because the team is still not good enough. And as soon as anything goes wrong, everything is likely to go wrong.

The Oval 1994 is not that long ago and South Africa's batsmen are still scared of Devon Malcolm. At any rate they are scared of the memory of Devon Malcolm, the man Nelson Mandela christened The Destroyer. It is a fading memory now.

The problem was not that he bowled especially badly. There was just no menace there. He ran up with the air of a man apologising to the batsmen for past wrongs, instead of trying to remind them. Miracles aside, it looks like the end of one era, anyway.

This remains a very puzzling Test match, right down to Brian McMillan's failure to heed the red light and depart when he was run out (though that at least fits with the normal behaviour of South African drivers).

Since there has never been a major match on this particular strip there is not much local lore to suggest how the pitch will behave from here. Possibly the batsmen's failings and the weather have had more to do with events so far than the actual surface.

One Capetonian knew South Africa were going to be all right yesterday because, when he woke up, there was no cloud on the mountain. Indeed, there was not a cloud to be seen all day – just a little afternoon heat haze and the plumes of smoke from the brewery. So there was not much chance of the ball swinging.

Last night another change in the weather was forecast: no rain but cooler. If batting conditions do deteriorate, England might plunge to defeat very quickly, leaving the hordes of spectators, already turning ozone-hole beetroot, plenty of time for sunbathing and chuntering. In the meantime they are indulging in the familiar British pastime of straw-clutching.

Guardian, 4 January 1996

New emphasis on coaching is first step to halting decline

John Woodcock

Cape Town is full of disappointed, not to say disenchanted, English cricket supporters, many of them asking the same question. How much longer do they have to wait for a genuine revival in England's cricket fortunes?

To blame the umpiring for the defeat in the fifth Test match last week, and the consequent loss of the Test series to South Africa, is to hide from the truth. England were beaten by a better side. In bowling and fielding, South Africa were a long way ahead, and their batting was more solid than England's.

From the start of the series, I could never quite understand why so many experienced observers saw England as the likelier side. One of them, Jack Bannister, no less, finished by eating his own words on live television, washed down with a bottle of Chardonnay. Maybe they were beguiled by the captain's optimism. On the eve of the tour, Michael Atherton wrote: 'The variety of our bowling attack is a major asset for us. We have, I believe, an attack suited to any kind of surface. We have pace bowlers, swing bowlers, nagging accuracy and spin. Importantly, we also have, in Cork, Gough and Ilott, excellent experts of reverse swing.'

More meaningfully, I am afraid, England are desperately short of wicket-taking bowlers. Not even Alec Bedser, when he was the heart and marrow of the England attack, carried more of a burden than Dominic Cork does at the moment. Now that Malcolm's confidence is in shreds, Cork alone has the knack of making things happen.

It was just as much England's batting that failed them, though.

The pitch at Newlands for the last Test match may not have been a particularly good one, but it was nothing like poor enough to explain England's totals of 153 and 157, even when some undoubtedly questionable umpiring decisions are taken into account. At Port Elizabeth, in the fourth Test match, they managed only 263 in their first innings on a pitch that gave no advantage to the South Africa bowlers, while in Johannesburg, in the second, a first innings total of 200 was the best England could do in reply to South Africa's 332.

Nothing was more certain when South Africa returned to Test cricket than that what they lacked in experience and flair they would make up for in commitment; and that is just as it has been. I doubt whether they have quite the flexibility to win the forthcoming World Cup, and they may well have a job coping with the spinners when they go to India next winter: but at least they have, in Paul Adams, a spinner of their own now, who is more than just a token. Their faster attack is as good and disciplined as there is. There is no more explosive bowler in the world than Donald, and Pollock has the whip and suppleness of a young Brian Statham.

One's sympathy goes out to Atherton. It is by no means the most urbane of teams that he leads, but that, unfortunately, is a reflection of the times. No captain ever set a more resolute example at the crease or was deserving of better support. It is ridiculous, when he has such gifted players as Hick, Smith, Stewart and Thorpe at his side, that, unless he himself makes runs, England collapse. It is absurd, too, that when, in English cricket, there is such a wealth of material, England should be a poor sixth in the Test rankings.

We have now had, successively, the Peter May era, the Ted Dexter era and the Raymond Illingworth era, the last being much the most authoritarian of them. In their contrasting ways, these dedicated men have given their all to make England into a winning side again. More expenditure and more acquired knowledge never went into an England tour than this one, and yet, so far, there is not much to show for it.

Basically, all Illingworth asks is that his sides should make the best of themselves, which, unlike South Africa, they too seldom do. The fact that, of the 35 catches that South Africa held in the series just finished, 20 were taken at slip or gully and eight others at the wicket, when the ball never moved about a great deal, is an indictment of English batting technique.

In the reorganisation of English cricket that is now under way, coaching must be seen as being of much more importance than marketing – coaching that puts orthodoxy and self-expression on a par. It is time, too, for a switch to more open government and a more constructive contribution from the best of England's former players, so many of them now surveying the scene from their ivory electronic tower.

If South Africa's victory helps towards the creation of a wider cricketing culture in their incredible country, that will be wonderful. At the moment, it is still very much a white man's game. On Christmas Day, I walked along a beach in Cape Province with such an expanse of flat sand that it could have accommodated every imaginable game. There must have been 5,000 people on it, virtually all non-white and a great many of them playing with a ball of some kind. In all that multitude, I spotted only two small black boys playing cricket.

Adams, however, took to Test cricket like a duckling to water. In a kind of way, he lifted the veil off it. He twinkled while he spun and there is all too little of both in the modern game. When he came in last in South Africa's first innings, cheered to the echo but looking vulnerably young, he had faced only 16 balls and scored four runs in first-class cricket; but, when Cork gave him a glare after bowling him a bouncer, Adams responded with a wink. When, eventually, the first African, as distinct from Cape Coloured, wins a Test cap, it will be of even greater sociological significance, but it could never be more disarmingly accomplished.

The Times, 8 January 1996

The World Cup

Introduction

Once more were the forces gathered – to play cricket? Nobody would have thought so at the outset. A bomb, death threats, refusals to play preliminary matches, fierce disputes . . . at one stage it looked as if the tournament might have to be cancelled. And then when the jamboree did eventually get underway, reported intimidation, crowd disturbance, and in the offing, potential riot and even war.

Thankfully, however, in the end, cricket won the battle with politics. And the ultimate triumph of the long-time underdogs Sri Lanka, with their uninhibited, adventurous approach was, for all true lovers of the game, a joy to behold.

War clouds ahead

Mike Marqusee

At Lord's, on February 2, 1993, Alan Smith blew his cool. Smith, a former England and Warwickshire 'amateur' wicketkeeper, now the chief executive of the Test and County Cricket Board, is a notoriously tight-lipped devotee of cricket's ancient cult of official secrecy. But on that day, seething after a record-breaking fourteen-hour meeting of the International Cricket Council, he called an unprecedented press conference to denounce what he considered 'by a long way the worst meeting I have ever attended . . . fractious and unpleasant . . . beset by procedural wrangling . . . there was no talk of anything like cricket . . .'

In reality, however, Smith was outraged not so much by the conduct of the meeting as its decision to reject England's long-standing bid to host the 1996 World Cup in favour of a joint proposal from India, Pakistan and Sri Lanka. He was joined on the warpath by virtually the entire English cricket establishment, whose feelings were summed up by Christopher Martin-Jenkins in a bewildered protest in the *Daily Telegraph*. Arguing that England was 'the ideal venue' whose 'advantages cannot be matched by the rival bidders from a vast and frequently unruly subcontinent', he decried the ICC decision as a triumph for 'money and politics' over cricket. In so doing, of course, he rewrote the previous 200 years of cricket history, dominated as they have been by English money and politics, but as so often when national pride is pricked, facts and logic were quickly superseded by myth and emotion.

Since then, English commentators have lost few opportunities to rubbish the forthcoming cricket jamboree. Last month an editorial in *The Cricketer* warned: 'No one knows what horrors lie in store as a result of total control of the arrangements for the 1996 World Cup devolving into the hands of the Asian host countries alone.'

Now in its 75th year, *The Cricketer* boasts on its masthead that it is 'the world's largest selling cricket magazine'. Untrue. The world's largest selling cricket magazine is almost certainly the 100,000 circulation Hindi monthly called *Cricket Samrat* (Cricket Warrior). And its audience is more diverse, and certainly more youthful, than the blimps and anoraks who make up the readership of *The Cricketer*. In recent years subcontinental cricket has spread far beyond its old metropolitan enclaves. It is played today by Afghan refugees in Peshawar, at the foot of the Khyber Pass, and by fisher folk in the old Portuguese colony of Goa. To a foreign traveller, the game seems ubiquitous. In narrow slum streets, village *maidans*, posh suburbs and cluttered middle-class housing blocks, boys and young men play the game in all kinds of awkward spaces with whatever implements come to hand.

Coming to cricket (from an American childhood and a love of baseball) at the advanced age of 23, I was entranced at first by the sheer strangeness of the game, by its placid rituals and mossy mysteries. When, soon after, I encountered Indian cricket, with its spin bowlers, raucous crowds and labyrinthine politics, it seemed an exotic variation on an exotic theme, an eccentricity within an eccentricity. In the years since then, I've grown wiser. I've come to see that if you want to understand cricket in the subcontinent, you've got to shed some hoary assumptions about both the game and the people who play and watch it.

Bombay, city of skyscrapers and squalor, is the spiritual home of Indian cricket. Here, more than 150 years ago, Parsi merchants first set out to beat the English at their own game. Here, for nearly half a century, the subcontinent's principal competition, the annual intercommunal matches between Parsis, Hindus, Muslims and Europeans engaged the emergent nation and enraged the secular nationalists. Here, legendary Test stars Vijay Merchant, Farokh Engineer, Sunil Gavaskar and Sachin Tendulkar announced their talents to the world. Today, Bombay is the capital of the western state of Maharashtra, India's commercial and industrial giant, whose long domination over Indian cricket, much resented by cricket-lovers in other regions, is the source of a classic Indian joke: Superman flies from Metropolis to offer his services to the Indian Test selectors, who are meeting at an expensive hotel in Bombay.

They look at him suspiciously.

'Can you bat?' they ask.

'I guarantee that I will hit a six off every ball bowled to me and that I will never get out.'

'Can you bowl?'

'I guarantee to take a wicket with every ball I bowl and to bowl all day if need be.'

'Can you field?'

'I guarantee to stop the other team taking any runs off any ball they hit anywhere in the field.'

The selectors mutter among themselves.

'Ah,' they ask at last, 'but are you from Maharashtra?'

Bombay's Shivaji Park, named after Maharashtra's great eighteenth-century martial hero, is India's field of dreams. Among the Test stars it has nurtured are Gavaskar, Tendulkar and Vinod Kambli. On the afternoon I visit its rough-hewn, stubbly acres, the park teems with white-flannelled boys playing, practising and talking cricket. I try to count the number of matches underway, but they are so crammed together it is impossible to tell where one ends and another begins. Everywhere parents and coaches cajole their young charges, threatening punishment, promising the earth – the fame and wealth of a career in international cricket. As the sun sinks into the Arabian sea, Shivaji Park is animated with the global sporting dream whose radiance lights up the basketball courts of Chicago housing projects and the football pitches of São Paolo slums, the dream that, with talent and luck, Anyone Can Make It.

That night, at a reception for the visiting West Indies Test squad held at the five-star Oberoi Hotel, I am lucky enough to catch a glimpse of the glitter which explains so much of the toil at Shivaji Park. The cavernous ballroom is packed with businessmen, politicians, movie stars, famous cricketers and attendant paparazzi. Champagne and whisky flow freely, and mountains of multicoloured ice-cream disappear in minutes. A flickering light show and live band draw a crowd of Bombay's gilded youth on to the dance floor. Some of the more fresh-faced West Indian cricketers cast longing glances at the bejewelled women in silk saris, but any thoughts they entertain of strutting their stuff are quelled by stern glances from puritanical tour managers.

Early the next morning, outside Wankhede Stadium, thousands of police armed with the long bamboo truncheons known as *lathis* keep nervous watch over jostling queues of cricket fans. Inside, I take my seat in the press box and gaze out over the freshly white-washed stands, where the swelling crowd roars at the merest glimpse of a cricket hero. In the middle, an American TV technician with bare, burly chest and turned-around baseball cap adjusts the stump microphone, watched with patient fascination by dhoti-clad members of the Wankhede ground staff, whose average yearly income would barely cover a week's expenses for the American.

A subcontinental cricket crowd in full cry is one of the great sights and sounds in the world of sport. India is batting today and every boundary is greeted with a barrage of firecrackers. Fifties are celebrated with rhythmic clapping in unison. Mexican waves rip round the stands a dozen times before petering out. Self-appointed commentators and comedians parody pop songs and political slogans. Handwritten placards display messages in English, Hindi and Marathi, and hundreds of fluttering Indian tricolours add welcome splashes of colour to the unadorned concrete oval.

The partisanship is flagrant but good-humoured, which is astonishing given the conditions the fans have to put up with. Outside the VIP enclosures (always packed with hangers-on), facilities are meagre and overcrowded. Toilets are few and mostly filthy. Drinking water seems largely unavailable. If you want to eat, you have to battle your way through the throngs surrounding the food stalls, which invariably seem to have run out of anything edible just as you finally reach the front. Security is heavy-handed. Anyone who steps out of line can expect a crack on the head with a *lathi*. Thousands of supernumerary police clutter the gangways and the balconies, obstructing the paying customers' views.

Suddenly, the crowd surges towards the press box, hundreds of faces pressing eagerly against the wire mesh that separates them from the privileged media. Wondering why, I look around to find the movie star Nana Patekar, Bollywood's reigning macho rebel and moody man of principle, talking to Gavaskar. Responding to the agitation in the crowd, Patekar rises in his seat, wiggles his hips and cries 'Jai Hind!' (Long live India!). Some of the closest spectators seem about to faint with the sheer excitement of it all.

Seated in a VIP box just below the media enclosure – and enjoying from there the best view in the house – is the president of the Bombay Cricket Association, Manohar Joshi. With his fixed grin and too ready handshake, Joshi is at once identifiable as a politician. He is, indeed, a member of the Maharashtra Legislative Assembly and one of the top bosses of Shiv Sena, a right-wing, virulently anti-Muslim political gang widely believed to be responsible for the communal riots which ripped Bombay asunder in January 1993.

One of the heroes of that horror was Sunil Gavaskar, who intervened to stop some Shiv Sena *goondas* (party political musclemen) from beating a Muslim family in the street. Even the *goondas*, it seems, were overawed by the matchless prestige Gavaskar enjoys in Bombay.

Today, Joshi, who also happens to be a vice-president of the Indian Cricket Board, looks smug in his perch, as bigwigs take turns congratulating him on the marvellous spectacle he has provided for the people of Bombay. Apparently, it is inconvenient for anyone to recall that the last time Pakistan were scheduled to play cricket in Bombay, the match was cancelled after threats by Shiv Sena to dig up the pitch. Joshi's boss is 71-year-old Shiv Sena founder and self-confessed Hitler admirer Bal Thackeray (pilloried as 'Raman Fielding' in Salman Rushdie's *The Moor's Last Sigh*, now banned in India). Thackeray has devised his own version of the Tebbit test, declaring that he wants to see Indian Muslims with 'tears in their eyes' when India lose a cricket match to Pakistan.

Today's opponents are the highly popular West Indies side, but sections of the crowd none the less amuse themselves during slow periods of play by chanting '*Pakistan hai hai*' (down, down).

Three months after my visit to Wankhede, Shiv Sena and allied Hindu zealots were to sweep to victory in local elections. Manohar Joshi was sworn in as Chief Minister of Maharashtra in front of a huge, saffron-swathed crowd in Shivaji Park. In attendance was the Sheriff of Bombay, one Sunil Gavaskar, whose offer to resign the honorary post following the election result had been craftily rejected by Joshi.

The Shiv Sena government quickly launched a crackdown on so-called 'illegal migrants' from Bangladesh (an excuse for police harassment of anyone with a Muslim name), a puritanical onslaught against allegedly pornographic advertising and a high-profile (and ultimately successful) campaign to change the name of the city to Mumbai – invoking Mumbadevi, one of the area's resident Hindu deities. Thus, delightfully cosmopolitan, chaotically multicultural Bombay is being hammered by political hooligans into homogeneous, religiously strait-jacketed Mumbai. Already, the transformation has cost the city its right to stage a World Cup quarter or semi-final (it had always been agreed that the final itself would be held in Lahore).

The Pakistanis play all their first-round matches at home, but should they qualify (as is likely) for the next stage, they may find themselves playing on Indian soil for the first time in seven years. Joshi made a direct appeal for one of the semi-finals to be held in Bombay, but even he must have known the Indian cricket authorities could not risk it, especially given Thackeray's recent pronouncements. The Sena führer has warned that the Pakistani Inter-Services Intelligence agency (which enjoys demonic status in India, something like the CIA in Latin America) plans to use the World Cup to infiltrate thousands of agents into India 'under the guise of being cricket fans'. Even all-conquering multinationals are not beyond the range of Thackeray's increasingly grandiose threats: 'If Pepsi stick to their plans of sponsoring Pakistani players, their bottles will be broken and banners torn apart.'

The Indian cricket authorities are desperate to shield the World Cup (not to mention its paying sponsors) from the stain of political violence, and in the present climate that means ensuring that the Pakistanis are kept well away from Mumbai. Accordingly, the erstwhile capital of subcontinental cricket will have to make do with an attractive but innocuous first-round tie between India and Australia.

Bombay's loss has been Chandigarh's gain. While one semi-final is to be played in Calcutta, the administrative headquarters of Indian cricket, the other goes to the capital of the wealthy, if also politically unstable, northern state of Punjab, which also happens to be the power base of I S Bindra, who is the president of the Indian Cricket Board.

I meet Bindra at the Delhi Golf Club, a sprawling colonial remnant, now one of the Indian capital's elite watering-holes. As waiters in livery hover and fuss, we help ourselves to the Chinese buffet, then sit down under the huge chandelier to discuss preparations for World Cup '96.

Soft-spoken but firm, the dapper, grey-headed Bindra dismisses dire English predictions of World Cup disaster as mere sour grapes.

'The reality was that the majority of ICC members opposed the English bid and supported ours. They did so because we offered a better financial package. The TCCB has not got over the Raj hangover. They seem not to like their erstwhile colonial subjects coming to London and beating them at what they still think is their own game.

'Remember we hosted the World Cup in 1987, which everyone agreed was a great success. There was not one delayed or cancelled flight; arrangements for passing through immigration and customs, for travel within the country, for accommodation, umpires and journalists were all smooth.' In 1996, he promises, they will be even smoother.

Throughout our conversation we are gingerly interrupted by deferential suitors seeking favours from Bindraji, who is polite and modest with all comers, though clearly a man in command. After all, Inderjit Singh Bindra is one of India's top civil servants, a former secretary to the President of India and currently Secretary for the Punjab Departments of Industry, Sports and Youth Affairs. He is the finest flower of the Indian bureaucracy, long accustomed to weaving his way around politicians, adept at wielding power and dispensing patronage. But the awe in which he is held by the well-heeled denizens of the Delhi Golf Club derives pre-eminently from his position at the apex of the national sport.

The Indians are nothing if not ambitious and are confident that the World Cup will boost their status as the new epicentre of a global game, commanding a huge internal market now linked by satellite and cable television to the vast Asian diaspora in Europe, North America, the Middle East and the Far East. Every facet of the Cup – from sightscreens to drinks trolleys – will be sponsored, and every new deal has been announced with fanfare. Not since the eighteenth century, when an entrepreneur named Thomas Lord realised there was money to be made from this peculiar game, has cricket seen such shameless glorying in commercial success.

Today, Bindra is beaming over news of the £8 million World Cup 'title sponsorship' deal stitched up with Indian tobacco giant ITC – twice the sum named by a top UK agency as the most the Indians could possibly hope for. This is the biggest single sponsorship deal in cricket's history and the biggest ever investment sponsorship deal in cricket's history and the biggest ever investment in a sporting event in the subcontinent. Accordingly, the competition has been officially dubbed the 'Wills World Cup', after ITC's leading cigarette brand.

In India, as in England, it is not hard to find people complaining that the game has become too commercial, that money has become the cricket authorities' god. Bindra insists all the revenue-chasing is solely to serve the game itself. He cites a 160 per cent increase in match fees for first-class cricketers and heavy subsidies for junior cricket and the Ranji Trophy, India's venerable four-day domestic competition, now virtually unwatched by the public.

'This is the purpose of our marketing activities: to promote and develop the game. Nothing else. The number of people playing cricket in India is testimony to the Board's ability to take cricket to places which had never seen it before. It is no longer an elitist sport. It is for the common man. Most of our Test cricketers now come from lower middle-class backgrounds. Because of this, cricket plays an important role in national unity. The whole country is now represented by the Test side.'

But everywhere I have gone in India, I tell Bindra, cricket fans have complained to me that Test selection is biased by religious, caste or regional factors.

'Of course, you cannot please everyone,' he replies. 'The biggest pastime in the country is discussing cricket. We have several hundred million armchair selectors out there. It only shows the degree of public involvement in our cricket.'

Bindra's vision of the future of Indian cricket is very much in line with India's current policy of economic 'globalisation'. He believes the World Cup will help unlock new markets for cricket in North America and the Far East. He goes so far as to suggest that it will spark a craze for cricket in China and Japan.

For decades, multinationals were largely excluded from India's heavily protected domestic markets. Readmitted now under the country's fashionably deregulatory regime and keen to reach its 150 million-strong middle class, they have seized on cricket as the most reliable avenue to the hearts and pockets of south Asian consumers.

What has to be remembered is that cricket in this part of the world (and in sharp contrast to cricket in Britain) is seen as trendy, youthful, modern. Not surprisingly, the first thing Pepsi did on its recent return to India was to invest in the game of 'the new generation', buying endorsements from famous cricketers and cutting a deal with the Indian Cricket Board to sponsor domestic and international matches.

In the World Cup carnival of globalisation, however, loyalty means little, and Pepsi found itself outmanoeuvred by Coke in the competition for the title of 'official drink of the World Cup'. Likewise, Visa has trumped Mastercard by paying £3,800,000 for the privilege of styling itself the World Cup's 'official credit card'.

WorldTel, the US-based company which owns television rights to the Cup, estimates its potential planetary television audience at 1.5 billion. Total television revenues have already exceeded £21 million, four times what the Australians managed to squeeze out of the last World Cup. Kerry Packer has outbid Rupert Murdoch for Australian TV rights to the 1996 Cup, but Murdoch's Sky has captured the UK market.

But globalisation is not as straightforward as it may appear. Even the composition of the competing teams will bear witness to its complexities. One of the three non-Test playing 'minnows' to qualify for the World Cup is the United Arab Emirates, whose talented team of immigrants has been denounced by rivals as a 'Pakistan Second XI'. Given that the majority of UAE residents are in fact migrant workers from the subcontinent, and that the indigenous population is both minute and indifferent to cricket, the criticism seems unreasonable. In any case, the UAE will not be the only side to offend those who hold antiquated notions of national purity. Holland's batting will be spearheaded by the 48-year-old, Barbados born and bred Nolan Clarke, New Zealand will enjoy the services of Englishman Roger Twose, and of course England will have Southern Africans Graham Hick and Robin Smith in the ranks.

Globalisation has already tripped up the mild-mannered, ultra-cautious Indian captain Mohammed Azharuddin. Having justified his purchase of a new Mercedes Benz by arguing that no Indian-made car could match it, he proudly asserted that 'there is one area in which our country excels and that is in sports goods'. However, he then abandoned the Indian sporting goods company whose products he had used and endorsed for many years in favour of a fat contract with multi-national Reebok – a deal which soon landed the popular Azhar in hot water.

A photograph of the Indian captain apparently autographing one of the company's training shoes appeared in an Urdu-language paper in his native city of Hyderabad. Muslim clerics and politicians howled in rage. How could Azhar insult the name of the prophet, which he bears, by affixing it to such a lowly item? Azhar, previously a favourite of the clerics and a hero to Indian Muslims, was quick to insist he had only initialled the shoes. 'As a devout Muslim I have the highest regard for the almighty and the prophet,' he insisted. Theologians, however, continue to dispute the fine distinctions.

Not surprisingly, given three wars since partition, unresolved conflict over Kashmir, ongoing nuclear weapons competition and mutual religious intolerance, the Indo-Pak cricket rivalry makes the Anglo-Australian Ashes look like an exercise in international hand-holding. Over the decades, competition has frequently been interrupted by military conflict, diplomatic impasse or political posturing, and when it has been joined it has been a fierce, emotionally charged, usually dour struggle. In recent years it has been impossible for the two countries to play each other anywhere on the subcontinent, so they have been forced to carry their cricket battle off-shore, to Sharjah in the Gulf, to Birmingham, London and Toronto. But wherever cricket goes, national and religious rivalry seem to follow, and with them flag-burning, spectator clashes and charges of umpiring bias.

George Orwell derided international sport as 'war minus the shooting', and the depressing history of Indo-Pak cricket relations might seem to bear him out. But cricket officials from both sides of the border remain confident that the game is a healer. 'Before the 1987 World Cup the problems seemed intractable,' Bindra recalls. 'Our armies were eyeball to eyeball on the border. But in the end it went off without a hitch. Our slogan then was "cricket for peace" and cricket does help bring peace.'

Bindra stresses that relations between the two cricket boards are cordial. 'We do not feel that we represent different countries. It is a single enterprise. Remember that the total population of the subcontinent is involved in the World Cup. It is too big for small politicians on either side to disrupt and any politician who tried to interfere would pay a heavy price.'

For ever cast as the bad boys of World Cricket, the Pakistanis would dearly love to vindicate themselves by retaining the Cup, especially as no host country has ever won it before. Acutely aware of the high stakes and possible political fallout, Benazir Bhutto's government has asserted control over the World Cup preparations (her husband sits on the organising committee), but seems unable to stem the continuing violence in Karachi – where 2,000 have been killed in the last year in the conflict between government forces and armed mohajirs (descendants of Muslims who immigrated from India to Pakistan after partition).

Pakistan Cricket Board chief Arif Ali Abassi has appealed to all parties to agree a truce before the World Cup in order to salvage 'the country's honour and image'. Of the three matches scheduled for Karachi perhaps the most intriguing, if it comes off, will be the encounter between England and Pakistan on March 3 – the first time the two countries have met since the ill-tempered 'ball-tampering' series of 1992. It has all the makings of a grudge match in one of the most violent cities on earth.

But for cricket fans in the subcontinent any fixture involving England is a mere sideshow. A meeting between India and Pakistan in the final at Lahore on March 17 would be the biggest sporting event in the history of the region and would be followed ball-by-ball by nearly everyone with access to radio or television in both countries – not to mention immigrant communities on four other continents. Inflammatory perhaps, but undoubtedly enthralling.

Finally, who will win the World Cup? The one-day format (still disdained by purists in favour of the rigours of five-day Test cricket) is a great leveller, which means that any one of six or seven teams (including England) has a fair shot at taking the title. For an outside bet follow Sir Richard Hadlee's advice and back Sri Lanka, which recently became the only side to win a series against Pakistan in Pakistan for fifteen years. And fasten your seat-belts, it could be a bumpy ride.

Esquire, March 1996

Mind games tilting balance of terror

Vic Marks

There was a time when Sri Lanka was considered a safe haven for international cricketers. In 1984, the England team were grateful to escape to Colombo when the assassination of Indira Gandhi five hours after their arrival in India had provoked violence and 500 deaths on the streets of Delhi.

But now cricketers head for Sri Lanka with understandable misgivings; they must balance the prospect of a successful World Cup campaign against the threat of violence jeopardising their own safety. Is it worth the risk? The Tamil separatists would provoke no public sympathy if they disrupted the World Cup matches being staged in Sri Lanka, but they would gain unprecedented publicity.

Four teams are scheduled to visit Sri Lanka for the World Cup this month: Australia, Zimbabwe, West Indies and Kenya. Of these, the Zimbabweans appear to be the most gung-ho. Their manager, Denis Streak, said last week: 'We come from a country which knows about war and we're not going to worry about a few bombs. You could get run over by a bus in the street.'

The Australians are more circumspect. Even before that deadly bomb went off in Colombo, they had expressed reservations about their expedition to Sri Lanka and Pakistan. Now they have pondered a most un-Australian solution: forfeiting their game against Sri Lanka. Moreover, the Australian Cricket Board's chief executive, Graham Halbish, has made it clear that any player is free to pull out without blighting his career; a sensible, pragmatic view, since we know from past experience that reluctant, fearful tourists do not perform on the pitch. There have been plenty of those in strife-torn Sri Lanka in the past dozen years.

Indeed, just two weeks after England had taken refuge in Colombo back in 1984, a curfew was imposed in the city after 130 Sri Lankan soldiers had been killed in the north of the island. At the time, England's tourists congratulated themselves on finally managing to avoid an international crisis.

In 1986, the New Zealand tour was abandoned after a bomb blast at the Pettah bus station in Colombo, which killed 100 civilians. In 1992, Kiwi cricketers witnessed the assassination of a Sri Lankan naval commander and three of his aides by a suicide bomber from the Tamil separatist movement just 50 yards from their hotel. This prompted several acrimonious meetings among the New Zealanders. It was eventually decided to continue the tour, but five of the team opted to go home. Replacements were hastily summoned, but the remainder of the tour was a cricketing disaster for the Kiwis. Their players were too preoccupied to perform.

With hindsight, it is easy to under-estimate the fears of players caught up in civil strife. I can easily recall the tensions of the England party on that 1984-85 tour to India. The team was imprisoned in a Delhi hotel for five days after Mrs Gandhi's death while smoke from fires in the city centre filled the skyline; tempers became understandably frayed in such a claustrophobic, uncertain atmosphere.

Had the atrocity occurred a day earlier, the team certainly would not have travelled to India. The majority of the players wanted to go home, and when this view was forcefully put by Allan Lamb, the

England manager brandished his passport and challenged him to take it.

In the end the tour proceeded after our week's refuge in Sri Lanka, despite another atrocity. On the eve of the first Test, the Deputy British High Commissioner, Percy Norris, was assassinated eight hours after he had regally entertained us at his home. Now we were certain that the tour would be cancelled. We huddled in groups, fiddling for the World Service on our radios and speculating wildly. We were then astonished when captain David Gower (yes, Gower of optional nets fame) toured the rooms, announcing that we were going down to the Wankhede Stadium in Bombay for practice. 'What? Target practice?' mused Graeme Fowler.

From this point on, Indian special branch officers, armed with Sten guns, were ever-present in our hotel corridors, on the team bus (which as a precaution used different routes to the ground each day), and outside the dressing rooms. It took a while to become blasé about their presence. Such security will no doubt accompany every team during the imminent World Cup.

The following morning, Fowler opened the batting. He was out for 28, and his dismissal prompted in him not only the standard feelings of disappointment but also an unprecedented tinge of relief. Before the match it had occurred to him that if there were any anti-British crackpots in the stands, he would be a prime target as England's opening batsman. That may appear unduly melodramatic now; at the time, 24 hours after a heinous assassination, such a reaction did not seem at all ludicrous.

This particular episode had a happy ending. England, who lost that match in Bombay, came back to win the Test series 2-1, and there were no further life-threatening incidents. But that experience should not prompt a gung-ho attitude now, nor will it allay the worries of those players travelling to Colombo next week. Bill Shankly's famous maxim ('Football's not a matter of life and death. It's much more important than that') does not apply in real life. If certain Australians, or indeed any other international cricketers, prefer to stay home during the next month, their decisions should be respected and fully understood.

With constant unrest in Karachi as well as in Colombo, this World

Cup is proving to be a potential minefield. To modify that old cricketing truism: it no longer matters who wins or loses, but whether the games can be played at all. Even the hosts of the World Cup, who 'hijacked' the tournament at an acrimonious meeting of the ICC in February 1993, must be wondering whether the original plan – playing in England in the summer of 1996 – might not have been preferable.

Observer, 4 February 1996

Drop-outs deepen Sri Lanka's sense of loss

Simon Barnes

If athletes don't cheer you up when your life is miserable, then what on earth is the point of them? And God knows, the people of Sri Lanka need cheering up. I am not suggesting for a second that a few cricket matches could diminish the horror of the Colombo bombing, but a spot of decent sport could, at least, allow the citizens of Colombo to set it aside for a few hours.

Yet Australia and West Indies are all set to drop out of their World Cup matches in Colombo. Thus they fail in their duty to Colombo, to Sri Lanka, to cricket and to the entire concept of international sport.

Sri Lanka is a sad and lovely island and, in 1981, I spent a happy couple of months there. I remember drinking the demon arak and talking late into the night with my late friend, Nalin: black sheep, as he told me, not without pride, of a famous family, a man who, among other achievements, pioneered the plays of Jean Genet in Colombo.

Over the arak, we talked politics and cricket, for this is an island full of both. While I was in Colombo the police, seconded from the south to the northern, Tamil areas, had rioted, raiding booze shops, attacking Tamils and torching the library in Jaffna, destroying a treasure-house of centuries-old Tamil manuscripts.

Jaffna was considered a no-go area so, naturally, I went, not brave but curious, eager for a damn good story (I wrote it up for the *Far Eastern Economic Review*). I encountered not violence but sadness, staying with a once-rich Tamil family reduced to taking in boarders, their home and property in the south destroyed by looters. They were not angry, certainly not supporters of the Tamil Tigers: just sad.

As I was returning south, waiting for a bus, a cyclist stopped, dismounting with that bewildering leg-flick that modesty requires of a dhoti-wearer. He asked me the all-important question of that year. 'How is that bottom?' Meaning, of course, Botham.

Politics, sadness, cricket. All part of Sri Lankan life. Cricket is important because, in the midst of troubles, nothing cheers as much as triviality. Tickets for the Australia-West Indies match in Colombo sold out in two hours: they cost as much as the Sri Lankan average monthly wage.

It is Australia's blessing to be free of war. As a result, they have come to a dreadful error of vision. They think that cricket is actually important. More, they think that *cricketers* are important, that cricketers have no duties beyond sport and themselves.

I am not saying that the idea of playing cricket in Colombo is a comfortable one. It remains true, however, that apart from the horrific exception of Munich in 1972, with the murder of the Israeli competitors, athletes have not, thank God, been the target of lethal political action.

It is also true that England's 1984-85 cricket tour of India was similarly affected by political horrors. The Prime Minister, Indira Gandhi, was assassinated; so, a few days later, was the British Deputy High Commissioner, Percy Norris. Naturally, the cricketers were upset and wanted to go home. Instead, they went to Sri Lanka. Then, when the official period of mourning was over, they went back to India, continued the tour and won the series.

Top international athletes are, on the whole, a xenophobic bunch. But it is not that they are uninterested in abroad; they are not interested in much outside the team or, if involved in individual sports, anything outside their own heads.

This is not really a criticism, it is simply an aspect of the sporting mentality. Call it single-mindedness. I remember when covering a tour of India, I visited the Konorak Temple. You would expect most cricketers to display a passing interest in this monument, a short drive away from the team hotel. After all, it happens to be covered – absolutely encrusted – with pedantically detailed carvings of bosomy girls in a series of elaborate priapic grapples. But I think only Derek Pringle visited it, though perhaps Robin Smith went too.

When West Bromwich Albion made their historic visit to China, only three of them went to visit the Great Wall. These, inevitably, were the three black players known as the Three Degrees, Cyrille Regis, the late Laurie Cunningham and Brendon Batson.

Xenophobia, then, is part of sporting life. It has to be: every time you visit a country, it represents the enemy. All this is inevitable, but those of us who are not international athletes should not make the same error. That appears to be what has happened to Australia and, by craven imitation, West Indies.

A suggestion, then. The New Zealanders, I am sure, are above such a xenophobic and pusillanimous failure in the duty owed to international sport. England and New Zealand should offer to play their opening match in Colombo. That way the poor, sad, bewildered Aussies will be able to play their own opening fixture against Sri Lanka in the comfort and safety of Ahmedabad.

Perhaps West Indies will meet Australia in the final of the World Cup. If so, we can only hope that they both lose.

The Times, 7 February 1996

Bamboozled in Bombay and plain mystified by Mumbai

Ian Wooldridge

The work ratios involved in covering this World Cup across the subcontinent are roughly as follows: 67 per cent reading novels in airports or railway stations, 24 per cent being told you can't get a drink on a plane or a train and nine per cent watching cricket.

It is being contested over 17 venues in India, six in Pakistan and two in Sri Lanka and the first thing that awes you is that only a century ago this entire territory was being administered by a few florid British generals and a handful of District Commissioners straight out of Harrow or Winchester. Etonians tended to hang on until a vacancy for Viceroy came up.

Surprises confront you every mile of the way. For example, this dispatch comes to you from a sprawling, over-populated city on India's west coast called Mumbai. That's how it shows up on the airline departure screens but will the Australians, due here to play India on Tuesday, ever find it?

It certainly baffled me yesterday, unaware that only a couple of weeks ago Bombay had severed its last link with the Raj by reverting to what it was called in the Marathi language in the days before Clive. Fair enough, I guess, since 80 per cent of the population around here speak Marathi. Doubtless any day now Bradford will become Bradalebad.

Happily, the natives are as friendly as ever they were and these include Mr Shripad R. Halbe, M. Com (Hons); LL.M; FCS, Grad; CWA Dip in Systems Management – I quote from his card – who has masterminded collecting £2.5 million to spend on bringing the

Wankhede Stadium, where Tuesday's game is to be played, up to scratch.

'You will note,' said Mr Halbe, 'that all the lower seats in the arena have been painted green. This is to represent grass. Likewise, the upper seats have been painted blue. This symbolises the sky. It goes upwards, you see.'

While I enthused about the aesthetic originality of the project, Mr Halbe impatiently summoned a minion to get a key. This, it proved, was to render access to the players' lavatories behind the locker rooms. Mr Halbe is very proud of the lavatories, and well he might be since they are lined with marble.

'Shripad,' I said, daring the familiarity of first-name terms on such brief acquaintance, 'this is better than anything they have at Lord's.' Shripad preened himself. 'I expect it is,' he said.

Meanwhile, 150 boys and girls aged maybe 13 to 16, were filing around the perimeter of the pitch with upturned basins of earth on their heads. Quite where they were carrying them from and to, and for what purpose, was not apparent.

'You see,' said Mr Halbe, 'all will be well on Tuesday.' He is probably right. The massive holes gouged out of the playing area when a giant crane crashed sideways into it last week have now been filled in.

I liked Shripad Halbe very much. I had to. I need my accreditation for Tuesday's match and this, after taxi rides to three offices, proved fruitless. Each was occupied by about 20 men throwing their arms into the air and recommending the address from which I had just come.

'No problem,' they asserted. And indeed there is no problem. Ten quid's worth of any hard Western currency will get you anywhere you want in the Wankhede Stadium on Tuesday night.

Money is what this sixth World Cup is about. What started as a sporting one-day cricket sideshow in England back in 1975 has in two decades, through global satellite TV, become a rip-off target for businessmen who wouldn't even know the name of more than five competing nations. It is swiftly following the Olympic movement down a road named Profit instead of Principle.

To stage the event in the subcontinent, where massive corruption at the highest level is exposed daily on the front pages of responsible newspapers, was an act of lunacy. Indeed, if what one hears on the cricket internet is to be believed, it was an act of corruption in itself.

I am old-fashioned enough to believe this is an appalling word to use in the same sentence as cricket. But here cricket chiefs are at one another's throats, container ships ride out in the Mumbai sea lanes containing vital equipment which won't be landed until unconventional reparations, for the want of a better phrase, are paid.

Meanwhile, those like our cricket correspondent, Peter Johnson, and myself are rushing around this subcontinental cricket parish lending credence to a form of the game which is actually no more than a fairground sideshow.

I have much admiration for Bishen Bedi, the former India captain, who, in a publication in his native country and defiant of much public opinion, has denounced any cricket match played without slips, gulleys and conventional field placings as meretricious entertainment for the great unwashed.

He is right. Unfortunately, since the days when he bowled like an angel, both the game and the world have changed. It is why we are here, watching world-class batsmen hit Third World bowlers for a couple of sixes per over, while ex-player commentators who should know better, but are well paid not to, analyse the bowlers as if, conceivably, they might have some hope of a future.

It's okay by me. I love the subcontinent. I adore Mumbai, now I know where it is. But, seriously, the World Cricket Cup is a competition that has gone off the rails.

Daily Mail, 24 February 1996

Pakistan should reach World Cup home final after usual shambles

Imran Khan

With the decline of the West Indies, Pakistan now have the most talented team in the world. Given that the World Cup will be played on the low-bounce Pakistan wickets, I make them the favourites to reach the final.

The question is, does Wasim Akram have enough time to mould the team into a fighting unit before the World Cup? He has already made a good beginning by coming back from two demoralising defeats to win the last Test in Australia.

No one can begin to understand the mess that Pakistan's cricket is in at the moment, unless they know the intricacies of the structure of the game in Pakistan.

Whereas in the rest of the cricketing world regional teams are sponsored by organisations, in Pakistan the organisations such as banks, airlines and railways compete in first-class cricket. Some regional teams play first-class cricket, but no one takes any interest because all the top players are contracted by the organisations.

This set-up gives rise to some major problems. Firstly, since the organisations are based in the two main cities, Lahore and Karachi, it is more or less impossible for either the rural populations (70 per cent of the country) or players from cities other than Lahore, Karachi and Rawalpindi to have any chance to represent their country.

Secondly, this system has led to favouritism and nepotism in team selections. There is no criteria of selection in the organisations. Selection depends upon who one knows. Players who are not influential have little chance of playing first-class cricket.

Because there is not a proper regional competition – as in the rest of the world – first-class cricket in Pakistan is non-competitive. Most of the stars do not participate in it. There is zero crowd interest because crowds are not interested in backing banks and airlines. It is because of disinterest in domestic cricket that some players started to make money by allegedly betting against their own team and 'throwing' matches.

Pakistani cricketers suffer a huge disadvantage compared with players in other countries – no first-class teams possess their own cricket grounds. Matches are played on rented grounds, which are not exclusively for cricket and, as a result, are over-used.

Hence the problem of Pakistani wickets. Most of them are under-prepared, where the ball neither bounces nor moves off the wicket. As a result, our bowlers always struggle to bowl on green wickets, while our batsmen never quite develop techniques to play on bouncy or seaming wickets.

Because of the low bounce, there are hardly any catches that carry to the slips – hence the number of dropped catches in Australia. It is significant that Pakistan beat Australia in Sydney – a wicket which in character is more like a Pakistani wicket. Yet Pakistani cricket produces some of the most outstanding cricketers in the world. It is important to realise that these players break through in world cricket despite the domestic structure in Pakistan. Top players such as Wasim, Waqar, Mushtaq, Aqib, Salim Malik and now the teenager Salim Elahi all bypassed the first-class cricket structure and, from under-19 (the only proper regional cricket in the country) or club cricket, jumped straight into Test cricket.

Perhaps the single biggest flaw in Pakistan cricket is the way the president of the Cricket Board is nominated by the president of the country. Clearly, the president of the country has neither the time nor understanding of the game to select the right man for the job.

Some of the heads of the Cricket Board do not have even a basic knowledge of the game. Once, one Board president told a bemused Abdul Qadir (considered the best spinner in the world at the time) that the reason he could not bowl as well as the West Indian fast-bowlers was because he had such a short run-up.

During the two-year tenure of the present chief executive, five captains have been changed. Firstly, a players' intrigue was allowed to succeed against Wasim Akram and he was removed as captain. Salim Malik took his place, but was removed on allegation of bribery – without there being a proper inquiry.

Then Moin Khan, a junior player who could not find a regular place in the team, was made the captain. He was removed after a one-day series, and Rameez Raja was made captain.

Raja had not been able to find a regular place in the team for almost two years. Was he unfairly dropped for the past two years? If not, then it was wrong to make him captain now.

After losing the series against Sri Lanka in October, Raja was sacked and, finally, Wasim was brought back. How can any team perform when five captains are changed in less than two years?

Had the Board taken a stand against the rebels in the first place, Pakistan cricket would not have been in its current state. I feel this team is far more talented than the one that won the 1992 World Cup.

Recently political appointees have been made in the Board, which means that, with the change of government, the whole Board is likely to be changed.

What ought to happen, as in the rest of the cricket world, is that the president of the Board ought to be democratically elected by the regional elected committees – and should be answerable to them.

At the moment, because the chief executive is nominated, he is answerable to no one – and is essentially a dictator who has access to enough patronage to manipulate dissenting voices in the elected council and the press. In my view, Pakistan's recent disastrous run in Test cricket is almost entirely due to the incompetence of the current chief executive. Apart from the five changes of captain, there have been equally bizarre team selections.

Ijaz Ahmed was the second-highest run-getter for Pakistan during last winter's tour to South Africa and Zimbabwe. Inexplicably, he was dropped from the team. He was called in to replace the injured Salim Malik – and had an immediate impact.

Majid Kahn and Mushtaq Mohammad, two of the best cricketing

brains in the country, were made manager and coach of the team for the series against Sri Lanka in October. After losing just one series, both were disgracefully kicked out.

The chief executive is also directly responsible for mishandling the bribery allegations. When Salim Malik was blamed by the Australian players for offering bribes, rather than immediately holding a proper inquiry into the allegations, the chief executive sacked the captain and the manager and banned Salim Malik from playing any first-class cricket. Ten months later, an inquiry was held and Malik, previously condemned, was cleared.

However, even more serious bribery allegations against the manager, Intikhab Alam, and certain players were made by Rashid Latif, the wicketkeeper. According to his comments at a press conference, the manager and players deliberately threw matches to make huge amounts of money from bookies.

Amazingly, this time the chief executive did not even bother to hold an inquiry; instead, within a few weeks of the press conference, Intikhab and Rashid Latif were travelling together to Australia with the team. The only explanation given was that Rashid had made an 'unconditional apology'.

It is not surprising that most people in the country are of the opinion that, just so that the team can win the World Cup, the Board are willing to overlook the fact that certain players might actually have taken money to make their own team lose.

Daily Telegraph, 6 December 1995

Cricket's new order is happy to embrace the commercial age

Robert Winder

If it is true that all publicity is good publicity, then the sixth Cricket World Cup has already been a resounding success. The refusal by Australia and the West Indies to go to Sri Lanka is only an unexpected promotional bonus, bringing extra sizzle to an already spicy event. Bombay (recently renamed Mumbai) threw the first spanner into the schedule by refusing to play host to Pakistan, and relations between India and its neighbour are so bad that only a special visa deal, announced a couple of days ago, will allow their fans to travel. When Pakistan came to Calcutta for the opening ceremony it was the first time they had visited India this decade, though it was not diplomacy that cost Wasim Akram his ear stud: a Lahore citizen took a petition to the High Court urging the captain not to look like a girl.

So the 1996 World Cup is historic even before a ball has been bowled. Anyone who complains (understandably) about the rise and rise of one-day cricket, or bemoans the cheap aesthetics of what will undoubtedly be a gaudy fancy dress gala, is missing the point. On the field, the tournament looks like being a showcase, despite all the hype, for traditional virtues. There are flamboyant batsmen (Brian Lara and Sachin Tendulkar), classic fast bowlers (Allan Donald, Curtly Ambrose and Waqar Younis) and, best of all, three wrist spinners (Paul Adams, Anil Kumble and Shane Warne). But it is off the field that the competition will break new ground. The inclusion of three make-weights (the Netherlands, Kenya and the United Arab Emirates) is not an accident – they are three new countries to sell television rights to. The 1996 World Cup is cricket's first big attempt to go global.

The first clue that the balance of cricketing power had changed came when India, Pakistan and Sri Lanka (Pilcom) won the right to hold this World Cup in the first place. The International Cricket Council had just been democratised – one member, one vote, with England and Australia losing their veto. Pilcom seized the chance, offering the associate members $100,000 for their votes. England offered only $60,000, and that was that. Suddenly it was clear that Asia was where the money was, and the organisers have been raking it in ever since.

In the last World Cup the television rights went for £700,000; this time, £20m. Add the title sponsorship (£7m from Wills) and stadium advertising contracts worth £8m, and you have a gold mine – the first cricket has ever found. For the first time in India there will be corporate hospitality, in air-conditioned tents. In cities across India, Tendulkar and Mohammed Azharuddin smile down from hoardings holding fizzy drinks or credit cards. Even Coca-Cola, not a noted cricket fan, has been welcomed to the party (for a mere £2.5m). Only the subcontinent sized cricket audience makes this possible. Pilcom expects to gross $100m (£66.6m) in all – not the Olympics, but not bad. The votes of those associate members look cheap.

The row over Australia and the West Indies only emphasises the gulf between the old cricket order and the new one. After Saturday's last-ditch ICC meeting in Calcutta, one dejected Pilcom convener wondered aloud whether Australia would have refused to visit England following the bomb at Canary Wharf, and everyone knew the answer. The organisers bent over backwards to provoke a change of heart. India volunteered to play their match against Kenya in Colombo, to prove it was safe, and even offered to helicopter the teams into empty stadiums. But there was nothing doing. The Pilcom chief, I S Bindra, told journalists at one point that the meeting had adjourned for a coffee break. 'Hopefully,' he added, 'we will not need a dinner break.' His hopes were dashed. The debate ran on into the evening, moving rooms twice to clear the way for wedding receptions.

The immediate result is that Sri Lanka (many people's dark horses for the cup in any case) have won two games already. Otherwise there are no favourites. India have wonderful batting and hysterical home support – the team knows that people may die if they lose. Pakistan have had an awful year of defeat, bribery allegations and in-fighting, but have the most dangerous bowlers in the tournament, as well as big scores to settle. Australia are probably the best and toughest all-round team, but will also be the most noisily disliked, which will be no fun. South Africa look strong, and are on the crest of a national sporting wave. Lahore is standing by for an emotional visit by Nelson Mandela on cup final day.

As for England, who can say? Their wretched fortnight in South Africa dismayed home fans, and they have begun in the traditional manner, with a batch of groin strains and wonky knees. But, so far as the rest of the world is concerned, England at cricket are a bit like Germany at football: they never look like much, but invariably make it to the final. They've been runners-up three times in five tries, which gives them about the best pedigree in the competition. If Michael Atherton, Graeme Hick and Graham Thorpe hit form, if Dominic Cork and Phillip DeFreitas get their tails up, if, if, if . . .

The one team no one is talking about is the West Indies, the only team to have won the World Cup twice. Sure, in the last 18 months they have been fractious and unhappy. But they still have hot bowlers, and also, more significantly, Lara. After his controversial autumn the man is rested and eager. He arrived a day late – the plane from Barbados developed engine trouble and had to turn back – but then started asking what the one-day record was (181, by Viv Richards in 1983). For all the talk of handy all-rounders, it is big batting that wins these games, and if Lara is in the mood – hell, if he plays to form – he will set impossible targets. If the West Indies do spring a surprise, it will be one of the most unsurprising surprises ever.

At least the opening ceremony is out of the way. The spectacle was designed for the benefit of overhead television, but the blimp failed to secure air traffic clearance, so the effect – 1,000 dancers in symbolic floral patterns – was lost. And the Italian-designed laser spectacular was blown away by a sharp Bengali breeze, which made the huge projection screens flap about like net curtains. Was that a mountain range, or a stormy sea? Was that a fast bowler, or a skateboarder falling over? Before the event, rumours that Miss Universe was going to strip caused a flutter in shy Calcutta. In the end she simply handed out flags to the various captains.

Eden Gardens looked terrific, though, which is more than can be said for the Wankhede Stadium in Bombay. At the weekend, three of the four light towers for the day-night game against Australia were unfinished, and a huge hydraulic crane brought in to speed things up toppled on to the pitch, knocking a 4ft crater in the grass and spewing oil over the outfield.

However, India manages such crises with superb aplomb. A spokesman for the Bombay Cricket Association remained calm. 'We are very much within the time schedule,' he declared. 'Horticulturalists have been summoned.' A pity, really. It could have been a first: crane stopped play.

Independent, 13 February 1996

Giants cut down to normal size

Tony Cozier

For a team with a far superior overall record in one day internationals than anyone else (66 per cent win ratio to Australia's 57 and England's 54), the 6-1 odds bookmakers are offering on the West Indies to win the World Cup seem unusually over-generous.

For a host of reasons they are also realistic.

The days are long since past when they were as invincible in the abbreviated form of the game as they were in Tests. Under Clive Lloyd and with strength in every department they romped to the first two World Cups in 1975 and 1979 and only surrendered their title in the 1983 final through complacency.

That established a dominance that endured well into the following decade. In the World Series in Australia in 1984/85, they advanced to the finals by winning all 11 qualifying matches and defeat was a rarity.

They carried great players in every category. Desmond Haynes (17), his perennial partner, Gordon Greenidge and the irrepressible Viv Richards (11) are still the only batsmen to have completed more than 10 one-day international hundreds. There were no more feared nor meaner fast bowlers than the towering giant Joel Garner, the Rolls-Royce Michael Holding or the bustling Malcolm Marshall.

The West Indies knew they were better than the rest and they intimidated everyone. But it could not last for ever.

Richards, Greenidge, Marshall and the high-class wicket-keeper, Jeffrey Dujon, all left the international stage within a few months of each other in 1991 and, while a new batting sensation by the name of Brian Lara emerged from their shadows, it proved a vacuum impossible to plug properly.

Suddenly the powerhouses found they were losing matches and to opponents they used to take for granted. They, and their demanding public, found it difficult to come to terms with their shift in fortunes.

The Australian Mark Waugh has identified one consequence of the decline.

'For many years they had this aura about them when you didn't expect to win when you played them,' he said. 'Now when we play them it's level ground and we expect to beat them more often than not.'

Wes Hall, the great fast bowler of the 1960s who has been team manager for the past year, blames the deterioration on lack of planning for the specifics of the limited-overs game.

'We won those first two World Cups on sheer talent,' he observed. 'Since then, the other countries have lifted. They have poured money and ideas into the one-day game and studied it. You don't win on sheer talent anymore. Even the average English county cricketer is steeped in knowledge of the one-day game where we in the West Indies have not been exposed to that.'

Only in the past two seasons that the West Indies have organised a separate limited-overs tournament, for the Shell-Sandals Trophy, have they concentrated on preparing players for the instant game.

'I know we're now on the right road but it's going to take time,' Hall said.

There are other problems that afflict the West Indies as they attempt to defy the odds and regain the Cup. Internal divisions appeared in the ranks through the much publicised exit of the temperamental Lara on last summer's tour of England after a dressing room spat with the captain, Richie Richardson, an unassuming man without the imposing personality of his predecessors, Lloyd and Richards.

Lara's further withdrawal from the recent trip to Australia emphasised the problem and the West Indies were unrecognisable to crowds who had seen their cricketers conquer their continent from the days when the high-powered environment of Kerry Packer's World Series Cricket added discipline and self-belief to their skills.

Lara has been grudgingly returned to the squad by selectors who might otherwise have felt that discipline for his tantrums was in order. But he is so essential to batting that has been a recent embarrassment that it was unthinkable that he would not have been included as soon as he said he was ready.

If his mind is on it, the dapper Trinidadian left-hander has the sheer presence to inspire a revival in the coming month, whether the West Indies play their match against Sri Lanka or not.

His return has been counter-balanced by the recurrence of malaria that has forced the late withdrawal of Carl Hooper, an outstanding and experienced one-day cricketer. The chaos that has caused was evident when Cameron Cuffy, a fast bowler whose use of the bat is strictly as a prop at the non-striker's end, was picked to replace him.

The recent trip to Australia ended with failure to reach the finals of the World Series tournament and even more intense demands for Richardson's head from a disenchanted public.

But there were a few significant advances. The 21-year-old left-hander, Shivnarine Chanderpaul, hitherto regarded as a pusher and nudger unsuited to the urgent demands of the limited-overs game, has emerged as a quick-scoring batsman, the veteran Roger Harper is back to near his best as vital all-rounder and Glamorgan's Ottis

Gibson has made an impact as a strong lively fast bowler and devastating lower order hitter.

But even with those pluses and Lara's reinstatement no one in this part of the world disagrees with those pre-tournament odds. They know their cricket here.

Independent, 10 February 1996

Exhilaration of great adventure

Mark Nicholas

The influence of cricket on the Indian subcontinent and the joy it brings to so many people are not to be underestimated, nor are the frustrations and the funny side of travel and communication.

There are more than a billion people in India alone, and the game is their overriding passion. Though there are fewer in Pakistan and Sri Lanka, emotions are aroused with the same intensity.

I spent most of the competition in India, an extraordinary and intoxicating country with a special character and spirit, and enjoyed every minute of this unique cricketing adventure.

Friday, Feb 9

Bombay International Airport, 2am: The place is packed and chaotic – a vignette of India. Doesn't anyone sleep? The flight was painless, which is more than can be said for customs. As the officer goes through my gear he asks what I'm doing here. 'World Cup,' I say proudly. He looks up. 'Vills Vorld Cup?' (Wills are the sponsors). 'Absolutely.' He is thrilled. Immediately the luggage is zipped up and I'm escorted into the arrival hall as if I were the captain of England.

So who's the first person I bump into? Mike Gatting, would you believe. He has just landed from Heathrow and is with umpire David Shepherd, so it would have been a big bump, and they too are heading for Calcutta and the opening ceremony.

Pleased at seeing each other we sniff out a few beers and talk of England in South Africa, of Devon Malcolm and Mark Ramprakash, and of the gloomy future, until five in the morning.

Calcutta: Indian Airlines Flight 936 landed in the City of Joy at 8.10am. By 8.20 a couple of hundred taxi drivers had offered a ride into town. The journey through the smog-filled sprawl is unique: Essential India. Exhilaration and shock mix with the eternal sound of the motor-horn and the unforgettable smells of cow-dung and curry. The 1950 Ambassador Nova hustles past those colonial reminders, the Tollygunge Club and the Victoria Memorial, and leaves the vast expanse of the *maidan*, which is already sprinkled with cricket matches, on its left before swinging into the splendid Oberoi Hotel.

Saturday, Feb 10

Pilcom, the Pak-Ind-Lanka Organising Committee, are having a rough time of it. Australia and the West Indies are refusing to play in Sri Lanka because of last week's bomb in Colombo. There will be a press conference tomorrow after the ICC meet.

More chaos. A crane brought in to erect the floodlights in Bombay collapsed and made a considerable dent in the outfield. Only India can stick up lights a fortnight before the biggest match of the tournament comes to town.

Sunday Feb 11

The press conference was emotive and unpleasant. Neither Australia not the West Indies relent, so their points are forfeited and Sri Lanka lose two grand matches and a lot of money. The good name of 'Oz' is mud.

The evening's opening ceremony is the baby of Italian art director, Gianfranco Lunetta, whose charge is more than $2 million – so it had better be good . . .

It was a shambles. The actor Saeed Jaffrey presented the supposed extravaganza and couldn't even get the teams right: South Africa became the UAE, for example, and he asked the West Indians to wave at us, in order to prove they were Zimbabwe. The much-hyped laser show fell flat because a gentle breeze disrupted the giant transparent curtains on which it was screened. An audience of 110,000 at Eden Gardens were privy to a farce. Two million bucks, I ask you. Think what the Untouchables, living in utter squalor beneath the Howrah Bridge, could do with that.

Wednesday, Feb 14

Ahmedabad, Gujarat State: The teams and media travelling to the opening match left the hotel in Calcutta at 4.30 on Monday morning and arrived in Ahmedabad after nine at night, knackered. Nice preparation for a World Cup, said a washed-out Raymond Illingworth. Same for both sides, said Pilcom.

Neither England nor New Zealand look likely winners of the tournament, and if England are to make the semi-finals, which they ought, they'll have to hold the odd catch. Something got into them towards the end of the South Africa tour – don't know what as yet, but it's not good.

Friday, Feb 16

Hyderabad: Been around the houses a bit but made it to the home town of the biryani and of Mohammad Azharuddin. Actually, he's just left home, the wife, the kids, and moved in with an actress in Bombay, which as the one Muslim and captain in a team of Hindus is causing quite a stir.

Hyderabad is also the home of the Sports Coaching Foundation, which houses the only bowling machine in India. The academy has floodlights, dual-coloured sightscreens and Astroturf.

There are 12 coaches, psychologists and nutritional experts. Its purpose is to train boys aged 6-16 in the fundamentals of technique and approach. Just like we've got in England.

Had a drink last night with John Hampshire, who is coaching Zimbabwe. He said that Wes Hall had read a report which wrote off both their teams. 'So we jus' gonna have a nice friendly game among ourselves.' The West Indies win easily and don't look as if they should be written off to me.

Saturday, Feb 17

Colombo, Sri Lanka: Travelled with Michael Henderson of *The Times*, and we are quite excited about our visit to this supposedly bomb-torn city. The airport is pretty new, so it was 21st century in comparison to where we've been, and security was tight. No cars within half a mile of the terminals, which was comfortable, as there was space to breathe.

This morning the Sri Lankan team made a symbolic appearance at the Premadasa Stadium, where today's match against Australia was to have taken place. By the time we got there they had left and all was quiet. The empty concrete stands echoed with the silence.

Wednesday, Feb 21

After a good snoop around, we would have to say the odds against being blown up are long.

Zimbabwe arrived late yesterday, play today and fly out first thing in the morning. They will see nothing of this lovely island, the coconut plantations and the paddy fields, and not have time to meet any of its enthusiastic and friendly people.

Their lack of preparation was exposed by Sri Lanka, who burst out of the World Cup blocks with a convincing win. After the immediate loss of the hit-or-miss openers, Asanka Gurusinha belied his stodgy nature and smashed half-a-dozen sixes, which equalled the World Cup record held jointly by the more celebrated Vivian Richards and Kapil Dev, and Aravinda de Silva brought back memories of his thrilling hundred in the Benson & Hedges Cup Final last July.

If Sri Lanka can fit another bowler into their line-up, they will put some noses out of joint.

Friday, Feb 23

Have just arrived back from dinner with Arjuna Ranatunga and Dav Whatmore. They took me to Beach Wadiya – sand between your toes as you eat – for terrific seafood, and the owner, once the chef, now the drunk, proudly displayed his visitors' book. The page with the autographs of Princess Anne, Richard Branson and . . . Phil Tufnell particularly delighted him, though I'm not sure he saw the joke.

Ranatunga left early. He was getting up at 4am to drive six hours inland in order to receive an upmarket Buddhist blessing. He was taking half his side with him, so I was tempted to rush down to the bookie. The Sri Lankan captain reckons that one of the three subcontinent teams or South Africa will win the tournament. I reckon Australia, but he says no chance – 'neutral umpires at the World Cup'. Not a lot of love lost there.

Saturday, Feb 24

Bombay: It's taken most of the day and half the night but we've made it, to the Gateway of India and the city of films. More movies are made in Bombay than in Hollywood which, incidentally, is where any comparison ends as the long drive from the airport is a salutary reminder of India's pavement poverty.

Naked heads in their thousands lie sleeping by the edge, and I mean the edge, of the main drag into town, inhaling God knows what and risking decapitation. We check in at the Taj Mahal Hotel, a world away from what's outside, and thank our lucky stars.

Tuesday, Feb 27

At last, a game to set the pulse racing. The revamped Wankhede Stadium sparkled under the new floodlights – they've got 'em up in time and fixed that hole in the ground – and the cricket sparkled with them. Australia, playing superbly, beat India by 16 runs.

Mark Waugh scored a dreamy hundred, his second in five days, and then surprised us all with crafty off-breaks and the wicket of Sachin Tendulkar.

I cannot recall a batsman since Barry Richards and Graeme Pollock who made my heart thump the way Tendulkar does, or, for that matter, a bowler so wonderful to watch as Shane Warne. Their duel, morally won by the leg-spinner, was sublime.

Wednesday, Feb 28

Walked in on an earnest discussion between Peter Roebuck and Ian Chappell this morning. What-on-earth's-wrong-with-the-West-Indies? was the topic, though it soon switched to England. Chappell laid in, as everyone is doing, and added that Mark Waugh was laughed out of the Aussies' drinking session last night when he laid a hundred bucks that the Poms would beat Sri Lanka in the quarter-final.

It's midnight now, and I'm just back from the cinema where 007 was at his indestructible best. The theatre was pretty run down and some of the ads were classics of their type but otherwise it was much like any old Odeon.

Thursday, Feb 29

Shock, horror. Kenya have beaten the West Indies. Easily. I hope this means they don't do something sensible like put Malcolm Marshall in power. We've just secured him to coach at Hampshire.

South Africa withstood Pakistan and won Group A, and I have just withstood a flight to Nagpur with Chappell and Tony Greig, whose potent views on English cricket are no secret. I'm a bit nervous as I've got my first commentary gig with the heavies tomorrow – these two and Richie Benaud – though not half as nervous, I'll wager, as the bloke I sat next to on the plane. Six foot four, goatee beard and ponytail, plucked out of his first year in the Sheffield Shield: Jason Gillespie, 20, Australia's replacement for the injured Craig McDermott. I didn't know him from Adam and nor do any of his team. Imagine England selecting a kid with a ponytail that no one had met to play in the World Cup.

Saturday, March 2

The plane journey: We left promptly, soon after 10am on an Ilyushin 76, a private charter that is ferrying the entire television operation around the subcontinent.

The plane comes from Ukraine and is flown by an unusual assortment of Russians who operate under some unusual rules. No photographs for a start, not before we land anyway, and no need for seat belts. You guessed it, there aren't any seats.

It's a big aircraft, fat like an Airbus. It has an odd curve to the rear end where the 9½ tonnes of telecast equipment is loaded. It has a cockpit for the pilot and two more for the gunmen. Inside is a dark, empty shell of dirty metal, exposed wires and rolls of cable, melting rubber tyres, vast static generators, ladders, computer kit galore, and about 30 of us, privately nervous, publicly confident, done with Nagpur, where Australia made mincemeat of Zimbabwe, and *en route* to Jaipur. One can't help thinking that the previous cargo might have been Kalashnikovs and the last flight path Afghanistan.

We are Unit B, one of four production units, two in Pakistan and two in India, assembled by Grand Slam Sports to televise to more than 600 million viewers worldwide.

We are a motley bunch from Channel Nine in Australia, SABC in South Africa, TVNZ in New Zealand, Sky and just about anyone else who fancied the work. We sit quietly, or sleep, on the benches that line the shell and on the stacked metal boxes, swatting at the mosquitoes.

Benaud is with us and so is Chappell but Greig has gone ahead to Delhi to sing the glory of his beloved Sri Lankans, who have pulled one out of the hat, cruising past India's big score with a display of electric batting. England must beware the names Kaluwitharana and Jayasuriya in their quarter-final.

The Russians came to check the strapping on the boxes, which seemed to signal our landing, and confirmed as much when explaining in broken phrases that the runway was short so we should hold on to our hats.

The Ilyushin hit the tarmac with shattering force and within a split second the jets were in deafening reverse thrust. This caused the tonnes of TV cargo to slide more than a metre and Unit B to roll their eyes and swallow hard. We had no idea exactly how short the runway was, but got a good idea from the sound then the smell of the aircraft tyres. We stopped sharply but in surprising control.

There were weak smiles all round. We climbed down to terra firma, damp from sweat and getting damper still from the drizzle. We had made it by 50 feet.

Daily Telegraph, 20 March 1996

First among equals

Peter Roebuck

Beneath the high, brilliant lights of Gwalior, under the ancient gaze of its astonishing fort and amid swarming scenes – but a part of cricket on the subcontinent – a battle had begun that seemed destined to play a fascinating part in this World Cup; a battle certain to be important in the decade to follow.

Lara against Tendulkar; a prospect to savour. A struggle between friends, between a genius and a master, a lonely child with a dazzling smile and a professor's son with an impish look, a man with a relish for life and another with a hunger for the game, a player with his head in the clouds, another with his feet on the ground. Both are millionaires, but Lara has been turned into a commercial product while Tendulkar has kept cricket foremost.

Lara is the most remarkable batsman to appear in decades because he can hit any ball to the boundary without apparent risk, and keep doing it, hour upon hour, day upon day. At the crease, the man within replaces the child without. But his game is all about attack, and there is a fragility about him absent in his contemporary from Bombay.

Tendulkar will, it may be forecast, last longer. Whereas Lara seems to summon his supreme powers in surges before retreating to his tent, exhausted, Tendulkar plays within himself. He has a technique that allows him to protect his wicket in hard times, but lets him strike as opportunity arises. Lara angles his strokes, plays shots square of the wicket with a flourish; Tendulkar moves into line and drives straight on murderously off his pads.

Tendulkar is the more settled character. It was his good fortune to appear with Indian cricket on the rise, but he has been part of it, helping his captain, fielding close to the bat, bowling if required and generally throwing himself into the thick of things. It has been Lara's misfortune to appear with the West Indies in decline and he has been unable to resist it, holding himself back, not seeming to enjoy touring or life as a cricketer.

Lara's contribution to the West Indies' pathetic and arrogant performance against Kenya was sorrowful. He was as bad as everyone else. Moreover, he is sensitive to criticism, the proverbial prima donna. Tendulkar is made of sterner stuff. The Indian was triumphant in Gwalior and so were his team. Lara was given out, caught behind; Tendulkar was dropped twice before taking his team near to victory.

Not for years, though, will the relative merits of these two extraordinary batsmen be decided, for longevity has its place. Indeed, no sportsman can join the ranks of the immortals by ignoring it. It is not a matter of doing it easily, it is a question of doing it regularly. And these last few days have told a tale; Tendulkar fighting on, trying to raise his team, Lara slowly subsiding, the man with greatness in his game but not in his head.

Tendulkar, resisting the challenge of the superb West Indian, was, however, beaten a few days later by a batsman late in maturing, in an epic struggle played out, this time, under the lights of Bombay. Such an innings did Mark Waugh summon that he scored 126 in 42 overs, losing his wicket only in the wildness and weariness of the closing overs. And he batted with ease and serenity, in such command of himself and the bowling that it seemed he could do it all again tomorrow. Tendulkar replied with a breathtaking innings, 90 in 36 overs, but he had to reach towards the very edges of his gift to match the Australian. And the last word went with Waugh, who out-foxed the Indian with an off-break that drifted wide as the batsman advanced.

Waugh is a changed man. A year ago he might have played such an innings, but it would not have been expected. On the surface he is the same, smiling sheepishly, doing it on his ear if he can, like a boy riding a bicycle and calling: 'look, no hands.' Now, though, there is a voice telling him: 'Take care – there are some rotten drivers around, and potholes, too.'

Occasionally, still, Waugh does something daft, as if to remind us that a fellow is only human, after all. But there is a weight of thought and stroke in his cricket now, a combination missing in the patchy erudition of his early years. Inevitably, a search begins for the moment that caused this change but it is seldom as simple as that. Lots of factors combine. Waugh's hundred and the decisive partnership with his brother in the final Test in Jamaica last April certainly helped, bringing the surges of confidence and self-respect upon which every performer depends. Taylor's leadership has played a part, too, giving Waugh a seniority and a status within a team committed to adventure.

But something deeper lies behind the hardening in Waugh's mind. During the shenanigans about 'fixed' matches in Pakistan, he realised that the world was not such a nice place. His brow furrowed, and this is not a man of frowns. His mind concentrated, too. Hitherto, Waugh had led an uncluttered life. Now he began to demand more, to impose himself on games, to take command of himself.

It came as no surprise to see Waugh batting so well in the early matches of this World Cup. It is easier for him, of course, because he has a lighter weight on his shoulders. Lara's genius might rise again once he is captain. Tendulkar is already magnificent but his present ambitions may be thwarted by the limitations of his team. For the time being, the world sits at the feet of the late-blossoming Australian.

The Times, 3 March 1996

A long way from stick and corn cob

Derek Pringle

A little less than a year ago, the cricket world looked and blinked, unsure of what it had seen, as the West Indies lost their first Test series for many years, to a deserving Australia. Yesterday, cricketers everywhere would have gawped in utter disbelief, as Kenya thrashed the West Indies by 73 runs. It was as decisive a victory as anything achieved by their brilliant and better known distance runners.

Australia's captain, Mark Taylor, had already warned that Kenya could be the ones to cause an upset but even he could not have had the West Indies in mind. In fact, Kenya outplayed them, grittily using up their overs when all looked lost at 81 for 6, showing a tenacity the West Indies now lack.

It was not pretty, but then you never go out to fight wearing your best trousers. When it comes to passing the Norman Tebbit Test, I fail every time where Kenya are involved and my only disappointment is that I was not there to witness what has been undoubtedly their greatest moment in cricket so far.

That wish has nothing to do with revelling in West Indian woe, and everything to do with celebrating Kenyan joy. It is a country I hold very dear, being the place of my birth and upbringing – a place where, among other things, my father captained the national team, and I learned to play cricket.

The game has long been popular, having long been played by colonial expats and Asians, almost exclusively on jute or coir matting, stretched over a firm murram (compacted gravel) base – though most club pitches in the capital, Nairobi, are now turf.

Indeed, the annual Europeans v Asians matches were the equivalent of 'Test' matches, and regularly attracted large crowds. There were touring sides too. Sides like the Commonwealth Cavaliers, captained by the likes of Ted Dexter, who in 1963 presented my father Donald with his England touring cap after he skittled Lord Ted with an inswinger first ball.

Black Africans did not really play, even at school, although the few that did usually came from Uganda. But then that is the truly amazing aspect of Kenya's victory. Unlike Zimbabwe – who have achieved full ICC status – Kenya have a team who not only have a black majority, but whose best players are indigenous Africans, most of them from the Luo tribe around the shores of Lake Victoria, where cricket has not been played since Kenya's independence over 30 years ago. Today, only Nairobi and Mombasa have cricket leagues.

But where have these brilliant black players like Maurice Odumbe, Steve Tikolo, Martin Suji and Kennedy Otieno, come from? Certainly there were none playing when I left Kenya to live in England back in 1977, and the story of their emergence is almost as fantastic as yesterday's victory.

According to Harilal Shah, who captained East Africa in the 1975 World Cup, and who is now the team manager, the story began during net sessions at Nairobi's Sir Ali Sports Club, where the young Odumbes and Tikolos would watch the club players practice, setting up their own impromptu game afterwards, using a stick for a bat and a dried corn cob as a ball.

Their obvious enthusiasm and skill eventually saw them invited to join in, snowballing their development until word eventually got around and clubs began to invite them to turn out for matches.

Word also got round the extended family – to which nearly all the current African players belong – that this static game with its expensive equipment was really quite fun.

There are of course other strands that led to yesterday's stunning victory. For a start, Kenya have beaten both England A and India A in the last five years. They have played here as if expecting to win, not in the slightest bit overawed by their opponents.

Credit must also go to the efforts of Jasmer and Hanumant Singh, tireless administrator and coach respectively, the latter arranging for England's bowling coach Peter Lever to stop off on his way back from coaching Devon Malcolm and Co in South Africa last November. It is easy to see who were more receptive to his ideas.

People have always gone to Kenya to see its wildlife and its runners. Soon they will be going to watch its cricket team play Test matches.

Independent, 1 March 1996

Indian hopes hampered by sense of anti-climax

Christopher Martin-Jenkins

It is soupy, hot in Calcutta; a good enough reason for today's first semi-final of the World Cup to be a day-night match, starting when the sun has passed its zenith. Year after year, they say, the weather starts to get seriously hot in India after *Holi*, the festival of colour, which took place on March 5, in accordance with the appropriate phase of the moon. Who knows what the stars foretell of the match between India and Sri Lanka. It is likely to be close enough, certainly, for chance to decide it.

It was not quite so hot when England were here on their last tour, late in 1992, nor is the pollution quite so obvious in the thick air, except when you risk the walk across the maidan from the ground, weaving through the on-rush of ancient, exhaust-belching Ambassador cars and the stomach-turning open sewers to the sanctuary of the Oberoi Grand. There it is all colonial splendour, air conditioned-cool and thick carpets which muffle the constant din and shut out the desperate race for existence beyond.

In Bangalore, on Saturday, even the beggars were smiling after India's victory over Pakistan, their hands filled with sweets if not with rupees as joyous spectators spilled out of the ground.

For cricket followers at least, that was the most important match in the World Cup and the hunger to win the trophy itself is no longer so intense. Perhaps when it comes to motivation, therefore, the Sri Lankans will have the edge. They have played so well so far that they have no reason to fear any opposition.

They beat India in the qualifying round and, in the space of eight days in Australia in January, they defeated the West Indies once and Australia twice. They have been winning both ways, too; batting first, or chasing.

As Arjuna Ranatunga said last night, before his team and the Indians practised 50 yards apart in nets impeccably presented beneath the Eden Gardens lights on a lush outfield, it may not matter if either Jayasuriya or Kaluwitharana should fail to pulverise the bowling again in the first 15 overs. 'We have seven experienced batsmen all capable of playing an attacking innings.'

Indeed, six of them have already played more than 100 internationals each. They may not be quite so confident against India if they bat first, rather than having a target in their sights as they did when comfortably overhauling England's 235 and India's 272.

There is little reason why, however, they should not be equally explosive in the first 15 overs as they were against England and Kenya, especially since India have conceded 120 runs in these overs in their last two matches. It will be no surprise if India try to prevent a similar damaging leakage of runs by giving Anil Kumble the new ball.

The pitch, bare and dry, looks little different from the usual Eden Gardens strip, despite the fact that it was recently dug up and relaid. A slow turner is almost guaranteed and spinners like Muralitheran and Raju may achieve sufficient turn for the recent run of very high scores in the tournament to be cut back to something nearer 250.

The doubt about Navjot Singh Sidhu's fitness, the fact that Mohammad Azharuddin is still having to plead with sections of the Indian press to stop writing about his private life – he has recently divorced after an affair with a model – and the feeling that India may have seen the Pakistan match as their real World Cup final, all suggest that Sri Lanka might win today.

It is the only match in this tournament to be staged at the scene of the 1987 final and 110,000 are expected to cram in somehow, some of them with the cameras, binoculars, thunder-crackers and tiffin boxes which are all supposed to be banned. Most can only dream of tickets in a city where even the No. 2 in the British High Commission finds that the six tickets he was promised have suddenly disappeared.

I was also asked for guidance yesterday by a man from Rochdale who has been in correspondence for six months with the Bengal Cricket Association for a ticket, in vain. He had just been offered one elsewhere for 3,000 rupees (£60). That is 10 times the face value but I advised him to take it while the chance was there.

Daily Telegraph, 13 March 1996

India and Pakistan revel in the recriminations

Henry Blofeld

In the space of five days first Pakistan's and then India's hopes of winning the World Cup have been shattered. Even though Sri Lanka have deservedly reached the final in which they play Australia here tomorrow, the subcontinent is in turmoil after the crowd scenes which caused the abandonment of the semi-final in Calcutta.

Although the transformed Gadaffi Stadium has been sold out, the last match of what will surely be seen as the least satisfactory of the six World Cups so far cannot now hope to fulfil local expectations.

After three days of extraordinary violent reaction to the defeat by

India, Pakistan were presented with gift-wrapped redemption when India were outplayed by Sri Lanka in a match which was ended by rioting crowds.

Pakistan's homecoming after the Bangalore defeat was all too predictable. The national anger and indignation were intense and the players first need was for a police guard. The perceived chief culprit was the captain, Wasim Akram, whose injured back had, at the last moment, prevented him from taking part.

The general feeling is that even if he was only 70 per cent fit he should, due to the special circumstances of this match, have played. According to reports, Wasim's house in Lahore has been stoned and effigies of him have been burned in the streets. In the search for scapegoats no player has been left out.

Another by-product of Pakistan's defeat was that the following day an indirect approach was made to the Pakistan Cricket Board to move the final from Lahore to Calcutta. It is said that the Cricket Association of Bengal made an offer of $6m.

Eden Gardens holds 110,000. The Gadaffi Stadium's capacity is only 28,500. The Bengalis sensed the chance to make an extra financial killing in a tournament which seems to have been thought up by people who, in the words of Oscar Wilde, 'know the price of everything and the value of nothing'.

Then came India's defeat in Calcutta. By the following morning Pakistan had reclaimed the moral high ground and is still busy rejoicing in India's sad lack of sportsmanship, not to say moral decline. Tomorrow the public will probably be saying 'come back Wasim, all is forgiven'.

It is against this furiously changing emotional backdrop that last minute preparations for the final are going on at the Gadaffi Stadium so named by the late Zulfigar Ali Bhutto, Benazir's father, at the time of a state visit by the Libyan president more than 20 years ago. Everything will be in place by the time the first ball is bowled and in Pakistan the administration of this competition has been excellent.

With a capacity of only 28,500 all too few tickets remain available for the public after the respective Boards of Control, the Government, the sponsors and all 12 participants have had their whack.

On Wednesday, I visited the ticket office and the demand, even after Pakistan's defeat, was unending. They varied from an individual's request for 10,000 to a nineteen-year-old girl from Cape Town who had come to Pakistan ticketless and on her own. She was given a seat in a VIP box.

In the final the Pakistanis should support the Sri Lankans who are playing a side which refused to visit their island for a qualifying match. But in this fiercely parochial part of the world their main feeling is more likely to be one of profound relief that they will not have to watch India lift the Cup from under their noses. Just possibly they will stay at home and watch television.

Independent, 16 March 1996

Sri Lanka complete fairy-tale success

Alan Lee

Out of a World Cup contaminated by suspicion and ill-will has come a result to make the spirit soar. Sri Lanka, who have reacted to every adversity with the style and smiles of pre-paranoia West Indies teams, yesterday crowned their improbable jaunt through the competition by overwhelming the most accomplished cricket side in the world, and the one they had the most personal of motives for beating.

It was a romantic triumph for a team of part-timers, most of whom are expected back at their day jobs tomorrow, and it was acclaimed by a crowd that took them to their hearts. Sri Lanka, who have won every match without being extended, are a team in every sense.

This game belonged to Aravinda de Silva. With 107 runs, three wickets and two catches, de Silva had the kind of day that belongs to dreams and dog-eared schoolboy novels, but very seldom to reality.

His wickets were a valuable bonus. His runs won the match, and reclassified his standing among the leading players of the world. Nobody had ever doubted his shot-making skills, but now he showed the capacity for batting through an innings with selectivity and without compromising his flair. Glasses will have been raised to him as far afield as Colombo and Canterbury, where, last summer, he was as popular an overseas player as England has known.

Australia must have felt that they had done the hard part by overturning a lost cause in their semi-final. Yet here, against a side entirely new to such a heady occasion, they were allowed no such indulgences. Where West Indies panicked unworthily, Sri Lanka proceeded with composure, reaching their target of 242 with 22 balls to spare.

Australia were comprehensively humbled, as has rarely been their fate in recent years. As the cup, for which they had long been favourites, slipped from them, strange things occurred. Three catches were dropped, and Shane Warne finished with none for 58. If Sri Lanka had pre-planned the purging of raw memories from their Antipodean tour, they could not have done it better.

Cup final day began with uncertainty. The weather had turned hostile, a spectacular overnight thunderstorm putting the start in doubt, and nobody could be sure that the residue of acrimony would not resurface. If the first fear was overcome by a morning of mopping up, the second was revived when the Australians walked away from the pre-match ceremony before the playing of the Sri Lankan national anthem. Apparently, they had mistaken the Pakistani anthem for that of their opponents, but it was an untimely gaffe.

The ground was far from full when play began, and by the time it had reached its 28,000 capacity, Australia were squandering a position of power. Midway through their innings, at 134 for one, they were on course for 300, but in the next ten overs they lost four wickets for 36.

This early cricket was a duel between the captains. One is known as 'Tubby', whereas the other really is. Mark Taylor, he of the nickname, batted with massive conviction for his 74 from 83 balls, but the control he had assumed, after the swift loss of Mark Waugh to a casual shot, was reclaimed, with breathtaking unorthodoxy, by Arjuna Ranatunga.

Thirteen overs from his new-ball pair had cost 68 runs, and so, with no regard for the accepted priorities of the one-day game, Ranatunga dispensed with seam and devoted the remaining 37 overs to spin. He shuffled his four slow bowlers with dexterity, never allowing the Australians to settle, and while the most impressive of them was Muralitharan, the most surprising success belonged to de Silva.

Bowling off spin is very much an occasional pastime for de Silva, but he had Taylor caught at deep square leg in his second over, and bowled Ponting through an ambitious cut in his fourth. There was no stopping him now. He took catches at long-on and gully to dismiss Steve Waugh and Law before Ranatunga gave him back the ball, and he obliged with a third wicket, as Healy played a head-in-the-air thrash indicative of a team losing faith.

By now, the nerves that had undermined Sri Lanka's fielding had given way to a joyful atmosphere in which nothing seemed beyond them. Bevan at least ensured that Australia batted out their overs, but, on a blameless pitch, 241 was 50 below par.

Sri Lanka did not flap when they again lost both openers cheaply. De Silva simply took control, first with Gurusinha and then, fittingly, with Ranatunga. The partnerships were worth 125 and 97, and while Australia may plead that they lost the toss and had to bowl with a wet ball as dew mingled with evening drizzle, it would do them no justice, for they would have batted first anyway.

It is part of Ranatunga's job to take players into remote parts of Sri Lanka to coach and play against the locals. He sees it as missionary work for the game. After this triumph, he need not work so hard to spread the word. Even England, whose attitude to Sri Lanka has been arrogantly lofty, must now recognise a serious new power.

The Times, 18 March 1996

County Crusades

Introduction

Even the longest memories were hard put to recall a season during which the County Championship had been in serious contention by so many for so long.

Towards the end of August six counties, Derbyshire, Leicestershire, Surrey, Essex, Kent and Yorkshire still had realistic chances of flying the pennant. At the beginning of September, Yorkshire's hopes receded into the realms of mathematical possibility and by the end of the penultimate lap Derbyshire and Essex had also been outpaced. But finally on the last-but-one afternoon of the season Leicestershire were in a position that could not be overtaken. The county of the running fox were a compact unit – only thirteen players used throughout – and, according to their captain James Whitaker, had won with collective leadership.

In the Benson and Hedges and NatWest competitions Lancashire, fielding a side largely composed of internationals, were unassailable. And in the Axa Equity and Law 40-over fling, Surrey deservedly had a trophy to hold after years of waiting in the wings.

Stewart puts Surrey in driving seat

Ivo Tennant

There is a common belief among self-confident sportsmen of all denominations that once their team has won one trophy, a second and third will swiftly follow. Surrey have achieved all too little in Alex Stewart's years at the Oval, yet even after another fractious winter he continues to hold that viewpoint.

It seemed yesterday that this was not empty talk. Surrey beat – overwhelmed – Hampshire in a way that suggested Dave Gilbert's emphasis on unifying the team is already having an effect. No longer do the capped players change in a different section of the dressing-room to the juniors. No longer, if the new coach has his way, will the Oval be a repository for doleful individuals.

Given that this was Surrey's first match of the season, Gilbert naturally looked to his captain to show some character. Stewart, an unabashed admirer of his kind of coaching methods in Australia, not only made 160 off 151 balls, but also gave his county such a rapid start that they made their highest total in the Benson and Hedges Cup, 333 for six – this in spite of the number of overs per innings having being reduced in line with World Cup regulations from 55 to 50.

The pitch accorded to the customary standards at the Oval and the Hampshire attack only affirmed Australian views about some of the bowling to be seen in county cricket. Yet this was a terrific way to start a season. Just as Michael Atherton professes to feel refreshed, so Stewart is as content as he can expect to be at such an early stage.

Surrey were put in by Stephenson, a bold move considering the conditions and the attack he commanded. There was no Udal (injured) or James (omitted), nor, alas, Liam Botham, who was made twelfth man. Later in the day, when Hampshire batted, one kept expecting Nicholas to walk down the pavilion steps. This is a changed club, and it will do well to prosper this season.

By the fifth over, Ward and Brown had put on 40. After 15 overs, the benchmark now in this competition, Surrey were 118 for one. Benjamin, Hampshire's best bowler, was proving as expensive as others lesser known. Milburn, who at least has an auspicious cricketing surname, was given the new ball ahead of the experienced Connor and struck all around the ground. Poor Thursfield had to bowl all his ten overs: there was no one else. Only Whitaker, who conceded only 33 runs and took two wickets, restricted Stewart and the middle order.

Stewart struck the ball more or less where he pleased, including one amazing six high over the extra cover boundary off the back foot, a great carry on this ground. There were three further sixes, 18 fours and a considerable number of other runs collected through his self-belief. He and Butcher, who hit 42 off 46 balls, enabled Surrey to beat their previous highest total, also against Hampshire, 331 for five, made on this ground six years ago.

Hampshire never looked likely to win. Smith also made a century, 123 off 114 balls, which would suggest that he was in as dominating form as Stewart. The difference was that his innings did not carry the same hopes. Three middle-order batsmen went for ducks, one of them to a neat catch by Stewart behind the wicket, and that was that so far as a contest was concerned. The margin of victory, 59 runs, rather flattered Hampshire.

That is not to say that Smith did not time his shots uncommonly well, opting to cut before the end of April, let alone May, and driving with characteristic strength off the front foot. He struck 19 fours and a six in his innings, which will have been noted by selectors and anyone concerned for his form in this his benefit year. Stewart rightly took the gold award and some succour for Surrey's future.

The Times, 29 April 1996

Patel takes his turn as Lancs lose their way

Christopher Martin-Jenkins

Denigrators of County Championship cricket should have been at Canterbury. This was a constantly absorbing day's play, sternly but honourably fought and keeping everyone guessing until shortly after tea when Min Patel, Kent's eventual match-winner, bowled Mike Atherton, who had looked likely to be Lancashire's for much of the day.

Atherton will no doubt reproach himself for his rather desperate attempt to regain a rapidly slipping initiative by aiming, two short of 100, to swing Patel to the big gap at deep mid-wicket. Lancashire, chasing 340 from a minimum of 96 overs, will certainly reproach themselves as a team for collapsing from 190 for two, with Atherton firmly entrenched and Neil Fairbrother in brilliant form.

Certainly there were some rash strokes against Patel's teasing flight as he bowled with Underwood-like accuracy from over the wicket. The fact is that Kent persevered diligently, that Martin McCague came back with great fire and spirit from the embarrassment of a poor second spell, and that the victory was genuinely earned.

Kent won by 64 runs, Patel finishing with an unchanged spell of 15 overs and two balls in which he took five for 28. In four games against Lancashire he has now taken 31 wickets, including eight for 96 here two seasons ago.

It was Kent's first win in the championship since McCague and Dean Headley bowled out Durham for 85 at Chester-le-Street last

June. If that rout owed much to the pitch, this one did not, but the wicket did have sufficient life to encourage McCague to bend his back and there was a little bounce, as well as gentle turn, for Patel's left-arm orthodox.

The absence of Dean Headley and Mark Ealham had threatened to give a thin look to the Kent attack. That proved not to be so, given the contrasting virtues of McCague and Patel, the ability of Julian Thompson to bowl a genuine outswinger, Tim Wren's willingness and the jack-in-the-box quality of Matthew Fleming. Indeed they bowled out a side with 10 batsmen who have made first-class hundreds despite calling on Carl Hooper for only one over.

One of the Lancastrians, of course, *should* have made another first-class hundred. At lunch, when Lancashire were 136, they were well placed and just before tea they were still favourites, at 223 for four. So well had Fairbrother played, however, that Atherton had remained in third gear and he could not take control when things started to go wrong.

Atherton and Jason Gallian had played with little bother through the first half-hour, but Thompson then produced an outswinger of the right length to find Gallian's outside edge.

John Crawley patiently laid a base for half an hour, played one impeccable off-drive, then received a pearler from Fleming which left him off a perfect length. Had Crawley been forward, not back, he might have got something on it, but although he needs some luck and runs, Lancashire were now put firmly on the right road.

Atherton drove on either side, but especially through extra, with discernment and perfect distribution of his weight. Fairbrother, meanwhile, was at his engaging best. If only he could play like this every time. He hit hard, with the full face of a bat which looked broader than is allowed, to all parts of the slope but especially in the safe area between mid-off and mid-on.

The match turned in the 48th over when McCague, working up a full head of steam, had him caught at slip off the wicketkeeper's gloves with a ball that lifted from a length. He quickly followed this by having Nick Speak caught at short leg.

Mike Watkinson, willingly compliant in Steve Marsh's declaration, was bowled off an inside edge, Warren Hegg and Ian Austin failed to look before they leapt and when Atherton was eighth out, only the shouting remained.

Daily Telegraph, 7 May 1996

Kent are back on title trail

Paul Newman

When Kent began their defence of the Sunday League with two defeats from their opening two games, another tilt at the title appeared unlikely. Now things have changed.

Kent's second score of 300 plus in consecutive weeks gave them their fifth win on the trot and took them above Middlesex, their crushed opponents, into second place. Kentish confidence, further boosted by a sharp up-turn in championship fortunes, could not be higher.

None more so than Mark Ealham. Last year he hit a Sunday century off 44 balls and now he was in similar mood, striking 89 off 51 balls with such effortless aggression that for Middlesex, unbeaten before yesterday, there was no way back.

The biggest of Ealham's four sixes summed up Middlesex's day. It sailed over midwicket, almost clearing the Canterbury lime tree, and left Angus Fraser, the aggrieved bowler, standing hands on hips.

Ealham, dropped by Paul Weekes on 17, was not the only Kent hitter to excel. Trevor Ward got the innings off to a rattling start, five sixes featuring in his 65, while Graham Cowdrey joined in the fun with 68 from 49 balls.

So limp was the Middlesex reply, Keith Brown apart, that the biggest cheer came when a streaker, imitating the athletes at

Birmingham, completed a lap of the ground in impressive time. Linford Christie, however, he was not.

Daily Telegraph, 17 June 1996

Yorkshire's faux pas lets in title rivals

Peter Deeley

They call themselves the Old Farts and it is their hard work and dedication that keeps Yorkshire first-class cricket ticking over in one of Bradford's deprived inner city suburbs.

The Friends of Park Avenue (FOPA for short and sometimes unkindly referred to as Faux Pas) bring to mind the characters from *Last of the Summer Wine*. Yet without their efforts Yorkshire would not be taking on Leicester here this weekend.

On the days and evenings before the game started, septuagenarians like Bruce Moss and Bill Boag were weeding the car park, sweeping up the litter and individually wiping down every seat on the ground. On match days the mainly-retired army of solicitors, surveyors, architects and businessmen run the gates and hand out scorecards.

Moss is a millionaire who owns a string of dispensing chemists and could be sunning himself in the Channel Islands.

But this is Yorkshire's annual pilgrimage to Park Avenue and FOPA guarantee the club a 10,000 crowd every time they play here. The Friends bridle at criticism of the ground and references to faded glories. 'It may not be perfect now but you should have seen the state of dereliction when we took over,' said Moss.

Leicestershire, showing the highest level of commitment in this game, would doff their caps out of mutual respect for the work put in by the FOPA. I am not so sure that Yorkshire enjoy being here, their performance suggesting ambitions of their first championship title since 1968 are misplaced.

Yorkshire came into the match top of the table but Leicestershire have looked much more like title aspirants. Skipton-born James Whitaker says he always enjoys playing against his home county and how he has rubbed their noses in the dust.

Like some FOPA he only got about two hours' sleep the night before the game, then won the toss and scored a career-best 218 to go with Vince Wells's 200.

Some Yorkshire bowlers showed little inclination to give their all on a pitch which they believed was too friendly to the bat but workhorse Gordon Parsons demonstrated the fallacy of that view with four hard-earned wickets.

When Yorkshire began yesterday still needing all of 531 to save the follow on, Parsons got early lift to remove both Craig White and Richard Blakey to scooped-up edges at gully. But Michael Bevan sailed on serenely above the common herd, hammering Phil Simmons for four successive boundaries. Eventually, he went to David Millns, edging again to gully, when he was 49 runs short of being the first batsman to the thousand this summer. Unbeaten second time round he was still four shy.

Darren Gough bravely hit Parsons back over his head for six and also collected eight fours in his 50. Then Leicestershire caught Yorkshire's chance-dropping disease – letting three go – as Richard Stemp and Chris Silverwood put on 79 for the last wicket.

Even so they still had a mountain to climb when they followed on in mid-afternoon and with Millns claiming wickets in successive overs were in deep trouble at 160 for five, still 179 in arrears.

Sunday Telegraph, 23 June 1996

Minor days a major appeal of the game

Henry Blofeld

Thirty-one years ago, in 1965, Norfolk went to Southampton at the start of May to play Hampshire in the first round of the Gillette Cup, the original limited-over competition which began in 1963. Today they retrace their steps in the first round of this year's NatWest trophy.

In that first encounter I was lucky enough to be chosen to open the batting for a Norfolk side captained by none other than W J (Bill) Edrich of Compton and Edrich fame. When WJ retired from Middlesex, he returned to the county he had started with before the war and captained us until well into his fifties.

In those far off days, a game against a first-class county was awarded to the top five in the previous year's minor County Championship. Nowadays most minor counties get their chance and their instant demise is an all too familiar occurrence. In 1965, it was new and breathtakingly exciting for the lucky few.

There we were, a group of part-timers, heading for a glimpse of the big-time. Our captain, whose optimism usually defied all – or most – known logic, was convinced that we could win. I am not sure that he did not convince us, too.

We were more than just a motley crew. Terry Allcock, who kept wicket, also played at wing-half for Norwich City when the Third Division South side reached the semi-final of the 1959 FA Cup and lost to Luton in a replay.

David Pilch, who used to bat and bowl the seam with equal distinction, was a direct descendant of Fuller Pilch of Norfolk and Kent in the 1840s. Claude Rutter, our other opening batsman, was a parson and the most formidable operator in the pulpit.

It would be stretching the truth to say that the County Ground at Southampton was full. The toss was conducted in some style by W J and Colin Ingleby-Mackenzie, now the president-elect of MCC, while we shivered in our boots at the prospect of Roy Marshall's flashing blade – he toured with the West Indies in 1950 – and Derek Shackleton, whose subtle medium pace offerings had been so successful against the West Indies in 1963, to say nothing of the tearaway pace of Butch White.

Hampshire won the toss and batted and W J assured us it was the best possible toss to lose. We took up our positions in the field; I found myself at backward short leg to Roy Marshall, and whenever our opening bowlers pitched short, which was not infrequently, the ball hummed over my head like a wasp in mid-season form.

We did our best and none of the Hampshire batsmen were greedy; they all got some and a few rather more than that. Even so, 295 for 7 in 60 overs did not daunt our gallant captain in the least. 'We can win this,' he assured us. And Ian Mercer and I set forth to do battle with 'Shack' and Butch White and Bob Cottam, another who was to have his chance with England.

It was Mercer and not Rutter who came in with me, because the gallant vicar had met with an accident in the field which must be unique in cricket. A tall man in rimless glasses, he was fielding in the covers and came striding in to try and prevent a quick single. At the critical moment he slipped and fell, hitting the ground and somehow managing to dislocate his jaw, which for a while made him a spent force in the pulpit.

When rain stopped play after tea 'Manny' Mercer and I had put on 50 in 17 overs and as far as W J was concerned the match was as good as won. As I came off I even got a 'well played' from Len Hutton, the man of the match adjudicator. It was heady stuff. Cricket on Sundays was strictly taboo in those days and so we all trooped off to the New Forest and took part in a Sunday benefit match for, I think, Butch White. Having a rest day at 50 for no wicket, even though we were chasing 296, made us all feel about eight feet tall and here we were in the New Forest on first-name terms with chaps who had played Test cricket.

Sad to say, reality soon took over on the Monday. Manny and I returned to the crease with our confidence now a trifle suspect. We took our opening stand, much too slowly, to 87 when Ingleby-Mackenzie played the trump card. He brought in the left-arm spinner Peter Sainsbury.

It is no compliment to Peter to say that we viewed his arrival at the bowling crease with enthusiasm. I was immediately stumped by a yard and a half and in the space of 13 overs Sainsbury took 7 for 30 and we lost by 148 runs. I remember W J saying that he thought we had been unlucky. In truth, we had bowled far too many bad balls; they had bowled very few.

At the prize-giving, Gordon Ross, the former editor of the *Cricket Monthly*, who had taken over as the adjudicator from Hutton, mentioned my 60. In addition to his 7 for 30, Sainsbury had made a small matter of 76 and he won the award. But I hope it means as much to minor county cricketers today to take part as it did for us that weekend in Southampton 31 years ago. And I hope, too, that Norfolk win today.

Guardian, 25 June 1996

Little threat to Lancashire's one-day reign

Scyld Berry

In the Benson and Hedges Cup final last year a famous innings by Aravinda de Silva could not halt the team of Lancashire. This year it will take another extraordinary individual performance – like Curtly Ambrose in his 'Trinidad 46 all out' form – if Lancashire are not to win the cup again on Saturday, in the first final of 50 overs.

Now, as ever, Lancashire and the other counties with Test grounds have an advantage over the rest, like Northamptonshire. Lancashire, with its larger population and greater resources, can command the loyalty of such experienced reserves as Nick Speak and Steve Titchard without whom prizes cannot be won.

What is more, Lancashire is the traditional home of one-day cricket. India may aspire to assume that title, just as it took over the cotton industry from Lancashire but for the moment, within English cricket, Lancashire's one-day team benefit from the strong and distinct culture of one-day cricket in the county.

Lancashire have won 11 one-day trophies, more than any other county. Five times they have won the 60-over NatWest or Gillette competition. Three times they have won the B & H Cup, and three times they have won the Sunday League, including the first in 1969, a success which launched the Lancasheer-la-la-lager era of Jack Simmons and David Hughes.

Geographical coincidence was responsible for the cluster of mill-towns on the windward side of the Pennines, peopled by able-bodied men who, following the introduction of the Factory Acts, had Saturday afternoons free. The Lancashire League was set up in 1890, the Central Lancashire in 1892, and as the cotton mill-owners cashed in they could afford to hire some of the world's best professionals for their clubs, and one-day cricket was taken to a higher level than anywhere else.

Warren Hegg led Lancashire to Lord's this year when the semi-final was going Yorkshire's way, scoring 81 off 62 balls and taking the man-of-the-match award. Hegg's speciality is the hit over extra-cover. John Stanworth, the county coach while David Lloyd attends to England, remembers: 'Hegg could already hit over extra when he came as a 16 or 17-year-old from league cricket.'

Thanks in varying degrees to this culture of one-day cricket, Lancashire have built up an array of strikers right down the order. Neil Fairbrother is still not far short of being the best English one-day batsman, and Graham Lloyd is his right-handed equivalent, both of them able to hit a straight ball into whatever gaps there may be.

If there has been a weakness in Lancashire's B & H run – they lost in May 1994, to miraculous hitting by Dominic Cork – it is that their top order has increasingly left it to the tail-enders to take them home. They defeated Yorkshire in their semi-final with one wicket and nothing else to spare. In their last match of the qualifying round, they secured a home quarter-final by again winning by a whisker and a wicket, creating the first holes in Warwickshire's self-belief.

The profit has been that Lancashire's lower-order batsmen have become ever more practised at pursuing the improbable. They have become the best chasers in the business, the county equivalent of Sri Lanka. They have their natural abilities, like Glen Chapple and his cover-drive, or Gary Yates and his 'No 9 iron off the spinners' as Stanworth calls it; and they do have one-day nets in which they experiment in hitting over the top. But it is all refined by match practice.

Last Sunday Lancashire's ninth-wicket pair of Chapple and Yates needed 21 off the last over. Would such a target have been attempted in bygone years? In 1932 Surrey hit off 57 in seven overs to beat Middlesex in a 'truly memorable' climax. In 1949 Yorkshire made 185 for four off 25.5 overs from Derbyshire's 'useful seamers', Bill Copson, Cliff Gladwin and Les Jackson. And these were once-in-a-career, mind-boggling instances.

This season Matthew Fleming has hit 63 off 20 balls for Kent. Imagine a side needing 63 off 3.2 overs and achieving them. As batsmen's skills increase more quickly than those of bowlers and fielders, the parameters of the possible are ever widened. Last Sunday Chapple and Yates fell one run short.

But there is a price. For all their virtuosity, Fairbrother and Lloyd are not in the Test side. Lancashire, winners of 11 one-day trophies since 1969, have averaged 10th place in the championship since then. Their own conventional excuse is Manchester's weather. But the record does not support this argument: in the last two seasons they have lost 48 championship hours at home and 45 away, around 10 per cent.

For the championship, Lancashire, like England, need, above all, an attacking spinner. But local pitches have not been conducive and neither has their brand of league cricket: young bowlers do not benefit from watching the overseas pro keeping one end going throughout.

Lancashire's leagues have surely to be reformed if the Red Rose is to grow into more than transitory, one-day blooms.

Sunday Telegraph, 7 July 1996

Caddick does his worst to claim hat-trick

Pat Gibson

The life and times of Mae West were probably not on the curriculum when Andrew Caddick went to school in New Zealand, so he was unable to quote the immortal lines: 'When I'm good I'm very very good, but when I'm bad I'm better.'

As it was, the Somerset fast bowler, who has been good enough in the championship this season to revive the interest of the England selectors, had to settle for admitting that he bowled 'absolute rubbish' in taking the first hat-trick of his career and only the ninth in the 34-year history of the 60-over competition.

The fact that his stream of long hops, wides and no-balls interspersed with the odd decent ball had sent Gloucestershire hurtling towards a humiliating NatWest Trophy defeat said even less for their batting. They were all out for 118 in 32.4 overs and Somerset had the match won by 3.45pm with five wickets and more than 27 overs to spare.

It was a quite extraordinary exhibition from the moment that Wright was leg-before offering no stroke in Rose's first over. Hancock did something similar in Rose's next over and lost his off stump, which tended to confirm the umpire's earlier decision, whereupon Cunliffe and Lynch thrashed 57 in the next seven overs.

At this stage, Caddick, who had needed a cortisone injection to ease a rib injury and was mostly bowling off a short run, had conceded 36 runs in five overs. It was almost embarrassing to watch and he looked ready to come off when he served up a rank long hop to Lynch, who had to stretch a long way outside off stump to edge it to the wicketkeeper.

Inspired by that, Caddick produced a good ball that lifted off a length to have Symonds caught behind and, with the first ball of his next over, he claimed Cunliffe, who tried to force him off the back foot and was caught low down in the gully by Trump.

Suddenly Gloucestershire were almost strokeless. Russell managed only three off 27 balls before Rose had him caught behind and Trump, getting some turn for his off breaks, cashed in with three wickets for 15, two of them in two balls, which were sufficient to persuade David Allen, a former off spinner himself, to give him the man-of-the-match award. It was an eloquent comment on Caddick's bowling, but the fact remained that his hat-trick had effectively decided the match.

At least Gloucestershire tried to make a fight of it. Hancock lifted their spirits with a magnificent diving catch at mid-wicket to get rid of Lathwell and Lewis took wickets in successive balls when he had Bowler and Harden caught behind. Lee averted another hat-trick, but, when Smith had him leg-before, Somerset were indebted to Ecclestone, who batted solidly for his 37, and Parsons, who settled the issue with three boundaries off Lewis.

Even then, Somerset's celebrations were strangely muted. Hayhurst, their captain, admitted that Gloucestershire were 'terrible' while Walsh kept his side locked in the dressing-room discussing how they are going to resurrect a season which is going from bad to worse.

The Times, 11 July 1996

Life in the old hangdog yet

Frank Keating

The hangdog gait may be more ploughman-plodding than ever; the shoulders more drooping, but in himself the old boy is in bright-eyed trim. The brow, for sure, is less care-worn and furrowed than once it was and he is palpably revelling in his ripe and contented anecdotage as well as in his still resounding batting.

Graham Gooch was 43 in July. Yesterday England's new Test selector scored his seventh Championship hundred of the season to overtake W. G. Grace in the all-time list of first-class century-makers with 127. Tomorrow he strides forth once again for his beloved Essex in the NatWest final at his almost as beloved Lord's.

'It's a huge game for me, probably my last great packed-house occasion – and against Lancashire, too, who rightly consider themselves the prime one-day operators.' He will be playing against his friend Michael Atherton, England's captain since Gooch handed in his seals of office in 1993. He says that definitely adds spice, 'Since the semis, Mike's been ribbing me, "No problem, we'll win just by keeping in the old man who can't get it off the square these days." I have a go back – "When we crowd you and cramp you and bat-pad you, what's the big shot that's going to get you moving and out of jail, Athers?" '

All good, matey fun. The fact is that much more spice would have been added tomorrow had Gooch been coach-elect of Lancashire. He very nearly was. When he announced last week that he would play one more season for Essex, in 1997, Gooch did not mention that he had turned down the Championship's plum job at Old Trafford.

'Atherton was genuinely appalled at that – "Goochie you're mad! It's the best job in the world, it's like Alex Ferguson turning down Manchester United." '

Gooch agrees, but turn it down he did. 'It was completely untrue newspaper talk that said I had been offered a job by Nottinghamshire. I was quietly sounded out by Durham, that's true. But the offer from Lancashire was firm after a super dinner with their chairman, Bob Bennett. Half of me wanted to leap at the job there and then. But you know me, I'd want to do it with 200 per cent commitment and, if not as far away from home as Durham, Old Trafford would keep me too far away from the girls [his three young daughters] because although Brenda [his wife] and I don't live together any more I aim to see the kids every single day. So I told Bob I couldn't say "yes" at this stage in my life.'

His parental duties will put up with one stretch of seven weeks away this early winter when he takes, as manager, the England A side to Australia. 'Seven weeks away is more bearable than a whole year,' he says. He has revelled this summer in scoring his runs and then turning up to the Test selection meetings. He has much time for Ray Illingworth, the departing chairman. 'He has been tremendous, put his heart and soul into it. We've always got on. He chides me about my foibles and I get back at his unfailing Yorkshireness. I might turn up to a meeting just after making another hundred and he'll say, "Don't get carried away, lad, you're nowhere in the frame any more – Atherton, Stewart and Knight are the top openers, then there's Martyn Moxon ahead of you, and David Byas can open, and young Anthony McGrath . . ." '

In fact, there is a serious case for nominating Gooch as the most prolific batsman the game has known. Every schoolboy knows that Sir Jack Hobbs's 61,237 first-class runs (between 1905 and 1934) make him the champion run-getter of all time. Gooch will end this season a little short of 44,000. Hobbs, of course, never played one-day matches – and if one adds Gooch's phenomenal 20,000 one-day runs he began this season with 62,528 runs in the bank, more than any man in history (the nearest first-class and one-day aggregates combined are Geoffrey Boycott, 57,981; Dennis Amiss, 53,950; and Gordon Greenidge, 51,753).

In other words, some time last season Gooch pushed a ball for an innocent single and became the most prolific batsman ever. You are not telling me that tomorrow at Lord's, or in one-dayers of blazing belligerence on foreign paddocks for England in his salad days, Gooch was under less pressure or facing worse bowling than the mighty Hobbs on, say, a pastoral Saturday for Surrey against the gentlemen bowlers of Somerset or Northampton?

When you put such sacrilege to Gooch, the traditional cricket lover in him blushes to the roots of his new twined thatch from the Advanced Hair Studio. 'Well, I suppose you've got a point,' he concedes, 'what is for sure is you don't try any less hard whatever form of cricket you're playing. I never have, anyway. In fact, I'd say the one-day game is more physically and mentally demanding. A NatWest match can take more out of you than three days in the Championship.'

In middle-age, he admits he needs his rest now. He has enjoyed being at slip for Essex this season after a couple of summers loping around in the country. 'I'm pleased, I've caught pretty well, too, touch wood.' Yet fitness remains his credo. Rest in between is crucial, but he still runs and cycles and carries dumb-bells in his bag. One arduous day, he says, needs a rest day to compensate. The day before the Oval Test a fortnight ago he helped with England's fielding practice, bowled for an hour or more in the nets, and had a net himself when the players had packed up because he was due to play for Essex at Bristol the next day. 'Silly, I was knackered.' He hit Courtney Walsh and Co for a century nevertheless.

In Essex's last match, against Yorkshire, Gooch reeled off 13 overs – 'and got Byas's wicket as well, although Raymond hasn't mentioned he noticed'. He says he has been urging Atherton to resume bowling his once-decent leg-spinners. 'I've promised him a case of champagne if he takes more first-class career wickets than me. He's got around 110 so far; I've got 240-odd. If he plays another seven or eight years, at 20 wickets or so a season, he'll get the bubbly.' What, England's captain will be in his mid-30s then. Couldn't his predecessor see him going on to 43? 'Not if he has any sense,' he says, wistfully at first before the face lights up and he laughs fit to bust.

Gooch's first Lord's final was 32 years ago. 'Sussex v Warwickshire. I was just 11. Dad and I went down in the second-hand Austin Cambridge. What a thrill. We sat on the grass in front of the curve of the old Mound Stand. Ted Dexter batted and Sussex won.' To illustrate the bridging of cricket's generations, the man of the match adjudicators that day were Herbert Sutcliffe and Frank Woolley.

His next Lord's final was 1979 – the B & H and Essex's first trophy in their century-old Cinderella history. Young Gooch made a century and won the gold award. 'I'll never forget walking out to open with Mike Denness through the gate and onto that springy summer turf, and it seemed the ground was full of Essex people. We had to do it for them. I'll think of that moment again this Saturday, all of 17 years on. I'll use the memory to inspire me. Most sportsmen use past memories to inspire them, you know. And at my age, I suppose I've got more than most of them.'

Guardian, 6 September 1996

Whitaker's wisdom shows Leicestershire the way

Martin Johnson

As Leicester City prepare to post the 'house full' notices for their first home football match of the season, Leicestershire's cricketers are bracing themselves for their own version of spectator frenzy as they launch their final push on the County Championship. There is heady talk of doubling the number of gatemen to two, and the caterers are rumoured to be getting ready for this week's crucial game against Hampshire by ordering an extra cheese roll.

Only the championship leaders, Derbyshire, whom they trail by

17 points with a game in hand, play their home games in front of fewer people, but no matter if the only difference between Grace Road and the surface of the moon is that the latter has more atmosphere, Leicestershire's players will not be short on adrenalin as they push for domestic cricket's most prestigious title.

There might be a good deal more tangible evidence of local support were the city not saddled with one of those local newspapers convinced that a footballer blowing his nose is worth more of a headline than a cricketer scoring a century, but Leicestershire's captain, James Whitaker, is not unduly bothered. 'It would be lovely if we did get some decent crowds in midweek, but it doesn't make any difference to how keen the players are to win this thing,' he said.

Whitaker, who returns for the match against Hampshire tomorrow after missing the last two games with a calf injury, is regarded as the biggest single influence in Leicestershire's challenge this summer. Capped by England for the first and only time in Australia 10 years ago, the 34-year-old Yorkshire-born batsman has finally rediscovered his focus with the captaincy after a decade of personal underachievement.

He has many times been tempted to follow the likes of Phillip DeFreitas, Chris Lewis, Nick Cook and David Gower through the player-exit gate, and turned down the chance to captain Somerset two years ago. However, since inheriting the captaincy from Nigel Briers last winter, Whitaker's uncomplicated approach to cricket – the first three balls he ever faced from the then-in-his-pomp Ian Botham disappeared for four – has rubbed off on his team.

Briers, a schoolteacher, was a naturally cautious pilot, while Whitaker, son of a wealthy chocolate manufacturer, is more inclined to fly by the seat of his pants. He is also less autocratic, embracing the notion that there are 11 players all in this together, and all worthy of an audience. 'Collective responsibility is my idea of getting the best from individuals,' he said.

During the match against Worcestershire at Grace Road, Whitaker was busy conducting one of his regular on-the-field conferences under the umpiring eye of a former captain of his, Peter Willey.

Willey, whose own idea of consultation generally involved

hanging a player by his collar from a dressing room peg, came out with a sarcastic 'Who the hell's in charge around here?' to which Whitaker promptly responded: 'We are. Take a look at the scoreboard.'

There is, though, a harder edge to Whitaker's captaincy, as pace bowler David Millns discovered in a match at Edgbaston. Millns threw a bit of a wobbler when he was not given choice of ends, and although his absence from the next game was officially given out as an injury, Whitaker dropped him.

Whitaker had also been lobbying for a couple of seasons to move Vince Wells up the batting order to a specialist position, and backed his judgment by promoting Wells to open early in the season.

Wells, originally signed from Kent as a player who bowled a bit, batted a bit, and kept wicket a bit, made two double centuries and 197 in six days.

Phil Simmons, the West Indian Test player, has also had a major impact, not least with his bowling when Alan Mullally has been on Test duty. Simmons irritates opponents with a geeing up routine involving near non-stop rattle and hand-clapping from the slips, but as far as Leicestershire are concerned, it is indicative of his commitment to the team.

Jack Birkenshaw, the cricket manager, was a member of Leicestershire's only championship-winning squad, in 1975, captained by Raymond Illingworth, and containing players of the calibre of Graham McKenzie, Ken Higgs and Brian Davison. Birkenshaw is in little doubt that the 1975 side were a better one, but inferior to the 1996 version in terms of team spirit.

'All the players love each other,' said Birkenshaw, doubtless still harbouring memories of Illy only asking him to bowl when the pitch was not turning. In those days, a local character known as 'Foghorn' would regularly circuit the ground clutching (or, to be more accurate, spilling) a pint of mild, shouting: 'Get Birkey on to bowl!'

Birkenshaw said: 'In 1975 we had players who knew how to win, but this lot have gelled in a team of lesser individual talents. Jimmy [Whitaker] is an inventive captain, Simmons has been brilliant, and a championship this year would be a better achievement than 1975.'

If Leicestershire are looking for omens, their only defeat this season has been to Surrey at the Oval, as it was in 1975. Birkenshaw said: 'If we bottle it, we bottle it, but we're certainly going to give it a crack. One of half-a-dozen sides could win it, and I don't see why it can't be us.'

Daily Telegraph, 21 August 1996

An Early Indian Summer

Introduction

Any feelings of 'after the Lord Mayor's Show' were quickly dispelled. England and India both put their disappointing winter behind them and played engaging cricket. There was much to admire: Ganguly and Tendulkar's batting, Srinath and Prasad's bowling, the confident re-emergence of Nasser Hussain and the continued tenacity of captain Mike Atherton with a series-securing century.

Were England beginning to climb back up the international tree in the five and one-day formats, or was it too soon to tell? Many were happy to forgo crystal ball-gazing and just enjoy the present.

Prasad right up with the early pace

Ian Hawkey

India have not had the easiest of introductions to their tour. Outplayed in the one-day internationals, hampered by the weather and then by a walkout, there were times last week when one or two of them wore faces as long . . . well, as long as the winter that has pursued them all around England and all the way into June. One of their number, the Sikh batsman Navjot Sidhu, has returned home, irredeemably miffed; the medium-pacer Salil Ankola has been called in from league cricket in the northeast, the summons apparently acknowledging that the original party set off a seamer or three light.

From all this, a sharp ghost-writer might conclude that the Indians have been busily cramming all the spice of an Illingworth paperback, a volume of Lamb and an Oslear opus into the space of a preface. When chapter one begins in earnest at Edgbaston on Thursday, the roles of hero, villain and saviour are ready to cast and, to plot them, sufficient motive to expect a sting in the tail.

England are the favourites, but warily so. In truth, the chance for some uncontrived, uninterrupted cricket would do a great deal to lift the Indian mood and change the flavour of the headlines at home. Sunshine in Birmingham will return smiles to faces for a start.

In between the squalls and the squabbling, the gains the Indians have made are concentrated on their pace attack, a needy area. India's new era with the new ball has been half complete, through Javagal Srinath, for two or three years; having departed for England without Manoj Prabakhar, the invitation was open. Ankola's arrival provides a cushion but few in the party have impressed more than Venkatesh Prasad, a latecomer who, barring injury or further internecine complications, will make his Test debut this week.

Two months short of 26, Prasad has waited a while for his coming, the queue having stretched more than a decade behind the protean, prolonged talent of Kapil Dev, Test cricket's leading wicket-taker, and Prabakhar, who has retired to politics. Ask Ankola, whose call-up to this series comes seven years after his sole previous Test, and you find he has been twiddling his thumbs around the fringes for most of the sabbatical. It hasn't helped that India's schedulers lean so heavily towards the limited-overs game.

'There's a generation of bowlers who have had to wait,' said Sandeep Patil, the Indian tour manager and contemporary of Kapil. 'Even Srinath had to wait and there have been many others. When Kapil left, Prasad had to wait too. But this tour has been very good for him so far and I've seen him improve with every game. He and Srinath have been bowling very well together. It's been one of the pluses for us so far.'

Colleagues at state level, Srinath, Prasad and Anil Kumble have done most to suggest it will be they, more than the more orthodox spinners, who ask the most searching questions of England. Srinath and Kumble will ask them in the more familiar tongue – they took 192 first-class wickets for Gloucestershire and Northamptonshire respectively last summer – while Prasad holds one or two surprises. Lean, six foot four with a high action and deceptive pace, he troubled England through the one-day series and has found a good rhythm and a searching line in the county games.

The three come as something of a package, all children of Karnataka in the mellow south-east, all of them close contemporaries. 'They seem to be growing taller and taller in Bangalore,' said Mohammed Azharuddin, the Indian captain. 'There are good bowlers there. I just hope they keep coming.'

Prasad's education was tougher than Srinath's or Kumble's, however. Not born to the great opportunity, he came to the game late, excelling first at hockey and practising his nascent cricket chiefly with a tennis ball until well into his teens. At 17 he was recruited into local league competition, and began to take wickets in his second season at the Dooravani club with an unencumbered combination of pace, height and native invention. Most of the time his game was still being developed on matting wickets in and around Bangalore but, with Srinath, he graduated to the state junior side. Srinath, though, always kept ahead and a sturdy Karnataka attack, built around the former Test all-rounder, Roger Binny, looked after itself without extensive recourse to understudies.

Prasad made his first-class debut five years ago, was in and out of the side thereafter but impressed for a Rest of India XI against Graham Gooch's declining tourists in 1992-93, and took 50 first-class wickets at 18 the next season. The breakthroughs came courtesy of, among others, Azharuddin, Prasad's captain in the zonal Duleep Trophy competition. As the young bowler gathered speed and studied guile, earning himself wider attention, Azharuddin took good note not only of his striking physique and ability to move the ball off the seam, but his fielding.

Dusty, raw surfaces are generally deemed poor schoolmasters to the young Indian fielder and the evidence of the tour thus far suggests outfielding is the least accomplished part of the repertoire of these tourists, Prasad among the exceptions. Fielding let them down in the one-dayers, but Prasad's run-out of Graham Thorpe at Old Trafford, a swift pick-up and direct hit from deep mid-wicket, was a rare moment to put one or two of his nimbler, lighter colleagues to shame. 'He is a good athlete,' said Azharuddin, 'very supple and flexible. He is hard-working and reserved and has put a lot into his game.'

The Indian captain attributes much of the development to Prasad's time at the Pace Foundation in Madras, set up to answer a need in the post-Kapil era and now preparing to celebrate its most successful native graduate. Srinath has been a peripatetic student there, but Prasad has become a project, not least for the chief coach, Dennis Lillee.

Prasad credits Lillee for his variety. An effective slower ball and a jagged leg-cutter have come with a shift up in gear. Aggression was more diffident in announcing itself, too diffident in Lillee's estimation, but at the World Cup, most notably, Prasad began packing a meaner punch. Against Pakistan in an electric quarter-final, he was a match-winner, arresting Aamir Sohail and Saeed Anwar's 84 off 10 overs with three quick wickets – not to mention a vivid parting gesture towards Sohail.

The rest is history and history that haunts India still. The tournament was to dip for them four days later with the semi-final defeat against Sri Lanka, the crowd protest and a public opprobrium so deep it will take until the next World Cup on the subcontinent to forget. In the meantime, India have much to play for over the next six weeks.

Sunday Times, 2 June 1996

Tendulkar unfolds his genius

Peter Roebuck

Not even a thrilling and courageous innings from Sachin Tendulkar could prevent England striding towards victory before a buzzing, boisterous and basking Birmingham crowd. Spurred on by occasional patriotic choruses, bowling on an ill-tempered pitch, taking their chances with unaffected glee and playing with an urgent and sometimes flawed passion, England overwhelmed their weakened and betrayed opponents.

Tendulkar alone stood long in England's path, a master summoning one of his most distinguished innings, an innings of craft, resource and skill, one of the greatest innings played in Test cricket. It took a tumbling of wickets at the other end to bring him down, a hook taken at mid-wicket. Even Horatio could not have held both ends of the bridge.

Tendulkar's innings was memorable and remarkable. Having resisted Lewis's early assault and checked Cork's exuberant onslaught, he took charge of pitch, opponents and situation, an achievement far beyond the capabilities of his colleagues. In defence, he offered the broadest of bats and in attack a range of strokes at once conclusive and correctly executed.

Nor was it an innings played in a vacuum. Craft was Tendulkar's servant, not his master, and he was sufficiently pugnacious to relish the battles of humanity to be found at the heart of every satisfactory sporting engagement. His duels with Cork were captivating, thrust and counter thrust, appeal and scorching stroke.

Only once did England think that Tendulkar had fallen. Having reached 76, the master batsman encountered a scorcher from Lewis that flew past a chin hastily withdrawn. On its way it flicked something, shirt or helmet, and all England appealed as the ball nestled in Russell's gloves. Fortunately, umpire David Shepherd was in splendid form and shook his head imperturbably, whereupon the home captain saw fit to leave his position at cover and to air his opinions on the matter. No less impressively, Shepherd promptly told him to attend to his own affairs.

Having survived this alarm, Tendulkar took command again, punishing Lewis and reaching his hundred in glorious style by stepping down the pitch to strike Patel over the straight boundary. At once the batsman turned to his colleagues in the pavilion with arms raised high. His eyes were still full of the fervour of competition. He knew he had produced something special.

No other Indian batsman could muster the combination of resilience and skill needed to survive against such hostile bowling on such a pitch. A torrid time was had by all, a time of bruised fingers and battered bodies as England sustained their assault.

To top it off, India found themselves playing on an unsatisfactory surface. The first ball after lunch skittled along the turf, the next ball spat up. It says much for Tendulkar's accomplishment that he survived, and for his temperament that he carried on as if nothing untoward had occurred.

Still, England were not to be denied the credit. Cork and Lewis bowled fiery spells in the opening and decisive hour of the day, removing a determined opening pair and bursting through a fragile middle order. Cork struck first, taking his 50th Test wicket in his 11th match with a withering ball that bit from the pitch to strike the shoulder of Rathore's bat before ballooning to Hick at second slip. Rathore stood his ground, convinced that the ball had not carried.

Jadeja was next to wend his weary way to the pavilion. Lewis had been bowling a swift spell, banging the ball into a helpful pitch. In the past, he was torn between bowling fast and relying on movement, and fell between the two stools. At least his approach is now clear. Repeatedly he directed fliers at the batsmen's bodies. Probably he overdid it. At last, though, he pitched his leg-cutter to a fuller length, defeating Jadeja as he pushed reluctantly forward.

India's next two men were more easily taken. Elevated by force of circumstance beyond his usual station, and appointed to the task of protecting the team's master batsmen, Mongia parried several lifters before hurling himself at a tempting half-volley and slicing the ball into England's alert slip cordon. Seldom can England have been better served by their close catchers.

Sadly, Azharuddin could not rise to the occasion, shuffling across his stumps and looking back in horror to see his leg stump lurching back. Mullally, who bowled him, produced some pace and bounce and might succeed overseas. To take wickets in England he will need to improve his inswinger.

India had declined to 36 for four and the end appeared nigh. Tendulkar was standing alone. Already he had played some memorable strokes, an on-drive and a back-foot force through cover lingering in the mind. He was joined by the doughty Joshi. Despite his broken finger, Joshi kept his esteemed partner company until Mullally cut a ball through his defences.

Manjrekar, whose enforced retirement in the first innings cost his team dear, hobbled out. By now, Tendulkar was in full flow, and Irani's appearance at the bowling crease was greeted with a flurry of pulls and drives. Irani is an odd mixture of cosmopolitan and rustic; here his agricultural side was to the fore. Manjrekar was batting on one foot, standing over his stumps and stunning Lewis's lifters. At last he could resist no longer, another bouncer thumping into his gloves and deflecting to the slips. Again, the end appeared nigh and again the Indians refused to buckle. Kumble showed the straightest of bats and Tendulkar collected runs as he could.

England tried spin, and Patel immediately bowled over the wicket and into the rough, a tactic certain to provoke the fury of connoisseurs and codgers alike. It is the most tedious of tactics and it is becoming commonplace.

Between them, this capable pair added 58 runs and Englishmen were beginning to frown by the time Tendulkar failed to respond to his partner's call. Never the swiftest of turners, Kumble could not beat Knight's smart throw.

Srinath was soon beaten by a shooter, whereupon Tendulkar felt obliged to open his shoulders. Caught at mid-wicket, he left to a standing ovation. It only remained for Mhambrey to strike some willing blows before Lewis brought the innings to an end with England needing to score 121 to win. Knight has fallen along the way, but by stumps, India were a beaten side. They have put up a fight, but have not been quite good enough.

Sunday Times, 9 June 1996

An age of mystery

Mike Brearley

The career of Sourav Ganguly can only go downhill from here. In the long history of cricket only one other player, Alvin Kallicharran, has scored centuries in his first two Test innings.

Ganguly has surprised everyone. John Barclay, who managed the England 'A' tour of India in 1994-95, described him during the Lord's Test as a batsman whose talent had caught the eye but whose hunger for runs was suspect. Geoffrey Boycott, during the same match, when Ganguly was 30-odd not out, said how helpful an innings of 40 or 50 would be for this young player in his first Test.

The Indian selectors clearly concurred; they did not pick him for the first Test, and he probably got his chance only because of Manjrekar's injured ankle.

Run-hunger may be the last thing to be expected from a boy whose garden in a suburb of Calcutta could comfortably contain its own cricket field. There are areas that size in Calcutta which house 5,000 people.

How wrong they all were.

Ganguly keeps things to himself. His age has been so much a matter of mystery that the official tour guide leaves his date of birth blank. Indian and Pakistani cricketers have been known for a certain ambiguity about their age. Sometimes this is due to a paucity of rural records; more often it has been down to a shrewd awareness of the advantages of being regarded as younger than you are.

It is better to be a 17-year-old of outstanding promise than 21 and useful; it is better to be a 25-year-old who may still develop than to be 30 and set in one's ways. Ganguly's age, in the press box at least, has oscillated between 29 and 23. The 'Maharaj', as he's called, presumably has a pukka birth certificate, but no one seems to have confidence as to its contents.

Whatever his secrets, his qualities on the field have been clear for all to see. He has a rare combination of a Gower-like fluency and range of strokes together with an immaculate defence. Like Lara, but unlike Sobers, Pollock, Edrich, Gower or Thorpe, he manages a full stride and bent front knee, even to the quick bowlers.

Even when bowling – and in this department he is decidedly friendly – he conveys an air of relishing the challenge.

The 255-run stand between Tendulkar and Ganguly displayed batting at its best – correct yet positive, dashing yet secure. Ganguly was the more secure. He looks, at least facially, more 23 than 29, but his batting has been as mature as that of Tendulkar, also 23 but who has played Test cricket for seven years.

India have improved steadily during their short tour. They must have drawn the short straw, as compared with Pakistan, in getting the first and not the second half of a summer which has been generally chilly. Their spinners have not quite blossomed. More important, I sense little conviction about victory in the Indian team.

This attitude was clearest on the last day at Lord's where England were, in effect, 85 for six on a pitch which was a bit uneven and which by that stage offered some turn to Kumble, who was bowling well. Even then Azharuddin was cautious. He gave Srinath and Prasad only two slips and a deep gully. To Irani, hardly off the mark, he immediately posted a deep long leg as well as the deep fine leg. For Kumble he never had a really attacking field, with a close silly-point.

As it happened, Irani immediately mis-pulled, spooning the ball to square leg, within reach of a short leg; and later he edged through third slip. Good sides, sniffing success, grasp it with both hands. India have not.

Nor have they grasped the chances that have gone their way. I cannot remember a series in which one bowler has so outbowled all others yet had, relatively, so little to show for it. Javagal Srinath has been that bowler. He has beaten the bat, even on this benign Trent Bridge pitch, with remarkable regularity. When he has found the edge, the slips – a sundry collection of rapidly rotating individuals – have, as often as not, dropped the sharp chances; or else the slip area has been left sparsely inhabited.

Srinath bowls with a fast, whippy arm, generating pace off the pitch. He hits the seam regularly, and moves the ball each way. But even his lbw appeals have usually been turned down. Stewart and Atherton – the latter's innings yesterday a triumph of determination over poor form – have been made to look stuttering novices. Yet he has taken fewer wickets than Lewis and the same number as Mullally – they have been the best of England's bowlers but are less skilled and varied than this man.

Srinath has been well supported by Prasad, but not by the Indian selectors who, though one Test down, selected a team with seven batsmen and only four bowlers for this true batting pitch. England's logic was sounder; they replaced a batting all-rounder with one whose main strength is in his bowling.

Since Edgbaston, India have lacked the courage of their attacking convictions.

Observer, 7 July 1996

Captain fights back to set up series victory

Scyld Berry

Whereas Lord's saw a rather tacky draw for England, this one should be honourable enough. With some style England have batted themselves out of trouble to secure, at the least, their first series victory against anyone other than New Zealand since India last toured here in 1990.

It is even conceivable that England have scored quickly enough – 290 in a day of 91 overs – that they can post a total beyond 600 and enjoy a few hours of putting the frighteners on India's second innings. But this pitch is showing no sign of wear and tear, and if the Indian bowlers are, they have the rare pleasure of a rest day in which to recuperate.

While Nasser Hussain provided the finest strokeplay yesterday, Mike Atherton was sufficiently obdurate to chisel his 10th Test hundred out of the most unpromising material, like a stained-glass window fashioned from milk-bottles. It was his fourth at Trent Bridge, which is no coincidence. This is a featherbed, as heartless to bowlers as Adelaide in The Don's day, which makes it all the more praiseworthy that England's bowlers should have dismissed half the Indians for single figures.

The scoreboard, however, can give no idea of Atherton's early troubles. He was so out of touch that when he reached 50, off a completely miscued hook, he laughed – at the sheer absurdity of cricket. What logic can there be in the game if a man in prime form can make nought, and a batsman all at sea can eventually reach a hundred?

Atherton's innings of almost seven hours has been testimony to what a stubborn will and a good eye – actually the best of eyes – can do; and to hard work. Yesterday, he was again in the nets by 8.30, to be beaten outside offstump by groundstaff lads, but it was there he got the worst out of his system.

Atherton considers that the first principle of his batting concerns his back foot. When he and Graham Gooch batted together so symbiotically, they would tell each other if their back foot was retreating towards square-leg as an initial movement: that was a sign of bad form. In the second half of last summer, Atherton's back foot was splaying a long way towards square-leg, and he still made runs against West Indies. Technical defect it may be, it can work for him.

At the start of this innings he was determined to keep his back foot anchored, even if it meant turning chest-on and bringing the bat down askew from second slip. He took many a thoughtful glance at the video screen to see a replay of his stroke. Above all he was wise enough to wait for the ball, not to go looking for extra trouble.

England's captain had luck too. He could have been caught in the slips on Friday evening. When 34 he fended a bouncer past third slip's fingertips, and he was reprieved a third time by umpire Francis when pinned right back on his stumps by Venkatesh Prasad.

The growing reluctance of Test umpires to dismiss batsmen has gone too far and been a factor in the sterilisation of this series. The Lord's Test should have been a nip-and-tucker. In two Tests, with the ball moving around and at Edgbaston keeping low, the visiting Australian Darrell Hair gave two lbws, one per game.

Test umpires now appear to fear they will lose their jobs if they raise their finger. At this rate, Test match draws will unnaturally proliferate, and Mr Jagmohan Dalmiya, of Calcutta, will have ammunition for his campaign to abolish the Test draw.

After his three 'lives', Atherton started to settle. A comic misfield by Venkat Raju at mid-off gave him a heartening four. When Raju offered his left-arm spin, a favoured dish, Atherton forgot his feet and fretting and played the ball, often and ever more crisply through the covers. By the close, he was allowing himself a half-twitch backwards of his back foot against the pace.

Stewart was almost as afflicted by the tormenting length and bounce of Javagal Srinath as Atherton, but he had no such luck, given caught behind off an inside edge. K. T. Francis, of Sri Lanka, is one of the best umpires in Asia, arguably one of the best 20 in the world, but there aren't half a dozen umpires at the moment who can officiate in a Test and stand up to the new levels of scrutiny.

The new, straighter Hussain, who cut out his open-faced steer at the start of last season, succeeded Stewart in the over after lunch and scattered the pecking pigeons with his driving. Not since Mike Gatting and David Gower were at their best a decade ago has an England number three made two Test hundreds, or been so assured in the position.

Again Anil Kumble dropped too short, to be worked to leg off the back foot by Hussain and Atherton – not that Kumble was alone. Tendulkar had to act as captain when Mohammed Azharuddin was hit on the shins at silly point, had to be X-rayed and spent the rest of the day in the pavilion.

There won't be pigeons waiting for Azharuddin when he returns to India. His situation will be more akin to that of the departed among the Parsis who are laid out on the Towers of Silence on Bombay's Malabar Hill for the benefit of vultures. But he will accept, with a wobble of the head, his fate. It was so different when Azharuddin began in Test cricket, reeling off his three hundreds against England, glittering through mid-wicket, late-cutting the spinners like a reincarnation of the Golden Age and sweeping with a vertical bat as only the best can. He might recapture some of it if permitted to remain as a batsman. Tendulkar, dictating from slip, was a tougher customer, alert to post a leg-slip when Hussain was sweeping.

Nothing revives a side like youth: if Sidhu hadn't gone home in pique, India would have had no space for Saurav Ganguly; if Manjrekar hadn't been injured, Rahul Dravid wouldn't have had his chance, and he looks more compact and classy than Ganguly.

England do not seem to have 23-year-old batsmen of such quick feet, calm temperament and orthodox technique. But two 28-year-olds did the job well yesterday, reaching the follow-on figure off the last ball, with nine wickets still in hand.

Sunday Telegraph, 7 July 1996

Late Pakistani Swing

Introduction

Any foreboding regarding the short tour by the Pakistanis was happily dispelled. Past differences were quickly consigned to yesterday's columns as everyone welcomed the visitors' diplomatic and good-spirited attitude.

The tourists were a potent force with a world-class bowling attack linked to a strong batting line-up. England were out-gunned in the Test series, yet collected crumbs of comfort when winning the Texaco one-day matches 2-1.

Hot pitch

Matthew Engel

It was February 1956. The scene was a run-down colonial hotel in Peshawar, near the North-west Frontier. The perpetrators were members of the young MCC A team who had been sent out to the infant country of Pakistan to play a series of games without Test match status, to help the game along there and breed a little goodwill. The victim was an umpire called Idris Bergh. The weapon was a bucket of water.

In 1956 Pakistan was not a country offering a great deal of entertainment to Englishmen in their early 20s. Throughout the tour the players had passed the time by throwing occasional buckets of water, mostly over each other. According to the MCC captain, Donald Carr, Idris Bergh had seen this happen, laughed like mad and been warned that he was next. Carr also says that Bergh took the whole thing in a spirit of fun. At first.

Unfortunately, two Pakistani players came in as Bergh was cleaning himself up. The story got into the newspapers. Official and public opinion was outraged. The incident turned into the greatest cricketing diplomatic row in the years between the Bodyline tour and the boycott of South Africa. MCC grovellingly apologised, offered to cancel the tour and pay compensation.

The tour did go on – just. In the old-fashioned way, Carr, who had not held the bucket, carried the can. He went on to become one of the game's most distinguished administrators, but he never played a Test match after that and, now nearing 70, still vaguely wonders if things would have been different had it not happened. He has been back many times to Pakistan. He thinks the incident has been forgiven – but never wholly forgotten.

If the symbol of cricketing conflict between England and Australia is the Ashes, then in the absence of a more formal trophy, the bucket of water must stand as the symbol for the conflict between England and Pakistan. Of all England's cricketing relationships, it has consistently been the most fraught and the least satisfactory.

At Lord's today the teams begin battle again, starting a three-Test series. The two captains – Mike Atherton and Wasim Akram – both play for Lancashire and are friends; everyone is expressing the hope that the series will, for once, be played in a good spirit. But as the game starts, three former captains – on the one side Ian Botham and Allan Lamb of England, on the other Imran Khan of Pakistan – will still be stuck a couple of miles away in the Strand, contesting a libel case that is turning into a legal Battle of the Somme. It is now entering its ninth day at a cost of about 15 guineas a minute. 'No one can deny,' Imran's QC, George Carman, said the other day, 'that this case is emotionally charged. Issues of race, class and country move in and out of it like black clouds.'

Court 13 is merely the latest spat in a deeply troubled relationship. On the surface, things were mostly quiet in the years after the water crisis. Pakistan, who actually won a Test in their first series here in 1954, were not good enough to beat England in the sixties or seventies. But behind the scenes, Abdul Hafeez Kardar, their first Test captain, was an abrasive figure who battled hard to undermine MCC's post-imperial dominance of the international game, something which did not end until the nineties. And in the eighties, when the teams were much more closely matched, open warfare began.

In 1982 the Test and County Cricket Board refused a Pakistani request to drop David Constant as a Test umpire. There was a similar dispute five years later involving Ken Palmer. It was against that background that Mike Gatting had his celebrated finger-wagging and shouting match with the Pakistani umpire Shakoor Rana the following winter.

Then, in 1992, came the row over ball-tampering, covered up by English cricket for fear of Pakistani wrath and litigiousness.

Why should England and Pakistan always produce such arguments? England and Australia have a perfect sporting love-hate relationship; English cricket has always been affectionate towards South Africa – too affectionate, which is one reason the game handled apartheid so ineptly; with West Indies any racial undertones are muted by mutual respect; England-India series are always amiable.

Somehow the Indians accept our national arrogance more phlegmatically than the Pakistanis. And from time to time English cricket has behaved very badly towards Pakistan. It was outrageous that their complaints about English umpires were treated so frivolously. 'Every mistake our umpires make is labelled as cheating,' says the former Pakistan captain Intikhab Alam. 'Every mistake their umpires make is an error of judgment.'

Umpiring is the usual overt *casus belli* but Athar Ali, the London correspondent of the Karachi paper Dawn, thinks the roots of the trouble lie in soil far deeper in cricket. 'You have to remember the background of Partition. Most Pakistanis came to feel that Pakistan was dealt with badly by Britain. Mountbatten remained as Governor-General of India and had a soft spot for India and the

Indian leadership. In matters of boundaries and sharing out the money, that came through strongly. That's why Kashmir was left in dispute.'

And the grievances have been reinforced by the post-colonial experience. Vast numbers of Pakistanis now have relatives here. They listen to the news, often obsessively. They know that Asian immigrants, Pakistani or not, are known as 'Pakis' and that hitting them is known as 'Paki-bashing'. They believe that many of the problems their migrants have here derive from religious rather than racial prejudice.

It is impossible to ignore the role of Islam in this. It is not a religion that most westerners find instantly attractive, as they might Hinduism or Buddhism. When cricketers visit Pakistan this is crucial to their experience of the country. There may be some hardships in visiting India but most intelligent tourists are captivated by the diversity and the charming dottiness of the place. Pakistan is a far more homogenous country: more dictatorial, less tolerant. The men dress identically; the women are hidden away. The bars were closed in the Islamic revival of the late 1970s, which means there is nowhere to congregate at the end of a hot day's cricket.

It certainly does not mean it is impossible to get a drink. The country is awash with malt whisky. I have myself drunk Johnnie Walker Black Label with a member of the Anti-Corruption Commission. If cricketers felt the official detestation of alcohol were more sincere, they would find it easier to accept. What they sense is national hypocrisy. And when Ian Botham came back and said that Pakistan was a good place to send his mother-in-law, his team-mates might have felt he was tactless, but he was voicing a general prejudice, about the country as well as about mothers-in-law.

The English are very insensitive, and Pakistan is a very touchy country. People there are convinced the western media treats them unfairly. Athar Ali points to a recent TV documentary about child labour. 'It pinpointed Pakistan. This is something that goes on in a lot of Asian countries, Taiwan, Korea, China, India. But this was all about Pakistan.

'Take BCCI. When it closed, a lot of people in Pakistan refused to believe it was corrupt. They felt it was a Jewish conspiracy against a

Muslim bank. They see double-standards whenever Muslim countries are involved.' In her book, *Waiting For Allah*, Christina Lamb described Pakistan as a country obsessed with plots. 'A plane cannot simply crash in the mountains, it has to be shot down by Indians or hijacked by Afghan secret agents. Even changes in train timetables are blamed on secret conspiracies.'

Inevitably, this has fed through to the country's most important sport. Cricket happens to be a game dependent on mutual trust between the combatants and the integrity of its officials. The reality behind Intikhab's umpiring paradox is that there really is a culture of anti-Pakistani feeling among English umpires. The best of them will hide it well, and try hard not to let it influence their judgments, even subconsciously. But many believe the Pakistanis have, more than anyone else, broken the laws about ball-tampering; that many of their players appeal aggressively and play argumentatively; and that successive captains have allowed these habits to fester.

At the same time it is beyond reasonable doubt that some Pakistani umpires have been corrupt. I have seen a visiting batsman become the victim of what may be a unique double; given out lbw, having hit the ball, in the first innings; and caught behind, having missed it, in the second. It was enormously redemptive that Pakistan recognised the problem and was the first to press for the system of third-country umpires that has now become mandatory throughout Test cricket.

There are two possible explanations for Pakistani umpiring. Athar Ali prefers the less discreditable. 'It is a new country with some complexes. It equates itself with India, which is much larger, and Pakistanis, including the umpires, don't like to lose.' The second point is that, uniquely, the Pakistan Cricket Board is appointed by the government and is thus dependent on political patronage. One can only speculate on the pressures that might have transmitted themselves to the umpires.

Four years ago, after a bad-tempered England-Pakistan Test at Old Trafford, Simon Heffer wrote a piece about the Pakistanis in the *Sunday Telegraph*, headed 'The pariahs of cricket'. It was a robust piece, which used the word 'cheating' a lot. It drew various writs, and the *Telegraph* nervously settled. Heffer, who has now changed employers, remains unrepentant. 'It wasn't racist, it was political. Pakistan is the only country where the cricket board is an extension of government.'

And it is intriguing that Heffer's view is shared, from a very different position on the political spectrum, by the writer Tariq Ali. 'The board became highly politicised during General Zia-ul-Haq's regime. That was a time when the country really did get pretty awful and he was a great believer in using cricket politically. In comparison, Indian cricket has remained fairly gentlemanly. In Pakistan it's always been more of a street sport, like football in England.'

The Heffer row came well before the revelations about the power of the Bombay and Karachi bookmakers, and the suggestions that they influenced Salim Malik, the former captain, to offer bribes to Australian players to throw a match. Malik was cleared by a Pakistani judge, who rejected the allegations without having actually heard them.

And so to Lord's. This Test will be under the control of two of the world's toughest umpires, the Englishman Peter Willey and the Jamaican Steve Bucknor. In the meantime events in Court 13 move inexorably towards a conclusion in which an honourable draw is no longer an option. Everyone hopes for a Test match of honest endeavour, without suspicion or rancour.

But there is something else that needs to be said about the Pakistanis. Most of the population are Punjabis – strong, brave people who in the old days provided the backbone of the Raj's army. They also make terrific cricketers. If they play anywhere near their capacity I believe they will beat England. Fair and square.

Guardian, 25 July 1996

My memories: Tom Graveney

John Stern

Tom Graveney's last visit to Pakistan as an England player was an exercise more in keeping limbs rather than wickets intact.

The tour of 1968-69 ended early when the third Test in Karachi was abandoned after three days' play because of rioting spectators. 'Every session there were disturbances,' Graveney remembers. 'On the Saturday morning, we saw a cloud of dust on the horizon and it was a mass of people coming to disrupt the match. We just left the pitch immediately although the one player who didn't want to leave was Alan Knott because he was on 96. The place was filled with police. We lay on the floor of the coach with bricks crashing against the side of it – it was terrifying.'

That Test was also noteworthy for a Graveney century, the debut of Sarfraz Nawaz and the last England appearance by Colin Milburn, who lost an eye in a car crash only a few weeks after the end of the tour.

'That 68-9 tour was a disaster because we were almost involved in a civil war,' adds Graveney. 'We were due to go to Dacca but there was so much unrest that we didn't want to go. We had a cable from the High Commission telling us that if we didn't go, the Embassy would be burned down. We decided to go on the promise of protection which didn't happen. We drove in from the airport and there were no police anywhere because the city was being run by students.'

Indeed the report of that drawn second Test at Dacca in the *Wisden Book of Test Cricket* simply reads: 'The only riot-free match of this rubber was played in front of crowds controlled by the student leaders of East Pakistan and without either police or army presence.'

That tour was Graveney's second trip to Pakistan. His first in

1951-52 was an unofficial tour because Pakistan had not been afforded full Test status at that stage. MCC played two games against Pakistan after their first official Test against India. Having drawn on a grass wicket at Lahore, MCC lost on a matting wicket in Karachi.

'I had played on coconut matting pitches for the Army in Egypt but it was a new experience for many of the players. Pakistan were masters at bowling medium-pace cutters that turned and bounced. Fazal Mahmood, who took seven wickets in that game, was virtually unplayable on a matting wicket. That was also the first time I saw Hanif Mohammad, who was only 16 then. He was Pakistan's first great player. There was something of Boycott about him in that he went on and on.'

Pakistan's first official tour here was in 1954 and Graveney, then 27, missed the first Test through illness. 'I had been coughing up blood a week or so before that game and was worried. I thought I might have TB. The doctor said I had to have three weeks off.'

He returned for the second Test at Trent Bridge in which a Pakistani leg-spinner called Khalid Hassan made his debut 14 days short of his 17th birthday to become the youngest Test cricketer at the time. According to Graveney, who made 84 in England's innings, he was 'slaughtered' by Denis Compton, who made his highest Test score of 278. Khalid took two for 116 off 21 overs and, for whatever reason, never played Test cricket again.

England won comfortably at Nottingham by an innings and 129 runs and, following a rain-affected draw at Old Trafford, went to The Oval for the final match in the four-Test series one-nil up. Unfortunately, selectorial minds were already turning to the winter tour of Australia and England slipped up.

Requiring a modest 168 to win on the fourth evening, England, led by Len Hutton, showed a remarkably unprofessional attitude to winning the match. Graveney explains: 'At tea on the fourth day, there was a feeling in the pavilion of let's get this over with and have an extra day off. A lot of us were having our medicals for the Australia tour the day after so we were keen to have a bit more free time. The batting order was changed with Godfrey Evans going in at five ahead of me. We made a tactical error and paid for it.' From 109 for two, England collapsed to 143 all out with Fazal Mahmood taking his second six-wicket haul of the match.

The 1962 home series against Pakistan was a successful one for Graveney and the team, England winning three and drawing one of the four Tests. Graveney's series scores were 97, 153, 37 and 114. England were captained by Ted Dexter whom Graveney described as 'not a great captain but a magnificent player – no one could bowl to him when he had the bit between his teeth.'

Five years later the Pakistanis returned, captained by Hanif, who made a superb 187 not out at Lord's in the first Test when Graveney and Ken Barrington put on 201 for the third wicket. It was also the occasion of Graveney receiving 'the best ball I ever faced', delivered by debutant seamer Salim Altaf. 'I was 70-odd not out overnight but the pitch was a bit damp. Bowling from the pavilion end, he pitched one on leg, it moved up the slope and hit off.'

Salim may not have achieved legendary status but he can be proud of Graveney's accolade. There were not many bowlers who bamboozled the great man.

TCCB Official Souvenir Programme, 22-26 August 1996

Atherton and Stewart steel themselves to save the day

Christopher Martin-Jenkins

Mike Atherton was a historian not a classicist in his academic days but in a foreword to a recent book he quotes Aeneas adjuring the Trojans to 'endure and preserve yourself for better things'. That is all that England could do, by no means for the first time in the Atherton era, once Wasim Akram had declared Pakistan's second innings just before tea yesterday, the fourth day of the first Test here.

What followed was a thrilling, highly-charged session in which Atherton's tremendous relish for a fight enabled him to lead England's struggle for survival into the fifth day. With Alec Stewart, another who likes nothing better than an innings for his country, he took England to 74 for one in theoretical pursuit of a target of 408 to win.

Well as Atherton and Stewart batted, both in more fluent form than during their longer stand at Trent Bridge, Waqar Younis's devastating inswingers and Mushtaq Ahmed's leg-breaks and googlies, turning substantially, came close to breaking through on several occasions. Atherton was dropped down the leg-side by Rashid Latif off Ata-ur-Rehman when he had scored 19. That would have been 39 for two because Nick Knight had already succumbed to Waqar, leg before on the back foot.

The forecasters predict a cloudy day with possible showers today. England will need all the help the weather can give them if they are to survive. They were given four sessions of play to win or save the game, but, like the Trojans, they could hope for no better than a draw and a chance to do better at Headingley. Against New Zealand here two years ago and India earlier this season, England saved Lord's Tests in circumstances not dissimilar to these, but their chances against a sharper attack than those two countries possessed will no doubt depend on whether Atherton gets set again this morning.

He had plenty to say during the early stages of his innings yesterday, first when the new ball was exchanged for another in only the third over after going out of shape – the fifth time in the match that this has been necessary – then when Moin Khan, substitute for Aamir Sohail, was warned publicly by umpire Steve Bucknor for yapping away at Atherton from his position at silly mid-off. Finally, Atherton complained, not without some logic, when the umpires also allowed a substitute for Inzamam-ul-Haq, who had earlier batted for three hours with a bruised knee and moved well enough to strike nine thunderous boundaries.

The atmosphere was intense but not nasty, which is as it should be in a Test. Atherton and Wasim were in friendly conversation as they left the field discussing where they would dine together last night, and the Pakistan team applauded Atherton and Stewart for a job well done. It is far from completed, however: Pakistan swept through England's tail on Saturday, taking four wickets for nine runs in one 16-ball period, a warning of what might happen even if England were to get to lunch today without further mishap.

A minimum of 124 overs remained when the fourth innings started, the additional four resulting from England's delaying tactics towards the end of Pakistan's innings. Up to lunch at least they had kept up a respectable rate, but by failing to separate Ijaz Ahmed and Inzamam-ul-Haq, both of whom batted comfortably and attractively on the still dead-slow pitch, they were obliged to go on to the defensive.

Dominic Cork took the two wickets to fall yesterday with the new ball, but Alan Mullally was the most economical of the England bowlers, keeping a tight line from both over and round the wicket and bowling a proper length consistently. He has settled down quickly at the highest level, and he will get many more helpful pitches than this as time goes on. Simon Brown bowled much better against the right-handers than the left but he swung the ball only minimally. Ian Salisbury bowled calmly, with good control and not much luck. His figures are neither better nor worse, at this stage, than Mushtaq's.

The slowness of the pitch has done neither any favours but Pakistan have controlled this match from the moment that Graham Thorpe played a ball from Ata-ur-Rehman on to his stumps just before lunch on Saturday. Thorpe and Jack Russell combined effectively, their left-handedness helping them to keep out Mushtaq's subtle probings and their ability to play the ball very late helping them against the swing first of Wasim then of Waqar. It was only when the junior professional, so to speak, came on that Pakistan found a way through a partnership which was threatening to bring the game back on an even keel.

England were 260 for five, only 80 behind, when the fresh and eager Rehman surprised Thorpe with a bit of extra bounce, much as he had Mark Ealham the previous day. Thorpe's bat had not quite reached a straight position as he defended off the back foot and the resulting play-on increased the number of Test fifties he has been unable to translate into hundreds to 17.

England, however, would have been in a pretty pickle without him. Russell remained, doughty and shrewd, to squeeze what he could from the brief remainder of the innings as Waqar joined Rehman in its swift destruction. No ball was more remarkable than the dipping, inswinging full-toss by Waqar to Mullally, a devastating Exocet for anyone to get second ball, let alone a tailender. It was exactly like a baseball pitch, delivered with a straight arm, of course, but with a certain twist of the wrist which produces a swerve unique to Waqar. If it is in working order this morning, England will need luck as well as skill.

Daily Telegraph, 29 July 1996

Wasim's happy band strikes the right note

Michael Henderson

The Pakistanis have recruited an unlikely ally on this latest tour of England: Dale Carnegie. Wasim Akram has led such a contented group of players that they appear to have heeded the American author's famous advice on how to win friends and influence people. Winning helps, of course, but the atmosphere on the field has been healthy and happy, with wickets and runs punctuated by smiles and laughter.

The last tour, four years ago, was fraught with misunderstandings, not to mention 'incidents'. The 'lowlight' of that acrimonious series was the bust-up at Old Trafford when that notable sportsman, Mr J. Miandad, failed to keep his players in check after Aqib Javed remonstrated about a trivial point of order with Roy Palmer, the umpire.

Indeed, far from restraining them, Miandad egged them on like a reckless schoolboy, who likes to goad the teacher but prefers other children to have their collars felt. It worked, too. In a feeble response to this unruly behaviour, Conrad Hunte, the International Cricket Council match referee, imitated Pontius Pilate, telling the captains they were responsible for what their players got up to.

How different it all is this summer. The relationship between Wasim and Michael Atherton has filtered down to the ranks, so there has not been any unpleasantness on the field – as opposed to off it, where those on the Western Terrace have lived down to their reputation. Even David Attenborough would think twice before venturing into that mephitic jungle.

When Nick Knight left the field yesterday, after completing his first Test century, nobody applauded much more vigorously than little Mushtaq Ahmed, the man whose catch ended his innings. 'Mushy' is having a whale of a time this summer, bowling splendidly and sharing a joke with anybody who wants to join in. Those smiles are a bracing antidote to the snarls and fisticuffs that Headingley witnessed yet again on Saturday afternoon.

Wasim can take much of the credit for the transformation of attitudes. His contribution may be compared with that of his mentor and fellow Lahori, whose name quite escapes me, and ultimately it might be more telling because he does not regard the team as his personal fiefdom.

The other chap (does anybody know whatever became of him?) is nothing if not self-important, and sounds increasingly pompous in his public statements. Wasim, who is more tolerant of less gifted players, does not see the point in brushing up his halo, and he has had much the more difficult job.

Captains of Pakistan, like Italian Prime Ministers and Newcastle centre forwards, are never around for long before another one comes along. Wasim found that out soon after he succeeded thingummyjig in 1992. Within 12 months he was unseated by a players' revolt and he got the job back only last winter, for the tour of Australia and New Zealand.

Before the first Test in Brisbane, which Pakistan lost inside four days, Wasim stated unequivocally: 'My main mission is to restore our reputation.' By the end of that series he had helped to do that from a cricketing point of view. Pakistan won the Sydney Test in fine style and, although they came unstuck during the World Cup, they have begun anew in England.

From the start of this tour, their players were smiling and taking time to talk to people. It may be that, having suffered the outrageous calumnies of their fellow countrymen after losing to India in the World Cup quarter-final, they realise that cricket, however important, is not everything.

So the manner of this series, established at Lord's, has continued satisfactorily at Headingley, although the big ball debate, frankly, has become tiresome. Predictably there were some ribald comments aimed at the Pakistanis on Saturday, when the ball apparently lost its shape, and the most ribald of the lot came from a former player who should know better. F. S. Trueman thought the ground was half-empty on the first day because there are 'no personalities' any more. Perhaps it is just as well.

The Times, 12 August1996

England selectors drawn into dilemma

Mike Selvey

Once England had failed to take the initiative on the first morning this was always going to be a difficult game for them to win and, as expected, it meandered to a draw yesterday.

After batting themselves to safety on the third day and then into the lead on Sunday they still had the vaguest of chances yesterday but victory depended on some incisive bowling. Although the seamers, in particular Andrew Caddick and Dominic Cork, operated effectively Pakistan were never in any real danger of collapse and, with half-centuries from Ijaz Ahmed and Inzamam-ul-Haq, reached 247 for seven – a lead of 196 – when Wasim Akram declared and the teams called it a day.

There is something vaguely familiar about the way this series is panning out. Two years ago South Africa won the first Test at Lord's and then played out a draw at Leeds. At The Oval Devon Malcolm produced one of the most destructive spells of Test-match bowling to level the series. England are now required to repeat that win to share the spoils in this series.

Although re-laying this pitch strangled the life out of it, making batting easier than anticipated, much fell into place during this game. Stewart's century which brought him the Man of the Match award showed that his feet are moving him into position better than at any time over the past two years, while the vitality and confidence shown by Nick Knight and John Crawley was a revelation.

The selectors have a dilemma on their hands, however. If they are to have a chance of winning at The Oval, they need all the bowling they can get. If a batsman has to drop out it will be Crawley or Knight and by no means is it clear-cut that the latter would retain his place purely on the basis that he had made a century.

Certainly his left-handedness helped to counter the threat of Waqar Younis in particular but there is a belief that Crawley is the only batsman in the England side who can read Mushtaq's leg spin.

Nor will the performance of the bowlers here have made selection any easier. Yesterday Cork bowled his best spell of the match up the hill from the Football Stand end, gaining some rhythm and late movement, and he collected the wicket of Saeed Anwar, caught behind off his second delivery. But with Darren Gough and, maybe, Malcolm waiting in the wings, Caddick did most to stake a claim for the next match, striding stiffly down the slope and taking the wickets of Inzamam, Salim Malik and Ijaz at a cost of 52 runs. His bounce and occasional hostility on a docile pitch would be amplified by the surface at The Oval. Lewis is the most likely to be rejected.

One player who is certain not to be relied upon as a front-line bowler is the England captain, although when the game was entering its death throes Atherton tugged off his cap and bowled seven overs of respectable leg spin. Given the state of his back, bowling is low on his list of priorities; he had not turned his arm over in a Test match since Sydney in 1991.

One wicket for 282 had been his career figures before yesterday and one good clump would have lifted him ahead of the Sri Lankan Wijesuriya for the worst average in Test history. But Wasim offered no stroke to the most gentle of leg-breaks and after long deliberation was given out leg-before by Steve Bucknor.

Inzamam's was the innings of the day, a knock played in much the same languid manner of those that had graced Lord's. At times he lived dangerously, such as when he spliced Caddick over the slips, but some thunderous strokes brought him nine boundaries, including a hook off Caddick that almost defeated the eye. In the same over, however, he top-edged an attempted cut to Stewart at third man.

The last day had been watched by a small gathering and it provided a contrast to the drunken debacle of the weekend when the behaviour of the Western Terrace once more put in jeopardy the future of international cricket here.

Limiting the amount of alcohol that can be brought into the ground is only a part solution and merely leads to larger bar profits for the Leeds Cricket, Football and Athletic Company. A complete ban seems more realistic.

However, the new England Cricket Board will need to look long and hard at its sponsors. Tetley put around £1 million a year into the England team but it is not morally right for cricket to encourage people to drink and then criticise them when they get drunk.

Guardian, 13 August 1996

Here's Looking At . . .

Introduction

The personalities of cricket are not always those with the most famous names. And while the flings and fumbles of any game reveal much, not everything can be discerned at some seventy yards distance or on the telly, particularly in this era of face-obscuring helmets.

That hackneyed line about 'those who stand and wait also serve' could well have been inspired by umpires, but they certainly need no excuse for the inclusion of two remarkable representatives.

Historical figures too, do not escape, those still with us and those now playing on the fields of Elysium.

But today's men take precedence. What have they done and what are they doing?

Master craftsman who turns his cricketing trade into an art form

John Woodcock

Wicketkeepers, as distinct from wicketkeeping goalkeepers, are a rare breed these days. The former are craftsmen, the latter gymnasts with gloves on: the former are mostly small, and neat and painstaking. Robert Charles Russell, known inevitably as Jack and at present playing for England in Port Elizabeth, is one of the former – as natural a wicketkeeper as Lester Piggott was a jockey or Barry John a stand-off half.

It is not generally realised, I think, how big a part timing plays in keeping wicket. In the days when he fielded at first slip for England, Keith Fletcher used to speak of the almost uncanny silence with which the ball entered Bob Taylor's gloves. That was because of Taylor's timing. Russell has the same gift. It is known, sometimes, as having 'good hands', which, again, wicketkeepers are either born with or they are not.

Russell remembers distinctly the moment when he resolved that one day he would keep wicket for England. It was his fourteenth birthday and he was watching England playing Australia at Headingley on the television, and he saw Alan Knott take a flying, one-handed catch in front of first slip off Tony Greig. In that instant, his ambition was fired.

From starting as Russell's hero, Knott is now his guru. Seldom a week has gone by on this tour of South Africa without Knott ringing Russell up, either because he has spotted something or other on the television, usually a technical point, or just for a talk. Ian Healy, Russell's opposite number in the present Australia side, is another who is regularly on the phone.

Russell and Knott are alike in many ways. Both are creatures of habit, and they are both fastidious. On one of Knott's tours – I think it was in Australia – the rooms on one side of this particular hotel's corridors had baths, whereas those on the other had showers. Knott's had a shower, but he is addicted to baths, so he came and used mine. After he had been closeted in the bathroom for an hour or so I felt compelled to ask him whether he was 'all right in there', and, of course, he was. All the powdering and the grooming and the soaping and the toning and the trimming and the towelling that went on was not vanity but orderliness. I cannot speak for Russell's ablutionary procedures, but in preparing to keep wicket he is every bit as meticulous as his mentor, and at the end of a day in the field he, too, is content with his own company, pursuing what amounts to his second profession.

Touring cricketers have much time on their hands. On his first overseas tour, to Pakistan in 1987-88, when he was the reserve wicketkeeper, Russell played two days' cricket in eight weeks. In Australia last winter, when he was sent for to reinforce the England party, he was there for 43 days without being given a game or even offered a net. So in his early touring days he took up painting, and he is now an artist of no little repute.

Russell has become primarily a landscape painter. Arthur Mailey, the illustrious Australian, as enchanting a wit as he was enticing a bowler in the 1920s, published some lovely cartoons and caricatures, and Bill Ferguson, faithful baggage-master-cum-scorer for most England and Australia touring sides between 1910 and 1950, made a little sketch into his book of the grounds on which he scored. Martin Speight, of Sussex, another wicketkeeper, is quite an artist now; but the sums which Russell commands put him in a class of his own.

In his first exhibition, some ten years ago, a work of his fetched from £50 to £200. Today, the range is from £500 to £12,000. His picture of the moment of England's victory over West Indies in Barbados in April 1994, the first on the ground for 50 years, is the most valuable of them all, being of account, of course, as a unique piece of cricketana, in view of the artist's identity and the fact that he played in the match, as well as for its other merits. Others are to be found in the gallery that he owns in Chipping Sodbury. Besides being a cricketer and an artist, our subject is quite an entrepreneur.

Russell is 5ft 8¼in, 'a quarter of an inch too short to be a policeman', he said. A wicketkeeper's shape is important. Indeed, if it were not for Don Tallon, I might say it is crucial. In the past 50 years, anyway, Tallon is the only one of six feet in height who has been absolutely in the top class. He was very thin, very deaf, very tall and very good. Keith Miller still puts him at the top of his list; but Tallon was the exception that proves the rule.

None of the other six-footers that I have seen, Clyde Walcott included, has looked quite right. John Murray and Johnny Waite, two great stylists, were probably 5ft 10in, but the best of the others have all been less than that. Here are a few whose height, or lack of it, suggests it helps to be near the ground: Herbert Strudwick, Bert Oldfield, George Duckworth, Arthur Wood, Godfrey Evans, Arthur

McIntyre and Wally Grout, together with Knott and Taylor. There have been some outstanding midgets, too, like Andy Wilson, of Gloucester, and 'Tich' Cornford, of Sussex.

Colin Metson, of Glamorgan, *proxime accessit* to Russell in England at the moment, and Keith Piper, of Warwickshire, who is making a reputation for himself, are not tall either; but I am afraid that, for them, the prospects of immediate preferment are remote. Russell, 32, is having the time of his life in South Africa. Despite the loss of almost five full days' play in the Test series, he has already claimed a remarkable 23 victims (21 catches and two stumpings). The 11 catches he took in the second Test in Johannesburg set a world record, and it was he, too, using a batting method never seen by man before, who stood by his captain through the heroic rear-guard action which saved that match.

I began this piece by saying that there are, these days, wicketkeepers and goalkeepers. That is because so much wicketkeeping work is now done standing back, diving this way and that, whereas it used mostly to be done standing up to the stumps, even to the medium-paced bowlers. Evans and McIntyre always stood up to Alec Bedser, for example. Russell, I am sure, would have been well able to do the same, but it is not of many who are playing today that I could say that.

No wicketkeeper has ever been remotely infallible. The drawback for them in this modern age is that every mistake that they make is picked up and endlessly repeated on television. Perfectionist though he is, Russell misses chances. He has had his critics, though at present they are silenced; he has been rusticated, and he has come back from rustication, still wearing the well-hung sun-hat that made its first appearance in 1981. It travels well; so does its owner.

The Times, 30 December 1995

In any crisis, send for The Specialist

Rob Steen

Any Martians on a recce in India over the next fortnight will be forgiven a sense of confusion. How, they might reasonably wonder, can a team's likeliest match-winner go into battle knowing that, no matter what wonders he performs, he will be jettisoned by June? But then no career personifies the schizophrenic existence of the late-20th-century cricketer quite so vividly as that of Neil Fairbrother.

Mr Hyde is the Fairbrother with 10 Test caps spanning six years, an intermittent, inglorious affair encompassing a solitary fifty and nine scores in single digits. In 51 one-day internationals, conversely, Dr Jekyll's average borders on 40, a terrain occupied only by the elite. While Lara may be about to make a few innocent bowlers pay for his recent miseries, Fairbrother's disdain for orthodoxy will get up just as many noses. Probably more.

The character explains the enigma. David Hughes, the former Lancashire captain, believes Fairbrother inherited his volatility and aggression from his mother. 'He's intense,' avers David Lloyd, the Lancashire coach, the tone a blend of mystification and awe. 'Tenacious, very busy, always on a flippin' high, eyeballs always spinning round his head.'

Few activities tickle an Englishman's fancy as much as pigeon-holing, and Fairbrother was consigned to his hole long ago. Flighty yet flinty left-hander, long on talent, short on concentration, ingenious with open face and slice, but stock the slips and watch virtue turn to vice. His canvases, none the less, are certainly more worthy of a spot at the Tate than any of Damien Hirst's dubious creations. An effervescent fusion of instinct and intent, daring and imagination, clarity of thought and speed of execution. Here, moreover, is infectiousness, the capacity to raise spirits as well as tempo.

Those attributes were in ample evidence during the last World Cup final, a lone, nerveless 62 almost denying Imran Khan his cancer hospital. The circumstances were not dissimilar at the Wanderers last month. Donald and Pollock were snarling, the ball swinging, the crowd baying. As usual, HMS England was sinking. Send for the elf with the oversized bat and the over-roomy helmet.

Lips pursed, chin jutting, brain whirring, Fairbrother was in his element. Full of nerve and verve, a master of angle and touch. One moment he was threading a cut through a five-yard gap between backward point and short third man, the next sliding head-long to complete a second that was barely a first. Neither was that the end of his derring-do. When Snell fired a shell towards cover, he misjudged the trajectory, staggered backwards yet still contrived to pull the blurring projectile down in his right, ie wrong, hand.

Call him a one-day specialist, though, and, such is the snobbery of his trade, he feels he is being disparaged. The typecasting, not unnaturally, annoys and frustrates. He is a professional cricketer, end of story. So he happens to have more good days with one skill than another. So what? In all, the lions have adorned his chest on 61 occasions – nearly twice as many as Washbrook. His 366 against Surrey in 1990 makes him joint 11th on the first page of the Wisden records section – ahead of Grace, Hobbs and Hutton, and both Richardses. Not bad for an alleged under-achiever.

At the same time, he has suffered more than most from the whims of superiors with as much grasp of human psychology as Freud's right knee. There he was in the Texaco Trophy at Lord's in 1991, scuttling to a match-winning century, driving Marshall, Ambrose and Walsh completely potty. Now, surely, was the moment for an extended audition as a 'proper' cricketer, to test his mettle while the heady taste of self-affirmation was still fresh. Come the first Test, he made way for the fading Lamb. As strategy, short-term or long, it was not so much blind as dumb.

Fairbrother's Test debut against Pakistan in 1987 was similarly marred. Out he marched into the Manchester murk, 20 minutes before stumps, a time when every good night-watchman deserves favour. Back he trudged five balls later, leg-before for nought, whereupon scores of three, one and one saw him shelved. Bone-headedness on the bridge never did do much for the confidence of the crew.

Lloyd prefers to dwell on the attributes that have enabled Fairbrother to claim centre stage by an alternative route: 'He's very brainy. He improvises, manoeuvres the strike, plays in areas that are hard to protect. He kick-starts the innings, takes the game away from the opposition, annoys the hell out of them. And he's a flamin' winner.'

All of which makes rather a mockery of England's insistence on sending him in at No 6. As manager of the England Under-19s, Lloyd may be destined for higher things, hence the cloak of diplomacy: 'At Lancashire, Neil's best position is probably four. That way, he can come in behind a solid platform but still have plenty of overs at his disposal.'

Fairbrother's occasional wilfulness may jar with Lloyd the coach, but Lloyd the fan would pay to watch him, any time, any place: 'It's unfortunate he's got this tag as a one-day player. If they'd put in a night-watchman on his Test debut, it could have been the making of him. He keeps his counsel about that, and at 32, would regard a recall now as a bonus. But he's played some wonderful, sustained knocks for us in the championship. There was a double hundred against Middlesex on a supposedly unfit pitch that cost us 25 points. Is that a temperament unsuited to Test cricket?'

The question, surely, is whether Test cricket, with its emphasis on self-denial at the expense of self-expression, suits Fairbrother. If those eyeballs are spinning in the Lahore final next month, who cares?

Sunday Times, 11 February 1996

Wally Hammond

David Foot

Why the compulsion, on my part, to write about Hammond? After all, I saw him play only a few times, and then on Bank Holidays when his imperious off-drives were relegated in my imagination and schoolboyish idolatry as no more than pale imitations of those sweet cover boundaries from Somerset's opener, Harold Gimblett, then my especial hero.

Gloucestershire were never warmly embraced at Taunton. It was rather more than neighbourly rivalry, something to do with the collective personalities of the two teams. I can certainly remember more smiles from the Somerset players as they cantered round the field in vain pursuit of the ball. Bill Andrews once told me: 'We didn't much enjoy our matches with Gloucestershire. They were such miserable sods. I'd pop my head into their dressing room before play started to wish them good morning. It seemed to me that dear old Reg Sinfield was the only one who came back with any kind of greeting.'

The gut reactions of the famously flamboyant Andrews were often extreme, as scathing as they could be wonderfully generous in spirit. Individually, there were in those distant days some delightful members of the Gloucestershire side. But when you put them all together and took them off to Taunton, their eyes glazed over and they could appear joyless. That at least was my impression, as a partisan Somerset native.

Jewish blood brothers, Bev and Dar Lyon, bared their teeth on one occasion, when Sinfield stone-walled interminably under orders and Gloucestershire won. Wally, like many of the finest stroke-makers, relished the Taunton wicket – and the food at The Castle. He had few friends within the Somerset club; indeed there was never much conviviality before or after matches.

It was Andrews himself who momentarily rearranged the chemistry. He was bowling at his own county ground, on a length, when Hammond braced the shoulders and hit him straight for six. It was the most exquisite and effortless of drives, demonstrating sublime mastery over a good county bowler who had done nothing wrong. The spontaneous reaction of Andrews was to shake his head in unreserved admiration and to applaud for ten seconds or more.

I have no idea whether Hammond noticed. The laconic Jack White, Somerset's captain, did. He walked slowly from mid-off and rebuked Andrews. Farmers from the Quantocks and beyond went to market and didn't concede sentimental ground when it came to buying a steer. Nor did bowlers go soft when opposing batsmen hit them for six. 'I didn't openly applaud Wally again although there were times when I wanted to, mostly off my bowling,' Andrews used to tell me. 'But Wally didn't return the compliment,' he'd joke. 'I'm pretty sure he vetoed my chance of playing for England just before the war.'

This isn't predominantly a cricket book, so my painfully limited experience of Hammond's batting is not important. By the time I first saw him, just after the war, the marvellous athleticism was disappearing. He had put on weight and, from my close-range observations at the lunch and tea breaks, the face was already looking middle-aged and blotchy. Was this 'the Bristol Prince' they used to talk so poetically about, I asked myself. Yet I still stood in fifth-form awe, just a few feet away, as he walked back on to the field. Tom Graveney and others talk unselfconsciously of how they worshipped him, of that extraordinary *presence*, and I know exactly what they mean.

I suppose I have wanted to write at length about Hammond since the mid-1950s, when I arrived to work in Bristol. That was when I first met Bert Williams, the Bristol Rovers FC trainer (or sponge-man, as these soccer craftsmen were still evocatively called). As a boy he'd steered the horse for his groundsman-father, Alf, to cut and roll the grass at the Eastville ground. By the 1919-20 season he was assistant groundsman himself. Bert was to live in a house just a few yards from a corner-flag. It was proudly painted in the club's colours of blue and white. Rovers never had a more loyal servant; he was with them for well over half a century. Hammond, who at school had shown exceptional gifts as a footballer as well as a cricketer, had signed forms for Rovers in 1921. Bert immediately took on a paternal role, which in fact continued when Hammond left football and concentrated solely on his cricket. Bert's wife did his laundry for 'a couple of bob a week'. There was always a pile of washing – the earliest signs of a clean and fastidious dresser were beginning to emerge.

Hammond had not benefited from a father who was emotionally close to him. There had been the strange nomadic army life in impersonal quarters. Then there had just been his mother. The gentle relationship between Wally and Bert could not have been more timely. Here was someone to confide in: whether about his sporting aspirations or the disturbing complexes of his emotional life. I gained the impression that Hammond talked more candidly to Williams than to anyone else in his whole life. The Rovers man was simple and yet wise. He was strong on human nature, with a sly East Bristol sense of humour.

'That's a smart old banger you've got, Wally. All the boys are envious of you. And they know why you've bought it.'

'Why's that then, Bert?'

'To take out them girls from the Prince's, the Hippodrome or the Empire in Old Market.'

Hammond would laugh. As ever, he gave nothing away. But his car, such a rarity among poorly paid young pros, would be spotted outside the local theatres late at night, as he waited for the chorus girls to do their final number and chase out of the stage door in perfumed high spirits. His romantic interest in one particular dancer was vaguely known to the Rovers boys.

The other players were never sure what to make of him. 'This lad's got something about him. But he won't stick to this – it's going to be cricket,' Bert told them. He himself puzzled over the enigmatic personality. It wasn't that Hammond was a good talker or particularly sophisticated, but his ambition, his eagerness to better himself socially, impressed Williams. And the handsome features appealed to the chorus girls.

Wally Hammond: The Reasons Why, David Foot
(Robson Books, 1996)

Dennis Brookes at 80

Andrew Radd

The lives of a few extraordinary men are history lessons in themselves. Harold Wilson picked up the theme when paying tribute to Sir Winston Churchill, recalling '. . . the shots in Sidney Street, the angry guns of Gallipoli, Flanders, Coronel and the Falkland Islands; the sullen feet of marching men in Tonypandy; the urgent warnings of the Nazi threat; the whine of the sirens and the dawn bombardment of the Normandy beaches . . .' Snapshots of great events, with the old statesman as the common denominator.

Which brings us to Dennis Brookes, who celebrated his 80th birthday, quietly and with an entirely characteristic absence of fuss, last October. As player, coach, administrator, officer and committeeman he has witnessed at first hand pretty well all the County's highs and lows since that momentous trial match back in 1932.

But he would never pretend to have experienced everything the game of cricket has to offer. Take last season, for example. 'It was a remarkable year, and as a watcher I was thrilled with it. There were so many times when we looked to be out of the reckoning but still came back to win. Extraordinary.'

The victory over Nottinghamshire in August? 'I've never seen anything like it before.' It's a judgement worth noting, coming as it does from a man who made 525 first-class appearances, 492 of them for Northamptonshire, and has observed a few hundred more contests from the other side of the boundary.

Similarly, he might reasonably be expected to know a half-decent cricketer when he sees one. And, certainly in the run-scoring department, he believes the club to be well-blessed at present.

'We've got some very good young batsmen. Mal Loye has bags of ability – he just needs to discipline it a little bit. But I think the best of them is Russell Warren who has all the hallmarks of an outstanding player.

'He has plenty of time, which is really how I judge a batsman. He never seems hurried, he can play all types of bowling and I can see a great future ahead of him.

'As for fast bowlers – well, it's hard work isn't it? But I think containment has now become more important than bowling sides out. No-one seems to pitch the ball up and let it run away or duck in. They're trying to bowl just short of a length to stop the runs, and I think that's having a detrimental effect. It's not just a problem at our county – it looks to be the case all over.

'I can usually make a fair assessment of a player pretty quickly. I remember watching Richard Williams bat for just one over as a fifteen-year-old and immediately telling Ken Turner to sign him up. Some stand out at once while others – by determination and strength of character – develop something that you perhaps didn't see at first glance.'

Dennis himself was snapped up young. After impressing as a triallist in '32 the Northamptonshire committee – according to the minutes – decided that the teenager should be '. . . offered terms, a clerkship and lodgings to be found, and so much pocket money paid'. He justified that faith with nearly 30,000 runs and 67 centuries.

The 'clerkship' reference is significant, for his ability to handle a typewriter during the winter months was, in those early qualifying days, at least as important as his skill with the bat.

'Eric Coley (the County secretary) was playing rugby up in Halifax and I was taken to see him. He said that if I came to Northampton could I type and would I help him in the office? I don't think I would have been taken on otherwise!

'When I first came on trial my aim was just to establish myself. But with the sort of games we had to play then – ridiculous Club and Ground fixtures when anyone who put their name down, regardless of a pot belly, got in the side – I couldn't quite see myself becoming a first-class cricketer.'

Those semi-social, mix-and-match affairs may have been far from ideal for training talented youngsters, but he is equally scathing about the amount of cricketing junk-food – the limited overs stuff – in the modern diet.

'Personally I wouldn't allow them to play one-day games at 2nd XI level. I've always felt that time is the most important thing in cricket, and if you take that away from a batsman you're taking away everything. Players can only develop by spending time at the wicket.

'I think back to Glenn Turner who couldn't hit the ball off the square when he first played for Worcestershire, but they allowed him to work on his game and he eventually became one of the quickest scorers. If you get the basics right, **then** you can go on to the one-dayers – but it's not necessary to play one-day cricket **in order** to develop those basic skills.'

Like most cricketers of his generation he feels the covering of pitches has taken an element out of the game: 'Batsmen rarely use their feet to the spinners now. If you played on a "sticky dog" you had to use them, or you didn't get any runs!'

And it comes as no surprise to hear him single out as his most satisfying innings one which tested his famed technique against spin to the full. Northamptonshire versus Kent at the County Ground in 1952; Dennis carried his bat for 102 out of 185, mastering Doug Wright on a pitch giving the leg-spinner every assistance.

He followed that with 61 in two and a half hours in the second innings, but couldn't prevent the County going down heavily. 'Brookes, acting captain, stood almost alone for Northamptonshire' reported Wisden; none of his colleagues reached 30 in either knock.

It was in that same year that the Indian tourists, off whom he made 156 at Northampton, named him as the best English batsman they had come up against during the summer. He finished the season with 2,229 runs and was still scoring heavily when he retired seven years later. But the England selectors didn't think it worth their while adding to his solitary Test cap, gained against the West Indies in Barbados on Gubby Allen's 1948 expedition.

Could it have been that the men from Lord's – not for the last time – regarded Northamptonshire as less-than-quite-the-ticket-old-boy? The concept of an 'unfashionable county' may be an absurdity, but it was a lump of mud which stuck for too many years, and Dennis Brookes would hardly be human if it didn't rankle a little.

'I don't think it helped, even to the extent that for years I didn't play in the Gentlemen/Players match at Lord's, which was the showcase.' He actually made his first and only appearance in 1959 – his final season – when, at the age of 43, he captained the professionals.

'Frank Chester said to me in 1946, when I was twelfth man for England in the first two Tests against India, that if I got picked for Gents/Players I'd go to Australia that winter, but if I didn't then I wouldn't. And I didn't!

'At the second Test at Old Trafford that year the chap from Simpson's came to measure the side for their tour blazers, and Wally Hammond told me to get myself measured too. So I thought I was going to be on the boat, but it wasn't to be.

'Then in 1951 Freddie Brown sounded me out about possibly going to India with the M.C.C. team that winter as senior professional, but I heard no more about it.' Personal disappointment notwithstanding, he is quick to praise the other outstanding batsmen of his time. He's seen them all, from Herbert Sutcliffe – who had a few encouraging words for the nervous Brookes when he made his Championship debut against Yorkshire at Bradford in 1934 – to the latest wunderkind, Andrew Symonds. And top of the list are Len Hutton, Denis Compton and Peter May.

'The ball never seemed to do anything when Len was batting. He was so sound in his method. If he got one that popped a bit it didn't go to gully – it went down at his feet. Denis was a great improviser who would have been marvellous in the one-day game, and I had a very high regard for Peter because he played at The Oval where the pitches were often poor, and he made batting look like child's play.'

And what of the leading purveyors? 'Alec Bedser was a great

bowler. If you played him on a day when the sun shone and everything was in favour of the batsmen then you thought you could cope. But if the conditions gave him a bit of assistance it was a very different kettle of fish.

'It's a funny thing but none of the spinners – except Tony Lock – seemed to bother me that much. I felt I was equal to them, and I used to really enjoy batting against people like Bruce Dooland and Jack Walsh, very fine bowlers though they were.'

Now, in retirement, he lives a life as neat and orderly as his batsmanship. Few County Ground match days pass without the former club president taking temporary leave of Freda, his wife of 56 years, (they married in 1940 – 'the best day's work I ever did') before heading for the committee balcony.

'I never get tired or weary of watching cricket,' he says. And if anyone deserves to be watching when Northamptonshire capture the Championship for the first time it's 'Mr Brookes' – Player and Gentleman.

Northamptonshire C.C. Handbook, 1996

Graham Thorpe

Tim de Lisle

Meeting me behind the pavilion on a wet day in Durban, Thorpe is affable, unaffected, down-to-earth. His tracksuit, tan, stubble and chewing-gum are standard-issue; his manners are not. He uses your name a lot, asks questions of his own. He has a slight lisp and a small, trustworthy smile. He seems as regular as his features, as uncomplicated as his game.

Thorpe laughs at the memory of that innings in Cape Town. He likes to pit himself against the best: 'When you've got a great quick bowler trying to intimidate you, it's like a boxing match,' he says. He won that one, on points. He made 59, and Donald had failed to dislodge him. Thorpe was eventually caught in friendly fire, run out by a jittery tail-ender. England lost, heavily, but the real Graham Thorpe had finally stood up. He had had a thin series, often getting a start, never reaching 50. This, he says, is worse than making no runs at all: when you do the hard part and then get out, it's 'sucker time'. But when England went on to lose the one-day series six-one, Thorpe was the team's best player, averaging 46 and hitting the winning runs in the lone victory. He was back in character. After Mike Atherton, Graham Thorpe was the man who emerged from this fiasco with the most credit.

A commentator once complained that Thorpe's batting had 'rather a narrow margin of error'. Half the point of sport is having a narrow margin of error. Caution and prudence are what we are paying to escape. Sport is brinkmanship. In cricket, this is true of batsmen more than bowlers, because one mistake can finish them. And it's true of left-handers more than right, because the ball is angled away from those players, taunting and tempting them. Brian Lara is a left-hander. David Gower was a left-hander. Boycott wasn't.

When Gower retired, in 1993, a nation muttered about not seeing his like again. In fact, England already had a left-hander who was a decent alternative: gravadlax to Gower's smoked salmon. Graham Thorpe can't match the blond curls or the public-school languor, but the shots are much the same. Even better than the cut and the drive is the pull: Thorpe sees the ball early, leans back, places his right foot on an imaginary ladder, swivels, and swats the ball off his right hip.

This unusual mixture, brilliance with resilience, is the nearest thing England has to Gower. In 26 Tests, Graham Thorpe has shown all the qualities that England fans love to bemoan the lack of: grit, flair, guts. He has faced only good bowling sides – Australia, South Africa and the West Indies, twice each – and has made runs against them all. The mark of a class batsman is a Test average of 40; Thorpe's is 41. Atherton said last summer that Thorpe was England's best batsman: no small tribute, even allowing for modesty. The Coopers & Lybrand Test Ratings agree, making Thorpe the fourth-best batsman in the world. And yet hardly anyone outside cricket has heard of him. The only time his private life made news was when in November last year he flew home from the warm-up in South Africa to console his wife on the loss of their unborn baby. He is cricket's invisible man.

Thorpe is a Surrey boy, born and bred in Farnham and still living there now. His father, Geoff, and his two brothers are all club cricketers. (This is the usual recipe; top players' sons seldom reach the top.) Toni Thorpe, a full-time mother, used to be listed by her son in the Cricketers' *Who's Who* as a 'full-time scorer'. At his comprehensive, Graham was as good at football as cricket, and he played in midfield for England Schools: 'I used to ruffle the opposition.' Brentford FC showed an interest, but Surrey CCC showed more. 'Cricket came to me really. It was my first offer, my first opportunity to earn a salary. Football, I wasn't quite on the ladder.' He thought he'd give football a go if he didn't make it with Surrey. 'I didn't want to be playing too much second-team.'

This was at eighteen – the crucial age for a cricketer: the time when, if English, something usually goes wrong. England's junior national teams are as good as anybody's, but their luminaries struggle to make the final leap. Not Thorpe: at age nineteen he hit a brave century for Surrey against Hampshire – ie, Malcolm Marshall. He finished his first full season with an average of 45, and a place on the England A tour of Zimbabwe, where, *Wisden Cricketers' Almanack* noted, he 'did more than hint at an emerging talent of the highest quality'.

Unsurprisingly, *Wisden* fails to record the nickname that his fellow tourists gave him. He was already, inevitably, Thorpey, and still is. But they came up with something more distinctive: 'The little c*** from Surrey'. The epithet wasn't because he was disliked, but because he was young, on the small side (5ft 10, with short legs) and tough. 'He was a right little shit, in the best possible way,' says Mark Nicholas, then captain of England A, now a commentator. 'A real fighter.'

Back home, Thorpe went down with sophomore syndrome, and his average sank to 27. The England hierarchy did what it is often berated for not doing – it stuck by its player. England team manager Micky Stewart and his successor, Keith Fletcher, saw his potential. Thorpe went on three more A tours, and when he finally made the senior side against Australia in 1993, he scored a century on his debut. This was storybook stuff, though the story does tend to have a twist: the previous two Englishmen to do this, John Hampshire and Frank Hayes, never managed it again. Thorpe had to wait for his second century until his fifteenth Test, but he would still recommend the experience. 'You look back and think, well, I can do it. After that, it's all about gaining consistency.'

His first senior tour took him to the West Indies, when they were still the best in the world. At first, Thorpe kept being clean-bowled – a boy's way to get out. But in the third and fourth Tests he made 80s, one slow, one quick, both helping to build winning positions. He rates the first of these matches as the low point of his career, as England were bowled out for 46; the second was the high point, as they bounced back with a thumping win. Tony Pigott says that tour was the making of Thorpe, and he agrees: 'I felt a different player after jumping those hurdles.'

The change was lost on Ray Illingworth, taking over as chairman of selectors. He replaced Thorpe with the all-rounder, Craig White. Instead of fuming or sulking, Thorpe made a resolution to become one of the five best batsmen in the country. He has been ever since.

Illingworth brought him back four matches later, after a heavy defeat in the Test against South Africa. He made three blazing 70s. 'That was a turning point. I played a lot more positively than I think I ever had. It was like people were then saying, "he's a strokemaker". Quite nice, because I feel I can be two players now.'

He has played in all eighteen Tests since, a run matched only by Atherton. Thorpe is only criticised for making too many 70s and 80s, but if the other batsmen shared this failing, the England team would be world-beaters.

Last September, Graham Thorpe married his long-time girlfriend, Nicola, an air hostess turned sports therapist. He calls her Nick, in a tone devoid of dressing-room chauvinism. The honeymoon was spent in Mauritius ('brilliant'). The couple returned from holiday to their new house in Farnham, but for Thorpe it was a fleeting visit before setting off for three months in South Africa.

As soon as he'd gone, Nicola discovered that she was pregnant. Within a month the pregnancy was found to be ectopic. The tour was at the warm-up stage, and Thorpe was allowed home. If he hadn't been, he says, he would have gone anyway. She did recover enough, though, to join the other wives and girlfriends for the Christmas period in Port Elizabeth and Cape Town. Illingworth blamed the influx for England's decline, and talked of banning the women and children from future tours. But Nicola Thorpe was there to see her husband hit top form.

After South Africa, Thorpe just had time to unpack before setting off for six weeks in India and Pakistan: another great itinerary from the Test and County Cricket Board. Later, when I spoke to him on the phone, I suggested that he must be knackered. But no, he was excited about playing in a World Cup. But the week off was unrelaxing, with bats to be tested, photographs to be taken, contracts to be signed.

He acknowledges that if he was better known, he would probably be better paid, but he is loath to surrender more privacy. When he rang, he reversed the charges, with suitable apologies, rather than let me have his number. His best man was an ex-cricketer, Ray Alikhan, but his other close friends are outside the game. 'I think that's important,' he says. 'Sometimes in sport there's a little bit of a false world out there – one which only wants you when things are going well for you.'

Asked what he likes most about his job, Thorpe says the travel – 'the way it's opened my mind up'. But that has its flipside. 'On tours, at times you realise that although you're honoured to be playing for your country, there are sacrifices to be made.'

You mean in your married life? 'Yeah. But also your career. Those qualifications I left college with would be absolutely useless now. A levels and O levels – they're only important to get into university.'

When he was struggling in South Africa, Thorpe sought advice not from Atherton, Illingworth or the England batting coach, John Edrich, but from his boyhood hero, David Gower – the most natural of talents, the least likely of coaches. Consulting him was tantamount to a decision in itself. 'His response was, "you're not playing badly, you're just getting out. Don't go into your shell, remain the way you are. It's a bit of fine-tuning, that's all." ' Wasn't Thorpe also getting advice the other way? People saying he should knuckle down? 'No. If it was being said, my ears were shut.'

This clarity is one key to his success. Another emerges when he talks about his friend Mark Ramprakash, a shining talent who has shown a baffling inability to shine for England. Thorpe's verdict is halting, but persuasive. 'Maybe he doesn't relax enough when he needs to, on the big occasion. You have to hover between a couldn't-care-less attitude and a real will to do well. And sort of not be afraid – if you fail, you fail, you know that generally you're trying your best. And once you get into a decent position, and you're settled, then you fight like a dog to win.'

GQ Magazine, July 1996

Angry Essex man becomes officer and a gentleman

Vic Marks

Chart the career of Nasser Hussain and you can construct a simple thesis to explain why English cricket is in such a muddle. Singled out at the age of 21 as a player of rich promise in 1989, Hussain was chosen – ahead of Atherton – for the tour of the West Indies when he had yet to complete a full first-class season.

In the Caribbean that winter he played three Tests. His contribution with the bat was modest (100 runs), but he had shown enough glimpses of a steely temperament to suggest a long Test career. Furthermore, in two of those matches, unbeknown to him and the England physio, he had been batting with a broken scaphoid (wrist).

Yet he had to wait until 1993 for another chance. In four Tests against the Australians he averaged 30, but despite another Caribbean tour he has not played for England since. Somewhere along the line the selectors lost the courage of their 1989 convictions.

If Hussain had been an Australian, you can surmise that by now he would either have played 40 or 50 Test matches or have been discarded as not good enough. Instead, we still don't know. He is now 28, at his peak as a county batsman (last year he scored 1,854 runs at an average of 54), and has just returned from a successful winter as the captain of the England 'A' side in Pakistan. Another recall is surely imminent, and with it all the agonies of establishing a secure place in the team. It is hard to avoid the conclusion that a lot of time as well as Hussain's talent has been wasted.

However, if Raymond Illingworth is feeling beleaguered this weekend, he can at least find some solace in his decision to give Hussain the captaincy of England 'A', for he was not an obvious choice. Hussain explains: 'This was a bridge-building tour, the first time we had been back there since the Gatting affair. Angus Fraser did say to me that "They might as well have picked Tufnell as you to captain the side if bridge-building was the main aim".'

Hussain is aware of his reputation for headstrong behaviour; he has had the odd tantrum on the field and in the dressing room, and was once dubbed, along with Ramprakash, as an 'angry young man' of English cricket. Has he mellowed? He is reluctant to admit that. 'One difference is that I'm now in a position of responsibility [he is vice-captain at Essex] and I'm now allowed to speak my mind.'

As if to prove the point, he mischievously instructed Graham Gooch, now an Essex foot-soldier, to hurry up and join the fielding practice going on at Chelmsford while we continued our conversation. Would the advent of Gooch the selector enhance his England prospects? Hussain raised his eyebrows enigmatically.

'Perhaps I have mellowed a little,' he eventually concedes, but he is adamant that he is as fierce a competitor on the field as ever, and that it is still wise to give him some leeway for five minutes post-dismissal. His leadership of the 'A' team suggests that he now has a longer fuse; the team were successful and there were no 'incidents'.

'I was more worried about the off-field demands of the captaincy,' says Hussain, 'but Embers [John Emburey, the 'A' team's cricket manager] was brilliant. He made it clear that I was in charge. He gave me responsibility, and I appreciated that.' He seems unusually philosophical about his stuttering England career – Hussain the diplomat? – saying that he is not the first person to suffer from untimely injury (in 1990) or selectorial whims (1994).

Does he regret being picked so early in his career? 'No. At no time in the West Indies in 1989-90 did I feel out of my depth on the field. I was a bit daunted in the dressing room. Gooch was there, though I hardly knew him then, let alone the likes of Allan Lamb.' David Gower was also around with the press corps (as usual, he had been controversially omitted by Gooch). 'Gower was my childhood hero, which made me feel a little uncomfortable when I was playing instead of him.'

His hand injury, acquired on a tennis court in Guyana, kept him out of cricket for three months in 1990. 'That was the year of small seams; stacks of runs were scored in county cricket and in the Tests [weak Indian and New Zealand sides were the tourists] and I could have established myself then.' When he was recalled in 1993 the opposition was stiffer, but he played Shane Warne better than most.

'I've always enjoyed the challenge of playing spinners, and it helped that I was once a leg-spinner [he was a teenage prodigy who lost it]. I also learnt a lot from Fletch: how to forget about the close fielders, how not to be intimidated by them, and the importance of waiting for the ball.' Just the sort of qualities that will be required against Kumble and Raju this summer.

Unsurprisingly, Fletcher and Gooch are batting mentors: 'Fletch for the mental approach to batting, Gooch for the technical side. In every net Gooch concentrates on one specific element of his batting. I used to go in there and have a thrash to entertain anyone who might be watching.' Not any more; he has tightened his technique. The face of his bat is no longer precariously open, and he is standing stiller when facing the quicker bowlers.

His second tour of the West Indies in 1993-94 was immensely frustrating; he played three first-class games and no Tests. Then, in 1994, with Illy taking the reins, 'I was very disappointed to be overlooked, having waited my turn. I scored two early-season hundreds, and when I was not selected for the one-day matches my mind went for a while.'

This disappointment has not affected his relationship with Mike Atherton. They have played together in Combined University sides and at under-15 national level upwards. His respect for Atherton is genuine, rather than diplomatic. 'He has not changed one iota in all that time. I can speak my mind to him and he will never bear a grudge.' The respect is mutual for Atherton likes men of intelligence and fire. Indeed, on the sporadic occasions that Hussain has played for England, Atherton has consulted him in the field before more 'senior' members of the team. This year they should be reunited on a more regular basis.

Observer, 21 April 1996

Jones broadens the horizons

Adam Szreter

Dean Jones had just made centuries on successive days for Derbyshire; the first helped them to a resounding 363-run victory over Middlesex in the Championship; the second was not quite enough to prevent defeat in the Sunday League. He might have been reasonably pleased with his form.

'I'm not worried about those type of performances,' he said. 'I'm just worried about getting results for Derbyshire, improving what we did last year and giving the club some future, some direction, and seeing where it wants to go.'

For someone who made 11 centuries in 52 Tests for Australia, and averages over 50 in first-class cricket and 46.55 for his country, a couple of hundreds at Derby probably are fairly small beer, on reflection.

Jones's dedication to his new post started somewhat prematurely, you might say. His wife was expecting their second child when he was about to leave for England in the spring. 'Jane said: "You're not going until you've seen this baby." So I said, "Well you better get it induced because I've got to go." '

Baby Isabella *was* induced and dad was on a plane within the hour.

Although his wife may not have appreciated it too much, you feel that Derbyshire are about to benefit from Jones's uncompromising personality. They have struggled to fulfil their potential in recent seasons, despite a regular battery of top-class bowlers, but now they are third in the Championship and have a number of young players who are catching the eye. Jones, however, is not satisfied yet.

'It's been good and bad,' he said of his first two months in charge. 'We're getting there, slowly but surely. I've inherited a squad and there's no doubt there'll be changes made to it before next year. I can't say which areas at the moment – that would be a bit silly of me, wouldn't it? But we are looking at a few guys and decisions will be made in the next month.'

Of the younger players at the club, Jones is in no doubt that they are generally behind their Australian contemporaries in terms of their overall development. 'At home, you get picked for Australia at 20 or 21 if you're any good. Here you're just playing the first game for your county.

'County cricket is a full-time professional job and therefore guys stay on longer, earning good money, and positions vacant are not readily available. At home, the turnover is better. We're not frightened of picking young guys. If they show potential, we just whack 'em straight in.'

Despite his nationality, as a county captain Jones is clear about his duty to the England team. 'I can't play Corky in the NatWest. He's just bowled 42 overs for England and I've got to make sure he does well for his country. That's my job. The club wants him to play well here, sure, but for his career, his life, it matters what he does for England. He wants to play against Staffordshire, which is the little minor county he's from, but I'll rest him.'

Even without Cork, Derbyshire are not short of big names. One, Devon Malcolm, is being nursed back to form after South Africa. 'We had to pick the pieces up from Dev, who was in bits after South Africa, but we've put him back together and he's a pretty useful bowler again.

'I think that what was done to him in South Africa was ridiculous. Dev can still play for England, without doubt. I've just got to keep him relaxed. He's a loveable bloke, very dry sense of humour, and I've just got to make sure he keeps running in fast and runs straight through the crease, instead of peeling off too quickly.

'Changing a guy's action at the age of 32 or 33, as one particular England fast-bowling coach advised, was bloody stupid. Absolutely ridiculous. I think they're trying to do things to justify their jobs.'

Despite the Malcolm affair, Jones believes England are at long last heading in the right direction. 'They've got some good selectors, they're starting to pick the right blokes, they're ringing captains up and speaking to players. A player might have got a hundred, but he might also have been dropped four times, so they're getting the right mail.

'Mike [Atherton] has done a good job and guys are starting to earn their coupons, like Goughie. He's starting to take wickets and make runs at county level. England caps used to be handed out, now they're getting earned, which is good. World cricket needs England. We need them playing well. We need a really tight series next year to keep lifting up the standards of Test cricket.'

As someone who spent a season with Durham under the captaincy of David Graveney, Jones has the ear of at least one England selector, and he has already had a say. '[Alan] Mullally bowled beautifully here, knocked us over and I thought, "He's ready." The major reason was that he swung the ball back in. But I've noticed in the last Test he's gone back to trying to bowl fast instead of shaping the ball. He's always been a fast left-arm medium, not a quick, and he thinks he's a quick again.'

As far as his own staff at Derbyshire are concerned, Jones can be proud of the way players such as Johnny Owen, Andy Harris and particularly Chris Adams have responded. 'It's a very unfashionable county. We've only won one Championship, in '36, so we're trying to change things. If you pick up the *Cricketers' Who's Who*, where it says "Least Favourite Ground", they always say Derby. So we're trying to clean the place up. The players don't like playing here because they always soup up the wickets, and they're facing Malcolm, Cork and Bishop, so I can understand there's a bit of hatred for it.'

Jones is quickly becoming something of a local hero in Derby, and if you ask him about his own heroes, he does not have to think long. 'Border without doubt. Toughest guy I've ever met mentally in sport. He doesn't care how he looks, he just goes out there and does the business. I've seen him facing the West Indians on wet wickets and he just takes them on. What I like about him is that he doesn't carry a grudge, which I think is very, very important.'

At 35, Jones remains one of the best batsmen in the world, but he accepts that his international career is over. 'I'm finished,' he says. 'It's time for the young punks to come in and play. Australia doesn't need me anymore.'

Jones has, however, signed to play one more season with Victoria this winter, despite losing the captaincy to Shane Warne, who he believes will be the next captain of Australia.

For the time being, he and his family are adjusting to their new life in the East Midlands. His elder daughter, Phoebe, is settling in to her school a little too well for her father's liking. 'She's starting to speak English, which worries me,' he says. 'She's got this Pommie twang and I'm going to knock the hell out of it.' You'd better believe it.

Independent, 26 June 1996

Glowing advert for amateur ethos

Sarah Potter

Audrey Collins is old enough to be a great-grandmother. She has done enough in women's cricket to have earned the right to call for her slippers. But do not be fooled; at 81 she is young enough to feature in an advertisement for the highest-profile company in sport.

Surprised? Well, maybe you should not be, for this woman has played for England, started clubs, coached children and served a decade as president of the Women's Cricket Association (WCA). So wholehearted is her passion and support that she has sold chocolate bars to spectators and even attempted to raise a personal bank loan when a home tour teetered on the edge of humiliating cancellation. In short, Audrey Collins is an amateur in the finest traditions.

Records are not extensive in the women's game. In Guildford today the hundredth women's Test match, between England and New Zealand, will grind to a halt. Talk on the pitch has centred on the debut of Charlotte Edwards, who, at 16, is the youngest player to be picked by England at this level, but Collins, watching keenly from the boundary, only just missed out on being part of the first recorded Test.

That was in 1934 when England sailed to Australia. She made her debut for England three years later against the old enemy at the Oval. 'It was my only match for England. We were due to go to Australia in 1939 but the war came and that was that,' Collins said, without bitterness: 'War is so much more important than anything personal. I had fun in other ways.'

Something in the watery-blue sparkle of her eyes says as much.

For Collins, fun and sport go together like bat and ball. 'I wanted games to be my fun, I didn't want it to be my work so I became a chemistry teacher and played cricket in my spare time,' she said.

Not that there was much of that. In the formative years of women's cricket, Collins was very much an organiser and leader. After the war she formed Vagabonds, the Hertfordshire club, played for them until she was 70 and still helps out by ferrying youngsters to and from the nets.

'I can't let the children down,' she explained with a smile that also suggested she cannot quite let go. 'The little 13-year-olds are so keen. I still get an enormous amount of pleasure out of it.'

Youth cricket is precious to Collins and has been the beneficiary of her surprise featuring in the Nike advert, where she follows in the lucrative footsteps of Michael Jordan and Eric Cantona. She used the £500 paid to her to buy a complete set of kit for an East Anglia under-17 team she is involved with.

The advertiser's motives, according to Collins – to 'persuade more women and girls to take up sport' – are distorted. Lipstick on a lined face is hardly likely to raise much more than a smirk, but if that is the status of women's sport in the eyes of the advertisers, at least Collins has put the money where it counts. She certainly did not do it to see her picture plastered on a billboard. 'They made me look 120!' she said, indignantly, 'but I never look at ads.'

Brand names which have youngsters running to buy, buy, buy have never mattered to Collins. 'In many ways we were so lucky to grow up between the wars,' she said. 'We had no money but we didn't have advertisements, we didn't have anyone telling us we should have this or that because our neighbours had it. There were none of those pressures on us. It is different now, but an advert has never made me buy anything.'

There is a defiant tilt of the head that reminds me of another time when I used to play. I had splashed a couple of thin blue streaks in my hair and with it had apparently strayed over the line of acceptable behaviour. As President of the WCA, Collins wrote me a chilling letter the day after the BBC half-jokingly featured my 'surprise' non-selection for an overseas tour in a news bulletin, suggesting that the streaks had led to my punishment.

'I was sorry that you saw fit to demean yourself in the way you did on TV last night and to express your conceit in such a public way,' Collins said. I ducked.

But after meeting her again I have the stirrings of a different feeling: the understanding that her passion for cricket is genuine and all-consuming. She radiates a trust in the presumed proper order of things that would be easier to parody than her warm gaze is to deflect.

Gathering years seem to have softened her edges, but she remains undimmed about her pleasures. 'I have made lots of friends all over the world,' she said. 'What more can you ask? This is what sport does for people. It is the important thing. That is what lasts.'

Collins is 'thrilled' that a 16-year-old has been picked for England. She wished Edwards a long, bright future. As I walked away from Guildford, I found I was smiling; thinking about Old Father Time, tradition and values. Collins, adopting Nike's advertising slogan, might be tempted to tell Edwards: 'Don't just do it, enjoy it!'

The Times, 15 July 1996

Dickie bows out at Lord's . . .

Michael Parkinson

This morning Dickie Bird will walk to the middle at Lord's to stand in a Test match for the last time, always providing he manages to arrive without being knocked down by a runaway horse or captured by an alien spaceship. If it were anyone else, the chance of being so discomfited would be laughable; with Dickie Bird it becomes a distinct possibility.

I once described him as a lightning conductor for misfortune, and it is a judgment based on a friendship going back 50 years. He was a worrisome youth when he joined Barnsley Cricket Club and we met for the first time. He arrived fretting about his suitability, carrying his possessions in a carrier-bag. Fifty years on, and although he might be the most famous umpire of them all, he is still fretful and able to carry all his worldly possessions in one hand.

In a long experience of observing fame and how it changes people (and I do not exclude myself from this investigation), I have not met anyone as unscathed as Dickie Bird. He is the Forrest Gump of cricket, wearing his innocence like a suit of armour. He is without guile or artifice, and throughout his 63 years has never seen fit to change his mind about living in the best country in the world, under the best Queen there ever was, with the whole thing presided over by a Great Umpire In The Sky, who was likely born in Bradford and loves cricket.

This simple view of life would be insufferable except for Bird's talent for not taking himself seriously. He would have made a marvellous stand-up comic. He has no need of gag writers. The humour comes from his daily battle with the world. Typically, when the BBC arrived to film the tribute shown this week, Dickie's false teeth were being repaired. It never occurred to him to tell the crew to come back when he was more presentable. That would have been bad manners. Instead he bared his gums to the camera, and explained what had happened, adding the fascinating information that he had swallowed the temporary replacements.

Although he made light of the matter (it would have been rude to have complained), I have no doubt the thought of what might eventually happen to his innards with seven teeth on the loose will become yet another concern in his life, another reason for wittering himself silly. This, after all, is the man who went to his doctor for an inoculation and, after telling him all his troubles, ended up strapped to a bed on a saline drip with cameras peering into every orifice. They found nothing untoward, which also caused the patient great concern.

When he was to appear on *Desert Island Discs*, he rang me up and said: 'Does tha know Sue Lawley?' I said I did. 'Does tha' think she'll ask me if I'm gay?' he said. 'Why on earth should she do that?' I said. 'Because she's just been interviewing Gordon Brown and she asked him,' he said. 'Why should she think you were gay?' I asked. 'Because I'm not married she might get the wrong idea,' he said. I told him to put the notion from his head, that Ms Lawley would not dream of such a line of questioning. He was unconvinced. 'I think I'll forestall her,' he said. At the beginning of the programme, when asked for his first record, Dickie Bird said: '*When I Fall In Love* by Nat King Cole, and before you ask, Sue, I must tell you it reminds me of an old girlfriend I met in Barnsley many years ago.'

Sometimes I look at him and wonder if I haven't got him wrong, that underneath the cap and the worried countenance there lurks a mastermind who constructed a disguise to fool us all. Then I feel a traitor to our friendship. Why should we be uneasy with honesty and naïvety? Why are we uncomfortable when confronted by an ingenuous and God-fearing personality? It is easy when discussing Dickie Bird to forget he made his reputation not because of his comic possibilities, but because he did a difficult job better than anyone else. As he says himself: 'I am one person when I am not on the cricket field. Quite another when I cross the rope. Then I am in charge.' What cricketers say is that he earned their trust and respect. They can say no more. Michael Atherton told me he believed Dickie's greatest gift was his ability to defuse a situation with a gentle word of admonition or a joke. He has melted the toughest reputations without fuss or ado. The paradox is that the career of the most human of officials has been shortened by technology. It used to be that the umpire's decision was not only final, but infallible. This basic tenet of the game has been challenged and changed by the use of cameras. Dickie Bird is not against change, but he sees more clearly than most how it will alter his life and the relationship he enjoys with his beloved players.

The thing to bear in mind as he walks to the middle today is that for all the change there has been and might come, only one game I know can produce and nurture a character as substantial and quirky as Harold Dennis Bird. He represents all that is worthwhile about cricket, and I can pay him no higher tribute. That being the case, he should not be allowed to wither in retirement, as he surely will if they don't find him something to do. He should be told to roam the world instructing umpires how best to do the job.

One further gesture before we send him on his way should come from Yorkshire County Cricket Club, which has yet to award him his county cap. He could wear it, along with his umpire's jacket and his MBE, when he eventually approaches the Pearly Gates. When this happens, he is bound to turn up early, and you can guarantee it will be raining.

Daily Telegraph, 20 June 1996

The Brown Bomber

Geoffrey Dean

Alistair Brown was banishing all-comers from a very early age. When, as an eight-year-old with a clearly remarkable eye for the ball, he smote an unbeaten 71 for his school side, Cumnor House, news somehow got to the then England captain of an innings highly rare for a boy so tender. He wrote the nicest of letters on June 15, 1978. It read: 'Dear Alistair, I hear that you scored a splendid 71 not out – I wish I could manage one myself. I remember my own first hundred against Forest School when I was 11. I hope you get one soon. Best wishes, Mike Brearley.'

Young Ally, as he has always been known, carefully stored away the letter and now has it framed on the wall of his south London home. He was also scoring hundreds very soon after Brearley wrote – indeed, about 10 a year at school, he recalls. The headmaster of Cumnor House, Duncan White, used to let Ally off some of his Latin lessons to go to nets instead, and England's newest maker of a one-day hundred still feels indebted to him. 'I didn't like Latin for a start,' he quips, 'but more importantly he never tried to change my natural game.'

Brown's natural game – a desire to despatch every ball unless it absolutely *had* to be defended – made schoolboy bowlers terrified of him, remembers Dave Twose who taught him at Caterham. Selection followed for Surrey Young Cricketers, but only at number seven in the order (with Graham Thorpe at six). Both were seen as all-rounders with Brown's leg-breaks considered useful. They still are, for when he turned out for his club side, Cheam, in the Surrey Championship last year, he took five wickets against Esher, including a hat-trick.

Surrey, recognising that here was a stroke-playing batsman with special talent, took him on the staff at 19 in 1989. Within a year he had made his Sunday League debut but despite averaging 48 in the Second XI over the 1990 and 1991 seasons, did not make his first-class debut until 1992.

The then Surrey coach Geoff Arnold was dubious whether Brown would make the grade at first-class level, being over-suspicious of a player so naturally keen to attack and so reluctant to defend. O ye of little faith! In his first 13 Championship innings he scored three hundreds (off 79, 71 and 78 balls respectively), topped the Surrey batting averages that year with 740 Championship runs at 49, passed 1,000 runs in each of the following three seasons and, as is well documented, began this season with a first-class average of 45. Let it be hoped, therefore, that the England selectors do not typecast him as a one-day player, as initially Arnold did.

Brown says he is desperately keen to play Test cricket and given that temperament is so vital to success at that level he believes that he showed he has the right one with that hundred against India in the Third One-Day International at Old Trafford. Who are we to doubt him, for none of us will know the pain that he felt following the *The Times*'s article on him immediately after his one-day debut at The Oval. He was under huge pressure at Old Trafford, knowing that 'if I failed that could have been it'.

That cricketers are affected by destructive journalism can be in no doubt. Brown takes up the story. 'I hadn't actually read the article but some of the boys said it was disgraceful and were upset. So, with the rain coming down at The Oval I sat down at lunch time and read it. It was a bit of a character assassination. I must admit I felt very flat for a while, very quiet. But David Lloyd said "don't worry about it, we know you're a good player". A lot of people spoke to me after that and John Morris rang up to say that all the Durham players wanted to complain to the newspaper. Dermot Reeve also called.'

Browney, as he is affectionately known at The Oval, was uplifted by the support from not just players but also a number of journalists. Ultimately, his own self-belief saw him through. 'I thought I knew what the Oval wicket was going to do in that game but I was wrong. There was sideways movement at pace and with bounce which made it very easy to play and miss as I did. I think I was perhaps trying too hard to go along with the press idea of being a pinch-hitter, and it wasn't on in those conditions.'

There were still some thumping good shots in his 37 but he admits that he was not completely happy with his technique that day. 'My head kept falling over and I would have liked to get back and across my stumps more rather than giving myself room to hit on the off side.'

Ironically at the Second One-Day International at Headingley, Brown said that he felt really good going in to bat before he was adjudged lbw second ball for nought. This confidence he felt about his batting persisted through to the Monday at Old Trafford, prompting Brown to tell Chris Lewis that he thought he would score a hundred. That he did so in such a responsible, controlled way marked him out as an international player of the future, making it, he says, the 'most satisfying day of my career, even if it wasn't the best hundred I've made'. For just as Don Bradman had been described as being 'not up to Test standard', after failing on his Test debut in 1928, by team mate Charlie Kelloway, so *The Times*' description of him as an international no-hoper had been made to look as risible.

'I was on a mission to prove I could play at a higher level,' Brown recalls. There should be no reason why he should not go on to play at the highest level of all.

Detractors will argue that half of his first-class innings have been on excellent Oval batting wickets but that has not stopped him from averaging more than Thorpe and Alec Stewart, nor from scoring five of his 11 Championship hundreds away from home. In any case, without a sound technique no batsman is going to average 45 on whatever ground he plays most of his cricket. Brown acknowledges he can still improve his technique and believes he can get his average into the 50s.

He does not quite understand where the notion that he is susceptible to fast, short-pitched bowling came from. 'It doesn't bother me as generally I go underneath it. I can't remember the last time I was caught hooking or at short-leg fending off. Normally, I get caught in the slips or am lbw. I look upon most short-pitched stuff as an opportunity to score – in other words, four-balls or if I'm in top nick, six-balls. In fact I think they should abolish the limit on the number of bouncers in an over.' Certainly, although he was looking to get forward in the one-dayers against India, he is a strong back-foot player.

He is much happier about his cricket now, feels happier about the way he is encouraged to play by Surrey's new coach Dave Gilbert. Being dropped from the Championship side last June after making 92 in a run-chase against Glamorgan at The Oval left him confused and demoralised.

He had been caught at deep mid-on, incurring the wrath of the then coach Grahame Clinton. 'Before the next match at Lord's Stewie tapped me on the shoulder shortly before the start and said he was sorry but I was being dropped but that he couldn't tell me why.' Clinton claims it was a committee decision but Brown thinks it was the coach's.

Brown was brought back after the Lord's game, immediately scored a hundred against Essex but was then dropped again at the end of the season without explanation.

This probably cost him an A-tour place, together with the fact, as he puts it, that 'everything was wrong at the club last year'. He says he was not surprised that he was not picked but felt more disappointed by the omissions of Mark Butcher and Adam Hollioake. 'For me, Butch is one of the best openers around.' All three could tour with an England side this winter and the selectors should not waste the chance to take the ambitious Browney with the seniors. Woe betide the Zimbabweans and New Zealanders if he is picked.

The Cricketer, July 1996

Sharp delights in the fun at the game's cutting edge

Mark Nicholas

By the time the bell rang at five minutes to 11, George Sharp was ready. He was not as nervous as he had expected and was even more excited, he supposed. But once he left his changing room and began the long walk to the middle, it felt different, he admitted, and his heart picked up its beat.

This was a first for Sharp, the ultimate for an umpire. A Test match, the highest honour in the game. Sharp has not been on the first-class list for long – only five years – so he has leapfrogged some longer-serving souls who would bite your hand off for the same chance.

Not that his colleagues are jealous; Sharp is not that type. In fact, they are thrilled for he reflects the salt of the earth, which is what umpiring is about.

The umpires' room at Trent Bridge is underneath the visitors' dressing-room, which is underneath the home dressing-room. It is alongside the public lavatories and hidden away behind the physiotherapist's lair. It is a small room, like most around the country. Even Lord's reserves a small, hidden room for the umpires. Fancy that in such a vast pavilion.

George was up and in the shower soon after 7 o'clock on Saturday morning. Half an hour later he threw himself at fruit juice, Weetabix and 'the full monte' – bacon, egg, sausage, tomato and gallons of tea. At a quarter past eight a taxi fetched him and he was at the main gate at Trent Bridge by a quarter to nine.

His first job was to supervise the daily mowing of the pitch. The blades must be even and level each morning, so that neither side gains advantage from a change of character in the surface.

On the first day, he and his fellow umpire – K T Francis – checked the distance of the boundaries and any local quirks in their placements before swotting up on regulations and chatting with the captains, the third umpire and the referee.

At 9.30 George had a cuppa and caught up with the newspapers before changing slowly into dark blue trousers, a white shirt and a National Grid tie supplied by the sponsors.

Into his socks went the foot powder and on to his feet went the whitewashed Doc Martens. He has three pairs of shoes, two pairs of Docs and one of Reeboks, one for each session of play. He chose his flat cap on Saturday because of the wind though ideally, in sunshine, he prefers the panama.

Into the pockets of his white coat he loaded pens, notebook, rules and regs, bails, coins (for counting the balls of each over), scissors, a rag, a light meter, lip ice and sun cream. It is a wonder he can walk.

Then the bell went, up the stairs from the dressing room, left and down the steps of the pavilion, and through the little gate to gentle applause. Sharp and Francis – the final arbiters – George standing for the first time, K T for the first time in England, their blood pumping.

Very soon the Indians – who bowled fast and straight – were appealing. Ventakesh Prasad asked George the loudest question when he nipped one into Atherton's front pad. ''Fraid not,' said George, with a lean of the head and a lift of the eyebrows.

'When I was a 'keeper, I thought most lbws were out, but being down the other end gives it a different perspective – particularly with those nip-backers,' he said at lunch, which consisted of two cheese rolls, two fags, a pot of tea and a change of shoes.

George Sharp was born in Hartlepool in the early spring of 1950. He moved down to Northamptonshire when Percy Davis, the assistant coach, invited him to a trial. Keith Andrew, a legend in Northampton in those days, watched him keep wicket for 20 minutes and offered him a contract at £10 a week. He was 15.

George says he could bat and averaged 21 in first-class cricket but I don't remember his batting like I remember his left-handed 'keeping. He was very good – Bishen Bedi, who could bowl a bit and who played at Northampton in the 1970s, said as much – though not especially elegant. Big and balding doesn't suit a 'keeper like it suits a centre-back. His heroes were his contemporaries, Alan Knott and Bob Taylor, and Keith Andrew used to impress him no end.

During the tea interval George had two cups, ignored the sandwiches and smoked a couple more cigarettes. He changed his shoes.

George finished playing in 1985 and went three years without seeing a game of cricket. He worked with a construction company and in fund-raising for the blind 'and played a lot of golf'. Then he was invited by a company for a day's county cricket and enjoyed watching so much that he resolved to watch from the best place possible. By 1991 he was on the list, the rest as they say, along with those days at a tenner a week, is history. He gets more than £2,000 for a Test but a little less than £20,000 a year as a first-class umpire. It's not a lot but it's all right with George, who is not one to grumble.

Play ended on time on Saturday and a sunburnt man pushed the peak of his cap to the sky, lifted the bails and headed for the pavilion. Back in the small room he slumped in a seat, lit a cigarette and cracked a beer. 'Aargh, got one wrong, Nasser [Hussain] nicked that one after tea, pity, all okay otherwise.'

Who cares? 'Well they did, not surprisingly, toys out of the pram stuff.' Perhaps, George, but it will be forgotten in the morning. It is not worth fussing about. 'Hmmmm, I hope so,' he said with a smile.

The giant screen had replayed it, of course, but neither Sharp nor Francis ever look. Television replays are neither here nor there because the next ball is what matters most.

The taxi picked him up an hour later and took him to his hotel and a light dinner that may or may not have included a glass of wine. He shared the evening with K T, Cammie Smith, the referee, and his pal David Constant, a classy old pro and the reserve for this match. He was asleep by half past ten.

George Sharp is a shining example of a band of thoroughly good blokes who are shining examples themselves. They should be both respected and applauded for their uncomplaining and unglamorous watch over the game we adore. It would be a loss if technology overtook them. Becoming an umpire was 'the best thing I ever did', he says. 'I love it.' Enough said, George.

Daily Telegraph, 8 July 1996

Prince of greatness

Jon Culley

Were it possible, just once, to travel back through time, it is difficult to imagine a destination more tempting in cricket's past than the couple of decades spanning the final years of the last century and the beginning of this, the era encompassing what was to become known as cricket's Golden Age.

If it were feasible to be more specific still in determining where to touch down, one might well conclude that, to bear witness to these times, no more agreeable vantage point could be found than a deckchair at Hove. Those fortunate enough to have enjoyed that privilege in the Sussex sea air between 1895 and 1904 would have seen, in his pomp, Kumar Shri Ranjitsinhji, the Indian prince known with affection everywhere he performed as 'Ranji'.

These years were indeed patterned with a golden thread, illuminated by the concurrent careers of some of the finest batsmen ever to have appeared on English cricket fields, names with a resonance that has, if anything, grown richer and deeper with passing years: Charles Burgess Fry, Archie MacLaren, F S Jackson, Johnny Tyldesley, Gilbert Jessop.

It was an age in which amateurs, unshackled by the mundane

requirements of professionalism, were able to approach their game with a carefree and daring spirit, unworried by such trifles as wages and contracts. In this climate, Ranji, of Cambridge University and Sussex, emerged as a star when the word still had some meaning.

As elegant a man as he was a cricketer, Ranji captured the imagination of the public as no other player had; and never more so than in this week 100 years ago when, at the age of 23, he made his debut for England against Australia in Manchester, the first Indian ever to play Test cricket.

It was a remarkable debut; he made 62 in the first innings and, when England batted for a second time, emulated W G Grace by scoring a century in his first Test. In the course of it, he established a mark of his own as the first to score 100 before lunch in a Test, moving from 41 to 154 in 130 minutes on the third morning.

The feat made Ranji the talk of the cricketing world, just as he had been on his debut for Sussex in 1895, when he scored 77 not out and 150 against the MCC at Lord's. In that first season he scored 1,775 runs at an average of around 50, which he was to maintain throughout his career. Effectively, this spanned fewer than 15 years and yet produced almost 25,000 runs in 500 innings, including 72 centuries, 14 of them turned into doubles. Twice he scored more than 3,000 runs in a season.

The cricket of Ranji, though, was not to be measured in statistics, impressive though they were, for he was a cricketer his contemporaries perceived as possessed of magic.

In part, this was due to his exotic countenance and to the impression most late Victorians held of India, as a land of conjurors, rope tricks, flying carpets and all manner of mysteries. But he brought a real mystical charm to the game with the way he played it. Blessed with the sharpest of eyes and timing which no other player of the day – not even Fry, his scientific Sussex team-mate – could match, he also had great strength and control in his wrists, which enabled him to drive with substantial power but at the same time execute the most delicate of strokes.

In this way he truly revolutionised batting, sending good length, middle stump balls to the leg-side boundary as if spirited away, perfecting the late cut and inventing what we now recognise as the leg glance, which enabled him to score runs in hitherto unexplored territory. He used the litheness of his body – or, as Neville Cardus put it, his 'fluttering curves' – to move across to the off side when the ball was pitched fast and short of a length, playing the ball off his hip with the full face of the bat.

The stroke tormented opponents and left spectators open-mouthed. Jessop, from whom a compliment was something to be treasured, described him as 'the most brilliant figure in cricket's most brilliant age'. Ranji's obituary in *Wisden* paid him what was, in the yellow book's estimation, the highest tribute, conceding that 'genius could with the greatest truth be applied to him'.

Never had been witnessed in a player such a natural ability as his and yet Ranji owed more, in fact, to practice than was probably appreciated by those who watched him, and who assumed from his unorthodox strokes that he played by instinct. In fact, until he went up to Trinity College, Cambridge, in 1890, he had no experience of organised cricket. At Cambridge, however, the game became an obsession. He hired Bill Lockwood, Tom Richardson and Tom Hayward, professionals on the Surrey staff, along with Jack Hearne of Middlesex, to bowl at him endlessly in the nets and insisted they bowl at their fastest, which in the case of Lockwood and Richardson was at fearsome speed.

By the time he qualified for Sussex he was ready for anything, at home on hard, fast surfaces but an expert, too, at playing rain-affected pitches, as he demonstrated against Middlesex at Hove in 1900 when, in the most unhelpful conditions, he made 202 in three hours. His career, in the end, was abbreviated by duty. On inheriting the title of Maharaja Jam Sahib of Nawanagar in 1907, he became increasingly pre-occupied with that state's administration and with other political distractions. He also had the misfortune to lose an eye in a shooting accident, despite which he returned to England to play a few more matches for Sussex in 1920.

He died suddenly in 1933 at the age of 61, after which India instituted the Ranji Trophy in his honour. Nowadays there is a clamour for greater recognition of his talents here, much of it coming from India, where commentators point out that for all that the English cherish Ranji's memory, they do not commemorate him as they do Grace, even though the good doctor, in 1908, said of him that 'you will never see a batsman to beat him if you live for 100 years'.

Cardus, more eloquently, said that 'cricket was changed into something rich and strange whenever Ranji batted. When he passed out of cricket, a wonder and a glory departed from the game forever.'

Independent, 17 July 1996

Sanath Jayasuriya

Thrasy Petropoulos

Sanath Jayasuriya is not the man he appears with bat in hand. Where on the cricket field, in the limited-overs contests at least, he looks to slaughter anything vaguely over-pitched, short of a length, or wide of the stumps, you would struggle to find a more genial and affable character off the pitch. Sanna (as he is known by team-mates and fans alike) is a devout Buddhist: a man who sleeps with a prayer book under his pillow at night.

His initial reaction with the media is one of distance: a little wary of what exactly you're after. But when he feels sure that you want to talk cricket, out comes that beaming smile remembered by all from the World Cup.

'What has it been like', I opened the conversation, 'since winning in Lahore in March?'

The ensuing sigh was as telling as his one-word answer: 'Hectic.'

A brief visit home did nothing to lessen the pace. Quite simply the Sri Lankan public treated the team, and in particular Ranatunga, De Silva and Jayasuriya himself, like gods.

In his home town of Matara, the streets were ablaze with people who had come out to greet the man who had left in relative cricketing obscurity and returned home having been voted the 'Most Valuable Player' of the World Cup and the double World Record holder of the fastest ever One-Day International hundred and fifty. Not bad for a few months' work!

Looking back on this golden period in his career, 27-year-old Jayasuriya is in no doubt as to where the turning point lay: 'The hundred in Adelaide was a big moment in my life. I proved to myself that I could play.' A century against any class of opposition is a feat in itself in Test cricket but to play such an innings against arguably one of the best bowling attacks in recent years: McDermott, Fleming, Reiffell and Warne, and then to follow it up with 48 in the second innings in the only Test you play in the series, is worthy of high praise indeed.

Followers of cricket could be forgiven for never having taken note of Jayasuriya before. In actual fact he toured England in 1990 and returned figures of 6-29 in a One-Day International against England on home soil in 1993. Having scored 140 against New Zealand he had, until De Silva eclipsed him with 145 in the World Cup, the distinction of holding both the best bowling and batting performances for his country in the international one-day game.

It is, however, undoubtedly for his heroics in the World Cup and in Singapore that he will be remembered most. A total of 212 runs off only 161 balls tells only half the story. He single-handedly caused the premature retirement of India's Manoj Prabhakar and took the England attack to the cleaners (that six off Defreitas on to the satellite dish during his 82 in 44 balls will remain in the memory forever).

It is important not to forget his contribution with the ball, too. Although nowhere near as dramatic, his spell of bowling in the infamous Semi-Final in Calcutta, after a failure with the bat, was vital to Sri Lanka winning through to the Final.

On being asked what he enjoyed more, his bowling or his batting, Jayasuriya revealed possibly the most important aspect of what he has to offer as a cricketer: he is a team man. 'Everything: batting, bowling and fielding. I love being involved and being able to contribute towards a victory.'

'Was there a time,' I added, 'when you thought that you got a little carried away with attacking, after your two failures in the Semi-Final and Final?'

The change in expression revealed an intensity that is carried over on to the cricket field: 'Yes, maybe. I was too tense. And I know against India I played a bad shot and then I came back for a crazy second run in the Final.' A deeply furrowed brow betrayed a lasting disappointment, almost an anguish. But then out came that sigh, and that smile: 'But at least we won.'

If Jayasuriya's exploits on the Asian sub-continent earned him cult status on a grand scale what happened in Singapore, although in a far more low-key event, was even more dramatic: the fastest ever One-Day International hundred, off only 48 balls – including 11 sixes and 29 off one over, records in themselves – followed by the fastest ever fifty, 17 balls. Granted, the Padang stadium in Singapore is not the biggest of grounds in the world, but it is worth noting that in an opening partnership of 70 in 5.2 overs against Pakistan, Kaluwitharana, his opening partner, was out for a duck!

Typically, Jayasuriya down-plays his feats: 'I didn't go out there to break any records. In fact, I didn't even know about the fastest hundred until a few hours after when someone told me. Some days you see the ball early; other days you struggle to time it at all. You can't hit every ball for four.'

A ball by ball view of his hundred suggests a different story.

For the moment Jayasuriya confesses to viewing recent events very much as if they were a very pleasant dream. It is a great shame that the English public cannot be part of that dream. Apart from a few hastily arranged exhibition matches on this current tour the public will have to wait until 1998 to witness a solitary Test match. Before then it is not inconceivable that a county approach Jayasuriya for the 1997 season.

One thing is for sure: if Jayasuriya does play county cricket more records are set to be broken, not to mention a few bowlers' hearts.

Cricket World Monthly, July 1996

Mushtaq keeps secret weapon for Test

Simon Wilde

Mushtaq Ahmed, Pakistan's cherub-faced but devilish leg spinner, is preparing a new delivery with which to torment England's batsmen when he meets them in the three-match Test series which begins at Lord's later this month. He was shown how to bowl the ball earlier this year by Shane Warne, the Australia leg spinner, with whom he has shared the secrets of their trade in the past.

Mushtaq, who has yet to employ the ball in a first-class match, was seen practising the delivery before play at Taunton last week. He was helped by Rob Turner, the wicketkeeper at Somerset, for whom Mushtaq took 225 wickets between 1993 and 1995 and to where he returns in 1997 and 1998.

'His new delivery spirals in to the right-handed batsman from outside off stump through the air,' Turner said. 'On pitching, it does not break so much as carry on its path.

'Batsmen will find it very difficult to pick out,' he said. 'The hand action is identical to that for the leg break, so that will be of no help. By the time they realise which ball it is, it will be on them.'

Two years ago, Brian Lara said Mushtaq presented a greater challenge than Warne because he possessed more variations. Asked at Taunton if he did not already possess enough deliveries which batsmen could not play, Mushtaq simply smiled in that disarming way of his and said: 'One can never rest in this game. You have to keep looking for something new. I like to experiment.'

According to one source, Mushtaq was planning to use the new ball in his first spell against Somerset but 'got shy'. In fact, he did not need it. By bowling his familiar repertoire beautifully on a pitch offering turn, Mushtaq was more than a match for his former county team-mates, taking five wickets – and adding five more in the second innings. Even Turner, with his insights into Mushtaq's methods, could not help twice losing his wicket to him cheaply.

However, provided that England's batsmen show more resolve than Somerset's when they play Pakistan in the Test matches, Mushtaq will surely test them out with his new delivery.

Mushtaq has made another change to his bowling since he was last in England and that, too, is down to Warne. During Pakistan's tour of Australia last winter, Mushtaq noticed how straight Warne ran to the crease, while he himself had long come in at a sharp angle.

By following Warne's lead, Mushtaq found greater comfort bowling his stock leg break, which had previously put great strain on his back. It was a ball that his Pakistan and Somerset team-mates believed he bowled too infrequently.

'We got on to him last year to bowl fewer googlies and variations to his leg break,' one Somerset player said. 'Part of the reason was that it hurt his back, but he also got excited if he saw a turning pitch and tried too many variations when all he needed to do was bowl five stock balls an over.'

Mushtaq so enjoyed bamboozling batsmen with his googly, though, that – even if he did not dismiss them – he was reluctant to use it less. The message got home partly by accident, after he had started falling away in delivering the googly. He was advised to bowl more leg breaks to get his action back and it was then, when the wickets came in even greater numbers, that he finally accepted the wisdom of his colleagues' words.

The reward for Mushtaq was not only 95 wickets for Somerset last season but also a recall to the Pakistan team for which he had previously achieved disappointingly little. This time he took 18 wickets in two Tests against Australia – after which Warne showed him the 'mystery' ball – and ten wickets in a one-off Test against New Zealand.

Mushtaq readily acknowledges what county cricket has done for him, which is why he had no qualms about re-signing with Somerset last week. 'The main thing I have learnt in county cricket,' he said, 'is to be patient.'

All this may sound like a strong argument in favour of the moratorium on overseas players in county cricket, but the failure of so many English players to learn how to play him may have more to do with Mushtaq's ability to keep on improving his game. At 26, he can only get better.

If England pay this summer for Mushtaq's latest modifications, it really ought to be their old foe Warne whom they should blame.

The Times, 8 July 1996

The Cat is back

Jim Melly

I'm in a corridor in the pavilion at Lord's. Phil 'the Cat' Tufnell prowls up and down like his namesake, warily eyeing the game going on outside the window. I get the impression that he's a tad apprehensive about the press. 'I'm a bit disappointed at the way that I've been portrayed. I think that most of the stuff that was said was very wrong. Okay, I've had a few little things off the field, but, y'know, that's off the field.' Ah, off the field. Tufnell's home life found its way into the tabloids throughout 1994, and led to time off from Middlesex to sort his life out. It's not the first time that he took time off from cricket: frustration with the club scene led Tufnell to give up for three years while he was at school. 'I just got abuse. I was the little fourteen-year-old kid who the old boys liked to have a go at – even though I was getting them all out. They were always, "Who d'you think you are? You're a bit flash, son." I couldn't see a full time career at it.' He spent the time working in the family business. 'My old man was a silversmith. I wanted to get fifty quid in my hand every week, and I just went out and did what normal sixteen-year-olds do: mucking around with motor-bikes and sneaking into pubs.'

Talked back into playing, Tufnell's ability and aggression brought him a place on the 1990/91 England tour to Australia within eight years. 'I was quite young and quite naive, and playing in front of thirty or forty thousand people at Sydney is quite nerve-racking first time up. I was a little bit nervous to be honest, and it was hard enough doing the bowling let alone anything else.' Though his poor fielding became legend, his second trip down under (in 1994/5) saw him in the TV 'catch of the series' competitions. Tufnell brushes it aside. 'It just comes with a bit more experience of playing at the top level. I went away and worked on my fielding.'

Things at that top level have changed. Spinners are now seen as attacking bowlers, with a certain Aussie leading the way. 'Shane Warne's a bit of a freak. He can take wickets on the first day of the first test and that's because of the way he spins the ball. A finger spinner is going to struggle to turn it so early on in a match.' So maybe there's something to be said for closing down one end? 'You've got to get wickets, but you've also got to gauge the game. When you've tied batters down, and someone comes on the other end and gets four or five quick wickets, that's as good as you getting them.' Does he feel that's not always appreciated? 'Yeah. People have got to be sensible enough to see that. Sometimes you've got to do a little more than just look at the wickets column.' Even Tufnell's batting is coming under scrutiny and – bizarre though it may sound – he is doing something about it. 'I'm working on my batting. Everyone's got to muck in and get a few runs here and there.' Yeah, right.

The winter was a long one for Tufnell. 'This is the first time in six years that I've had six months off, so I had a bit of time to sit back and think about a few things.' He says he's matured, but it could be the shock of missing South Africa and the World Cup with England. 'I felt gutted – you see it on the telly and you wanna be there, you wanna be involved. That made me even more determined to play well and keep fit and get back into it this summer.' So what's changed? 'It's just having a belief and a confidence in your own ability. I'm going to try and play well for Middlesex, get my wickets for Middlesex, and get back in the England team.' He's had to take on more responsibility since John Emburey left Middlesex. As the senior spinner, he'll be expected to take up where 'Ernie' left off. It's a lot to ask. He thinks he can do it. 'It's about being positive, growing up a little bit, being a bit more mature.'

Tufnell seems to bring something odd out of people. It's as though they see a 'cheery cockney chappie' and think they've landed in the set of *Mary Poppins*. Tufnell sees the problem. 'It can be quite good up to a point, that "cheeky chappie" thing. But it started to get on my nerves last year when they said that I wasn't a good tourist, and was disruptive and bad for team spirit. That hurt me. It was as if they were saying "we don't want him cos we think he's a bit of an oik".' All that 'cheeriness' shouldn't be mistaken for a lack of knowledge or commitment. For some, becoming a 'cartoon cockney' can be a convenient mask. Tufnell now feels that he has to carry its burden wherever he goes. 'I always seem to have to get twenty more wickets than everyone else or work that little bit harder.' Unlike his image, Phil Tufnell is an articulate man. The six months he had off over the winter have focused his mind on the job at hand. And probably broke his heart.

Phil Tufnell is the best spinner in England. He wants to play for England, and it's a desire so tangible you could put it in a sandwich. 'I love playing for England. It means 150% to me, playing for my country, playing for the team, playing for the supporters. It annoys me a little bit when people say, "his body language isn't right": my heart and my soul and my mind are focused on playing for England.' When Tufnell says that he wants to get wickets for Middlesex, it may be true; but his heart is looking towards the three lions of England. Claims that he is 'difficult to handle' seem weak. 'If wanting to go out and win every game of cricket that you play in – and wanting to win it passionately and aggressively and positively – well if that's "hard to handle", then I think that that's good.' If he's prepared to bend to the whim of the England management – to 'duck and dive' – just to get a place on the starting blocks in the running for

England, that doesn't mean that his performance on the field will be any less intense. 'I'm a believer in letting your character come out – you should show a bit of yourself out there,' he says.

So is he difficult to handle? Phil Tufnell's eyes light up, and he grins that roguish grin. 'Nah,' he says. 'I'm just a pussycat.'

This should be the Year of the Cat.

Inside Edge, June 1996

Issues Contentious and Polite

Introduction

The moral sanctity of cricket was upheld for such a long time it is not perhaps surprising that when the politics and marketing of the game gain the upper hand the mud smears furthest on the page.

Thankfully not all the years' issues were laced with venom. Genuine concerns and constructive criticism to bring about improvements were also aired.

Only a kangaroo court could find Malik guilty

Omar Kureishi

The Australian Cricket Board have rejected the findings of the inquiry which cleared Salim Malik of bribery charges levelled by Shane Warne, Tim May and Mark Waugh, and have done it with more concern for the reputation of the players than for the truth. In doing so, they have provided aid and comfort to the Australian media, who have already declared war.

One writer has warned that Salim Malik should bring his best flak jacket, another has hinted menacingly that a number of Australian players will be incensed that Malik is a member of the Pakistan team, and for good measure branded the International Cricket Council 'lily-livered'. Even the O J Simpson verdict did not provoke this kind of hysterical reaction.

It is important to recount certain facts. Alan Crompton, the president of the Australian Cricket Board, visited Pakistan in October 1994 when his team were playing a Test series. He profusely praised the spirit in which the matches were being played. So did Mark Taylor, the Australian captain, at the end of the tour. Neither appeared to know that three of their players were carrying a dark secret, and apparently nor did the tour manager and the international match referee, John Reid. It is intriguing to say the least.

On a tour one expects players to exchange gossip, not to mention an offer of a substantial amount of money to throw a match. Yet the officials and most of the Australian players were unaware of such an offer.

Five months later, the dark secret was made public through the Australian press. The Pakistan Cricket Board learnt of the allegations by reading about them in the newspapers. Graham Halbish, the chief executive of the ACB, did not see fit even to telephone his Pakistani counterpart. Why this lapse of good manners and protocol?

One cannot award high marks to the Pakistan cricket establishment for their handling of these allegations. They did protest to the ACB, but half-heartedly, and the impression they conveyed was that they tended to believe the allegations. Salim Malik was at first suspended until he could prove his innocence, thus turning the law on its head. The onus of proof lies with the accusers. They then fired Salim Malik as captain and dropped him from the team on the rather flimsy grounds that he had failed to maintain discipline on Pakistan's tour of southern Africa.

Under intense public pressure, the PCB appointed Fakharuddin G Ebrahim as inquiry officer. Ebrahim is a man of impeccable credentials. A retired judge of the Pakistan Supreme Court and a former Governor of Sindh and Attorney-General, he is known to be a person of integrity and is widely respected for being his own man, not given to taking 'instructions'.

At the outset, Ebrahim established that he would be guided by the basic norms of justice; that is, that the accusers must substantiate their allegations with proof, the sort that would hold up in a court of law, and must submit themselves for cross-examination. The accusers had refused to confront Salim Malik, expecting their say-so to be treated as gospel – a position, unfortunately, taken by the ACB as well. Shane Warne, Tim May and Mark Waugh had turned down an offer to visit Pakistan and testify. The ACB went further. They wanted Justice Ebrahim to go to Australia instead, at the same time maintaining that he would find very little, or nothing. It was an arrogant response and showed a contempt for the inquiry.

Thus the allegations against Malik were reduced to just that – unsubstantiated allegations of a kind that would be thrown out of any court of law except a court that dispenses kangaroo justice.

One would have thought that the ACB would have carried out an investigation of their own and submitted the accusers to the most gruelling cross-examination to get at the truth. Apparently this was not done and I am not even certain whether any attempt was made to hold any kind of inquiry, even of the most perfunctory kind. The ACB obviously have great faith in their three players and the question of their being economical with the truth or guilty of exaggeration does not arise.

At the same time, the ACB do not hesitate to dismiss the findings of a distinguished former Justice of the Supreme Court by stating that they find most regrettable the innuendo that the statements were concocted and the players were liars. Are we to believe that Salim Malik, by denying the allegations, is a liar?

I might point out that in the infamous Shakoor Rana-Mike Gatting slanging match in Faisalabad in 1987, the then Board of Control for cricket in Pakistan set up an inquiry and asked Mike Gatting and a few of the England players to appear before the inquiry board, of which I was a member. The England team management readily agreed, and Mike Gatting and the players did appear and were asked searching questions. They did so without compromising their dignity. They showed a respect for their hosts and for the law.

At the best of times, a tour of Australia is hard. Australia are not only a very good team, they are fierce competitors too. There are fears now that this tour could turn nasty. One hopes that good sense will prevail.

Sunday Telegraph, 29 October 1995

Malcolm's case sparks renewed pressure for right of reply

Christopher Martin-Jenkins

The England team return home from South Africa this morning to news that their representative body, the Professional Cricketers' Association, are seeking on their behalf a right of reply to any criticisms aired against them in the media.

The *cause célèbre* is Devon Malcolm, who felt strongly enough about the derogatory remarks of the England manager Ray Illingworth and his bowling coach Peter Lever to break his tour contract by telling his side of the story in a tabloid newspaper, for considerable reward and at the risk of what might have remained of his international career.

Dermot Reeve's public admission yesterday that he was 'angry and hurt' at being left out of the World Cup party showed that Malcolm is not the only disgruntled man among the 21 who represented England at various times during a tour which disintegrated dismally in the last three weeks after a long build-up and during which much of England's cricket was perfectly respectable.

The empirical evidence is all too clear that the policy of introducing four 'one-day specialists' – Reeve, Fairbrother, DeFreitas and Neil Smith – towards the end of the first-class programme disrupted team spirit and made no difference to the one-day results.

Reeve's complaint was that he was given too little chance to remind Illingworth and Mike Atherton, who between them chose the teams on tour and for the World Cup, what a potent force he could be in limited-overs cricket.

Reeve said: 'I have played just twice, bowling 19 overs and facing just 18 balls when batting. Last night was awful after Mike Atherton told me I was not in the World Cup party. I was angry and hurt, but I will bounce back.'

Reeve felt that it was unjust he should have been given only two games when he had played no cricket since last summer.

It seemed, certainly, that Illingworth and Atherton decided very early on that Craig White was the better bet as an all-rounder, although his record cannot compare with Reeve's as a one-day cricketer. Reeve has often been a match-winner, certainly at county level; White, so far, has been a useful contributor.

Illingworth has had unswerving faith in White's ability from the moment that he plucked him out of the Yorkshire dressing-room into England's two years ago, and it would do the chairman's much-reduced stock a great deal of good if his protege were to have a successful World Cup.

Warwickshire's effervescent captain was gracious enough to admit that White is 'a good cricketer and he has played better than me'.

Reeve thereby managed to get his message across without offending anyone, which is what both Illingworth and Malcolm palpably failed to do in the continuing affair of the discontented fast bowler.

The PCA's financial adviser, Harold Goldblatt, said yesterday that the association wanted to meet the Test and County Cricket Board after the World Cup.

They are seeking a revision to the draconian regulations about players speaking in public. Choosing his words carefully. Goldblatt nevertheless made it plain that the PCA believed the rules to be unbalanced.

'They are regarded by some as an infringement of the rights of individuals and the rules of natural justice. We discuss a number of things with the board. This particular matter has been highlighted by the Devon Malcolm case.'

Illingworth's relationship with Malcolm started badly in South Africa with the perfectly reasonable attempt to make his action more consistent and with the subsequent clumsy public undermining of a bowler viewed with respect and apprehension by the South Africans. It ended with the manager apparently blaming the fast bowler for the loss of the Cape Town Test and with it the series, in full view and hearing of the rest of the team.

Illingworth's plain speaking is often refreshing, but it was a dramatic failure in Malcolm's case. The fast bowler held the high moral ground while he maintained his dignified silence, but he conceded it by telling his story for an estimated £10,000 and broke his tour contract, which forbade unauthorised public comment on the tour before the end of March.

When the dust has settled on the tour, the TCCB will inevitably have to punish this most sweet-natured of fast bowlers.

It was already unlikely that Malcolm would play for England again, given the loss of Atherton's confidence in him, regardless of whether the board decide in March to renew Illingworth's contract as chairman and manager for two more home seasons.

It was among many tidying up duties in South Africa of the conscientious administrative manager John Barclay, a man of peace sandwiched in this case between an unmoveable object and irresistible force, to keep an eye and ear on what players said to the press, but he could hardly shackle the chairman of selectors nor indeed the bowling coach Peter Lever.

Daily Telegraph, 23 January 1996

The Devon Malcolm affair: Illy's response

Ray Illingworth and Jack Bannister

Illingworth
The thing that annoyed me most about Malcolm's reaction at the end of the tour was that he never mentioned the fact that he was the one and only England cricketer I told at The Oval that he would be going on tour. I did that to try to settle and encourage him, because I knew what he had done once to the South Africans and they would not forget The Oval in 1994 in a hurry. Also, I was told that the first three Test pitches would be the quickest of the five, so I was desperate to get him right for the first Test at Centurion Park.

Remember he had bowled only a handful of overs after The Oval Test against West Indies, when he developed fluid in the right knee. I arranged a net session at the Headingley indoor school in late September and got Peter Lever there at short notice. He needn't have bothered. Devon was half an hour late and did a bit of skipping because he said he didn't want to bowl indoors on the hard surface. The Derbyshire physiotherapist was there and I asked her, 'Can he bowl?'

She replied that he could. We did manage to get him out of doors once and he bowled well. Peter didn't have the video with him, but he followed through properly, which was all we wanted. It was rubbish for Kim Barnett, and other people who should have known better, to say that we were trying to alter his action. What was the point of that?

What I wanted was for him to attack the crease properly, and let his natural body and arm action lead him down the pitch in a proper follow-through, instead of bowling off the left foot, taking one more pace with the right and then cutting off sharply in his next left stride towards cover. That made him purely an arm bowler with no pace, no aggression or hostility, and no chance of controlling where the ball was going.

The right arm cannot find direction, length and pace on its own. Those have got to be generated by the body with the left arm playing a big part. Devon has never been a classical sideways bowler, looking at the batsmen outside the left arm and elbow, but few bowlers are. Allan Donald does not use the left arm to wind up his body action, but at least he makes it lead him down the pitch. And just remember how Devon out-bowled Allan at The Oval, although I know he was struggling with a toe injury.

That was all I wanted from Devon. A recognition of a basic fault which we all wanted to cure. Anyone would think that no Test cricketer had ever been told about a fault before. Devon either would not, or could not, work it out for himself, and we were soon in trouble when we got to South Africa.

I know that much of the first month was a political exercise in which we were thrilled to take part. I also know what an honour all our boys felt it was to meet President Nelson Mandela in our first four-day game in Soweto, so I can guess the extra pride and excitement Devon felt when he walked around the ground with the President.

I tried to make allowances for that but, in the next few days, it seemed to me that Devon had got carried away a bit, and it was difficult for him to focus on the job in hand. We had so little meaningful match practice available before the first Test, and all on slow pitches completely different from what we could expect in Pretoria, that I wanted to get as much hard practice into all the players, not just Devon.

During each day of the Soweto game, I organised with Peter Lever and John Edrich that the players not in the Soweto game would travel to Centurion Park for practice, because their net facilities are top class. That is why, when the home side had nine wickets down at the start of the third day, I reckoned that Devon would be better off having a hard net than staying with the team and spending most of that day doing nothing.

He was not picked out, but was told to go with the others which, after a few moans, he did. I remember once in that first month telling him that his bowling arm and hand were not right. He told me that his arm was so explosive that I had no chance of knowing whether it was right or wrong. I told him straight. 'Even from 70 yards range, the all-important position of the palm of your hand is clear to anyone who knows what he is looking for.'

Graham Gooch once told me: 'If you want Devon to do something, tell him the opposite.' I was beginning to know what he meant. We spoke to him on his own twice. We spoke to him in nets, but we got no clear response. I was beginning to wonder if he was unfit, because he seemed so reluctant to run properly in matches, and would often try to bowl off a short run in the nets.

South African coach Bob Woolmer had this to say to me after the series was over: 'We reckon Devon was never fit during the tour. That is not just my opinion, nor that of our players who faced him, but the view of all our medical staff, including physiotherapist Craig Smith and our exercise expert, Paddy Upton. They said that he showed every clinical and physical sign of carrying his right knee. They watched how he trained, how he practised and how he ran and walked. They were in no doubt that he had a problem, even if it was only a subconscious one.

The storm clouds gathered quickly, and broke together with the arrival of the rain that washed out the final day of the game in Soweto. The travelling journalists were short of copy and were understandably keen to find some. Lever and Illingworth obliged them in a manner which took little embellishment to generate lively – even lurid – headlines in their newspapers.

The now-famous press conference was not called – it came about by chance, so much so that several of the national correspondents were not present when the manna started to fall into their laps. It was an open secret that all had not gone well between Malcolm, the manager and the bowling coach, but now the 'classified' tag was removed when questions were answered honestly as far as Lever, in particular, was concerned.

He and Illingworth were approached by no more than six of the media to comment on remarks it seems that Malcolm had made to them about the attempts to change his action. The first question put was about the claim of Malcolm that the management were trying to turn him into a medium pacer.

Illingworth
Peter's reply was that Devon couldn't bat, couldn't field, but he could bowl quick. He then asked why anyone would therefore try to take away his one attribute by asking him to bowl slower. *He never used the word 'nonentity'*. That was used by journalists when they wrote the articles. The point that needs emphasising is that we were responding to remarks Devon had already made. We did not instigate the press conference but, when asked questions, answered them honestly.

The criticism of the press conference came flooding back from writers in England, including Ian Wooldridge of the *Daily Mail*. A reason for the attitude of Lever and Illingworth was that their patience – and that of the captain – was now exhausted after the softly-softly approach of the previous few weeks. Public kicks up the backside have been known to work, but not this time.

One-Man Committee, Ray Illingworth and Jack Bannister
(Headline, 1996)

Botham or Bolus? A poll that does not matter

Graeme Wright

When it comes to elections you have to hand it to the Americans: they make a show of it. Bands, badges and bandwagons, and that's only the Primaries. The Test and County Cricket Board goes about its elections in a much more English way – too much secrecy and too many leaks. When Ray Illingworth defeated M J K Smith in a postal ballot in March 1994, for example, no voting figures were given. Indeed, it would have come as no surprise had waiting journalists been kept outside the Grace Gate until a Vatican-style puff of smoke emerged from the cathedral of cricket.

With the forthcoming election of selectors, of course, we've already had the smoke by way of a smokescreen: a bonfire of vanities, so to speak. By putting up an unprecedented number of candidates, the counties have effectively – intentionally or unintentionally – clouded the most important issue. This is that England's cricketers have been poorly equipped (with the exception of sponsors' dogtags) to compete in international cricket. And Illingworth, the man who has understood this all along, is the man under attack by some of the counties.

'The players work hard enough running round the ground,' he said when he was appointed chairman, 'but not hard enough at the basics of cricket.' Perhaps the chairman has been getting too close to home truths for the liking of some counties.

The time for getting back to basics is not a few days before a Test match, as Illingworth should have been wise enough to know with regard to Devon Malcolm in South Africa. The right time is when the players are with their counties. Indeed, getting the basics right is the counties' responsibility, and that means employing first-class coaches who understand the mental and technical demands of the modern game. The modern international game, that is: not the modern county game.

Unfortunately, when you utter words like technical and technique, people go rather glassy. On a sports programme recently, the panel was advised not to get too technical lest the listeners wouldn't understand – in which case they'd do a double turn-off. Yet technique is an important part of most sports and essential in cricket.

Last May, for example, covering a Surrey match for our Sunday paper, I remarked on Alec Stewart's uncertainty when playing on the front foot. Having had consecutive winters in the West Indies and Australia, he looked every inch a Test cricketer on the back foot, but worryingly vulnerable when bowlers drew him forward.

That weakness was still obvious during the winter in South Africa, where accurate, intelligent seam bowling always sought to exploit it. This was something his Surrey employers should have sorted out, but the county appeared more occupied with the business off the field than on it.

In today's world, however, it is personalities and 'issues' that sell sports and newspapers. By throwing such headline-making names as Ian Botham and Graham Gooch into the field for what is, in effect, a pretty irrelevant contest, the counties have cleverly drawn the spotlight away from their own shortcomings as the providers of England's Test cricketers. Immediately, the most important issue in the media became not England's poor showing in South Africa and in the World Cup, but whether 'Illy' can live with 'Beefy'.

The Tories should be pounding a path to the county grounds for lessons in spin-doctoring – not that spin is on the county agenda all that often.

When Illingworth was appointed the chairman of selectors two years ago, high on his agenda was winning back the Ashes, something he achieved as England's captain in Australia in 1970-71. He didn't do it attractively, but he did it effectively, and no one worried whether he smiled or not. Yet if the counties have their way, England could go into next year's Ashes series in complete disarray, with

Illingworth concentrating more on his own back than, say, Stewart's front foot.

All the kerfuffle over Illingworth's countenance – likewise Mike Atherton's – is also a red herring. There's something inherently Protestant in the seemingly dour way they reduce the game to their own level, instead of raising their sights to the level of the spirit of cricket exemplified by Sri Lanka in the World Cup. It's a national characteristic.

So what about this eight-man exercise in democracy that comes to a head this week? Does it matter which two get the votes of the counties and MCC to join Illingworth, David Lloyd, the new coach, and Atherton, assuming he is captain, on the selection committee? No, not in the short term. It's not as if the selectors are spoilt for choice when picking the England team, even if they do manage the occasional baffling selection. What it might indicate, however, is how the counties view the long-term ambitions of men like Botham, Gooch and David Graveney – should we be told how the voting went.

What it might also show is just how much, or how little, the county managements know about the game, as opposed to the business, of cricket. They offered some evidence of this in 1993 when, after only one season, they abandoned the 50-over format in the Sunday League. True, it was initially foolish to choose the one competition that has the full fury of a County Championship match raging either side of it. But if the counties were serious about England's prospects in the World Cup, surely one of the three limited-overs competitions could have been played under World Cup rules?

This season the Benson and Hedges Cup will be played over 50 overs. But it's a little late. The horses have long bolted and you can't see them for the smokescreen.

Independent, 13 April 1996

Spinning over gets out of hand

Vic Marks

Brisbane, 29 November 1994, and Graeme Hick is battling to save the first Test. He has batted almost five hours for his 80 when Shane Warne bowls another leg-spinner from around the wicket.

The ball pitches in the rough outside the leg stump and bounces wickedly; it hits Hick's left pad, which has been thrust down the pitch. From there the ball balloons on to his chest and then the back of his bat. Wicketkeeper Ian Healy steps around the stumps to take the catch. If only Hick had had the presence of mind to toss his bat away in the manner of Dermot Reeve, England might have saved the Test.

Alternatively, Hick might have been declared a cricketing pariah for flouting the spirit of the game. That is how some observers have interpreted Reeve's eccentric method of combating the left-arm spin of Hampshire's Raj Maru in the championship match at Edgbaston three weeks ago. The Test and County Cricket Board have requested Warwickshire's observations of the episode.

Fifteen times in his innings Reeve thrust his left leg down the pitch and tossed his bat four feet to the off side, just missing Hampshire's Giles White at silly point. Maru said he had 'never seen anything like it in 16 years of first-class cricket'; Reeve pointed out that John Emburey had used this method. Reeve had also used the ploy successfully before, when facing Ravi Shastri.

Bear with me in a quick rummage through the law book, which suggests that Reeve is in the clear. Law 32 explains his actions: 'The striker shall be out caught if the ball touches his bat or if it touches below the wrist his hand or glove, *holding the bat*' (my italics).

Law 37 – Obstructing the Field – states: 'Either batsman, on appeal, shall be out if he wilfully obstructs the opposite side by word or action.' 'By word' covers the devious – or desperate – batsman, who yells 'Boo' when a catch is being attempted: 'by action' is there to stop the batsman physically impeding a fieldsman. In Reeve's case, his bat avoided the fieldsman; perhaps Maru, who was captaining Hampshire at the time, should have stationed another close catcher in the usual flightpath of Reeve's bat and then lodged an appeal.

Reeve could be stymied by Law 42 and its all-embracing clause of 'bringing the game into disrepute'. This becomes a matter of interpretation. For example, Greg Chappell's decision to instruct brother Trevor to bowl underarm in a one-day game against New Zealand was universally agreed to be contrary to the spirit of the game, and the law was changed.

But A. R. Wingfield Digby's tactics in a minor counties match, tactics which raised eyebrows at Lord's, were, in my view, legitimate. That famous cricketing cleric of Dorset once contrived that 60 runs should be donated to Cheshire in one over by ordering one of his team to bowl 14 wides, all of which went for four. He wanted to resuscitate a run-chase (he did, and Dorset won).

As for Reeve's eccentricities at Edgbaston, I have no qualms about them. He was not making a protest about Maru's line of attack – indeed Ashley Giles had bowled a long spell for Warwickshire in the same vein. His response was a rational and legitimate ploy to eliminate the risk of being caught.

Indeed this little episode can do us all a service by highlighting a trend that is liable to blight the game – namely the increasing use of left-arm spinners bowling over the wicket and pitching the ball 12 inches outside the leg stump. Fifteen years ago, this was rare; Norman Gifford occasionally taunted batsmen by lobbing the ball into the rough in this vein, often when they weren't looking. Derek Underwood disliked bowling over the wicket; Phil Edmonds, who regarded himself as a classicist, was also reluctant to use this strategy, on aesthetic grounds.

Now all our leading left-arm spinners – Patel, Illingworth, Stemp and Tufnell – frequently operate in this mode. It is legal and can be effective, as Jayasuriya proved in the World Cup. If the ball lands on the line of the stumps it can be an aggressive strategy. But when the ball lands a foot outside of leg stump it can produce the most unedifying of spectacles. The most likely outcome is a stalemate as the batsman pads the ball away. Alternatively he can play just one risky shot, the sweep, to a heavily guarded leg-side field.

The lawmakers have intervened in similar circumstances before. When a batsman was restricted to one attacking shot – the hook – by persistent bouncers, they imposed a limitation of two bouncers per over. The laws are not immutable. They are there, in part, to protect the aesthetic values of the game. Over the years the lbw law has been changed to combat negative pad play. Rather than fussing over Reeve's bat-throwing, the authorities should be addressing the problem posed by the current batch of left-arm spinners.

It is a tricky one. Restricting bowlers to just one fielder behind the wicket on the leg side would cure the bane, but would be unfair on off-spinners and inswing bowlers. Insisting that one of the two fielders currently allowed behind square on the leg side is in a catching position is too contrived and open to dispute.

I've been thrashing around for a simple solution to spare us this ugliness – without success. Any suggestions?

Observer, 9 June 1996

Gentlemen please, let's just play the game

Allan Massie

Just over a hundred years ago a Cambridge undergraduate and Indian prince, K. S. Ranjitsinhji, determined to improve his batting. So he hired a team of professionals to bowl at him in the nets at Fenner's. They included Tom Richardson, perhaps the greatest of all English fast bowlers and Ranji's future Test team-mate. Nobody thought it odd, and Richardson was probably glad of the money. That was in cricket's golden age, when an amateur and professional were quite different things.

You have to be middle-aged to remember the last Gentlemen v Players match, but in the past few days a whiff of that old division has wafted to Lord's from the High Court. The ill-advised libel case that Ian Botham and Allan Lamb brought – and yesterday lost – against the former Pakistan captain, Imran Khan, was only partly about the issue of ball-tampering. It was Imran's accusation of racism and class-induced chippiness that seems to have got under their skin.

Imran – himself an Oxford Blue – lined up the Gentlemen on his side, and the Players have been bowled out. That, at least, to judge from his earlier remarks, is how he may see it. Worse for Botham and Lamb, it is how the jury has seen it too.

Class has always mattered in cricket. The reason is obvious; unlike football (working-class) and rugby union (middle-class), cricket has always drawn its players from across the social spectrum. This has created tensions, not always smoothed away by the camaraderie of the game.

Others, besides Imran, remain aware of class differences. The journalist Frances Edmonds (Italian contessa, Cambridge graduate, and wife of former Middlesex and England spinner Phil Edmonds) once remarked, not entirely in jest, that in ordinary circumstances she would have expected to meet someone like her husband's county and England captain, Mike Gatting, only if she had had occasion to call a plumber. For all that, one can't help thinking that Imran is a bit out of date.

The gap between the Gentlemen and the Players started narrowing a long time ago – about the end of the First World War. There were still grandees such as Lord Tennyson, who captained Hampshire and made the wicket-keeper his valet (or was he valet first, wicket-keeper second?) and martinets like D. R. Jardine (Winchester & Oxford), whom Harold Larwood (Nottinghamshire coalfields) talked of as 'Mr Jardine' to the end of his days – but the respect in which Jack Hobbs was universally held raised the status of the profession. His England opening partner Herbert Sutcliffe – holder of a wartime commission and later a successful businessman – was a new-style professional.

Young professionals in the Thirties such as Cyril Washbrook and Denis Compton soon, consciously or unconsciously, adapted their accents to speak smooth BBC English. The successful cricketer was becoming middle-class. In the 1950s, the chief complaint of many pros was that the nominal amateur, with a sinecure as a county assistant secretary, might be making more from the game than they were.

Since then class distinctions in cricket have become blurred as in society at large. There has been a levelling-down as well as up. David Gower (King's, Canterbury & couldn't-be-bothered-with-university) modified his public school accent to fit in with his fellows – though it seems to be creeping back in the commentary box.

Mike Atherton (Manchester Grammar School & Cambridge), reacting perhaps to colleagues' labelling of him as FEC (which the gentle-minded took to stand for Future England Captain, until it was revealed that the E was for 'educated' and the F and C for less polite words), seems to go out of his way to present himself as a classless scruff.

As for racism, England's cricketers would have to be unreconstructed Afrikaners to feel any sense of racial superiority considering how often they have been thumped by the West Indies (and Pakistan too, for that matter).

Botham pointed out in the witness box that Vivian Richards is his son's godfather; he might have added that he flounced furiously out of Somerset when the club committee got rid of his mates Richards and Joel Garner.

Cricketers such as Botham and Lamb give the impression of being egalitarian, typical modern celebrities, who are as much at ease in a stately home or swish nightclub as in a public bar. What unites them with Imran is surely greater than anything that divides them: a love of cricket and a fierce pride in performance and achievement.

It is that pride which they all share that has been wounded, and led to this sad and unnecessary case.

Daily Telegraph, 1 August 1996

Best of English stifled by teams feasting on glut of foreigners

Simon Hughes

Money and sex are destabilising influences in life and sport which is probably why domestic football and cricket seem to be heading in opposite directions. [Soccer is rich and glamorous, cricket isn't. So . . .] More people turned up at Alan Shearer's press conference than attended the first two days of the second Test; while Premier League salaries and win bonuses are perking up luxury-yacht vendors, an increasing number of county cricketers are on performance-related pay, and violent terrace skirmishes are more common at Headingley than Highbury.

But the Premiership air still reeks of danger. Foreign footballers are infesting the leading teams and at least 200 have been registered in the four main divisions, more than ever before. Chelsea's starting line-up could read: Kharine, Petrescu, Gullit, Vialli, Di Matteo, Johnsen and Leboeuf, for instance. Yet last weekend five counties fielded an entire team of English qualified players in the Britannic Assurance Championship. A polarisation of views is emerging to the question: are foreign sportsmen good for the nation's health?

The Institute of Professional Sports is concerned and will hear from worried representatives of football, ice hockey and basketball when they meet next month before confronting the Department of Employment. Gordon Taylor, of the Professional Footballers' Association, will point out that there have been 400 free transfers in 1996 as football clubs cast off their fringe players predominantly in favour of cheap imports.

In cricket the overseas issue has come to head because of the hurried departure of Australia's Stuart Law and Michael Bevan from their counties immediately after last week's NatWest semi-finals to join a training camp back home. The gradual expansion of the international cricketing circuit has set many clubs wondering if the investment is worth it. Middlesex have ceased negotiations with Javagal Srinath because his commitments to India would eat into a large chunk of next summer.

The result should be extra opportunities for a home grown player, but the decreasing availability of foreign Test players is a mixed blessing. Overseas cricketers have made a vast contribution to our game for 36 years (Ron Headley was the first, joining Worcestershire in 1960), a fact that will certainly be recognised when the officers of the TCCB gather tomorrow to discuss, among other things, the proposed moratorium on overseas players in 1999, the summer of the World Cup.

Lancashire's chairman, Bob Bennett, tabled the motion. 'Remembering that the nine Test playing countries in the World Cup would each have a squad of 14, taking away the world's greatest players, we felt this was an ideal time for the domestic game to look at itself without overseas players,' he said. With a membership of 14,000 and a large catchment area, Lancashire can afford to be slightly gung-ho on the subject; they often choose to leave out their current overseas player, Steve Elworthy.

But the minnows in the championship pool will not be easily lured. Peter Anderson, Somerset's chief executive, was adamant. 'We think it's unreasonable for the TCCB to suggest we can't sign an overseas player for the latter half of the 1999 season if we want to,' he said. 'Call me Parochial Pete if you like, but players from the sticks are migrating to the larger clubs with more money, so the only way people like us can remain competitive is with overseas players.'

There is a dichotomy here. The presence of the Wasim Akrams and Courtney Walshes does raise the standard and entertainment value of county cricket, but the development of local players can become stunted if they are denied opportunity. And there is no doubt overseas players absorb all the idiosyncracies of English conditions and players, then subsequently undermine our performances at Test level.

Figures assembled over a longer period tell a vivid story. The chorus of overseas players in English cricket reached a crescendo in 1980 when there were 42 sprinkled among the 17 counties, though only two could play at the same time. It was not until 1988 that regulations and wastage restricted all counties to one. Between 1980 and 1988 England played 95 Tests, and won 19, a success rate of 20 per cent. This compares unfavourably with the decade before (35 per cent), the 1990s (25 per cent) or England's overall 34 per cent record (1876-present: Tests 728, wins 247).

Obviously this discrepancy is not caused purely by the influx of Asians, West Indians, South Africans and Australians. But a scenario we will call the 'hide and seek factor' is damaging. When counties field imported match-winners, many home-bred players take shelter behind them, scavenging on the scraps left by the predators. If there is a Malcolm Marshall or a Richard Hadlee in the side, the average English professional does not seek to change the course of a match, but tends to hide until the job is three-quarters done. Sometimes there is little choice. Cardigan Connor, no shirker, owed last week's nine for 38, the best figures ever achieved at

Southampton, to the advantages he enjoyed (new ball, choice of ends) as a result of Winston Benjamin's enforced retirement.

While it is tremendously exciting and challenging to scrap with the world's greatest players, it is a fallacy to think these stars *always* have a beneficial influence on their English colleagues. The fearsome pace of Wayne Daniel won Middlesex countless matches in the 1980s, but the technique he discussed after the game had nothing to do with cricket. Last week Walsh conceded that he spends too long in the field to have the time or energy for much tuition, and he is not alone. At least former greats like Malcolm Marshall and Desmond Haynes have now infiltrated England's tired coaching system to pass on their expertise.

Australian Dean Jones is another rare exception. His inexhaustible supplies of energy and bravura, his ruthless aggression and his verbal diarrhoea have taken Derbyshire to the brink of their first championship since 1936. He is immersed in the team goals and refutes the suggestion that his nationality compromises his objectives. 'I want to see England do well, it's important for world cricket,' he said, 'and I'm concentrating on trying to help Derbyshire bring on youngsters in a winning environment – that's the ultimate route to producing good Test players. I'm trying to help get Corky right.'

After 30 years of trial and error then, cricket has got its overseas equation just about right. One per county bolsters the weak without usually encumbering the strong and should not hinder the national side. Overall, the galaxy of foreign stars has transformed the county scene into the most prestigious cricketing circuit in the world.

The benefits of this sudden influx of foreigners in English football are less certain. In the short term they will offer the public, the sponsors and the directors the succulent fare they crave. But when the 'hide and seek factor' takes effect, the prowess of the England team could be impaired. Ruud Gullit is anxious for Chelsea to 'play the European way' so has filled his squad with skilful Europeans, wonderful for ticket holders, but not necessarily welcomed by Glenn Hoddle wearing his England hat.

The Premiership is awash with £22.2 million booty, and the top 11 finishers will all receive in excess of £1 million. The FA neglected to convert their projected prize money into lire or francs but Gullit echoes the thought of all managers when he says: 'English players cost too much money.' If the superior taste of Swiss chocolate was more affordable, we would consume the odd extra bar with no ill-effects. But those who gorged themselves would eventually be sick.

Daily Telegraph, 19August 1996

Outrage in the Long Room

Pete Clark

The news that the Marylebone Cricket Club is to offer 250 life memberships at £10,000 each to finance the construction of a new grandstand is a fitting end to a dismal season for English cricket.

To MCC members already reeling from the shock of seeing artists' impressions of the proposed media spaceship to be built at the Nursery End, bang opposite the hallowed Pavilion, this may well be the final straw, dammit.

The prospect of Lord's Cricket Ground bristling with futuristic architecture paid for by used-car johnnies topping up their vintage port with slugs of lemonade is not one that can be easily borne.

Membership of the MCC is entry to the Elysian Fields. Like all of life's deepest and most enduring pleasures, it has to be worked at with singular intensity. As with other gentlemen's clubs, you must first find a proposer and seconder from the existing membership.

Although members are readily identifiable from their dyspeptic club ties, getting two of them on your side involves an arduous courtship process during which the ardent applicant is required to pass muster on a variety of topics ranging from the difference between a Chinese cut and a Chinaman, to the exact degree of pink in the perfect pink gin.

If and when these delicate negotiations are completed in a satisfactory fashion, the name of the applicant will be forwarded. A letter bearing the famous crest will shortly drop on the doormat.

Do not be fooled by the speed of its arrival, as this will be the only significant communication from the MCC in rather more than a quarter of the average lifetime.

Even in a nation famed for its queues, this is a prize specimen. It is the queue's queue. There are 30,000 people in front of you, and the existing membership show no sign of relinquishing their grip on life.

This is important, because membership is a strictly finite affair: quite simply someone has to pop their brogues before the waiting list is trimmed by one.

Those on the waiting list therefore find themselves becoming addicted to the obituary pages, speculating on whether this baronet or that lieutenant-colonel may have been a member. The amount of patience demanded goes beyond the requirements of sainthood.

Although the wait at times seems endless, it is the nub of membership. This is a purifying experience, a shriving of the spirit. When full membership is finally conferred, it will be fully appreciated. The sense of belonging is palpable.

This is why queue-jumping is anathema to the principle of the MCC, especially when it is achieved by handing over 30 pieces of silver.

The 250 new boys will have no idea of what it is like to count down the years, the most demanding form of clock-watching known to man. Therefore they cannot experience the catharsis of that final acceptance.

They will not have acquired, by a process of relentless questioning, the arcane secrets of the Pavilion; how to bag a seat; where and where not to eat; how to avoid the charge of a berserk major; the correct moment to uncork the first bottle of Pouilly Fuissé; the guilty pleasure of watching the match on a television set in the Long Bar.

These 250 new members, although they do not represent a

significant proportion of the membership, will weaken the moral fibre of the MCC.

It is a common misconception that the MCC is somehow elitist. This is incorrect. Beyond the necessity to find two sponsors, there are no other qualifications required for membership other than a love of cricket.

Social background is of no account, wealth – until now, that is – is immaterial. The annual membership fee is modest and as it includes free entry to all Test matches and one-day internationals at the greatest cricket ground in the world plus the two knockout finals, it actually pays for itself.

Rather than elitist, the MCC is exclusive: it excludes all those without the patience to join.

This is what gives the club its special character. All cricket fans are to some degree fatalistic – a lifetime of washed-out games, dodgy lbw decisions, stubbornly dull tailenders, missing the shot/wicket of the day while attending a call of nature – but those who belong to the MCC are a breed apart.

They face all of life's vicissitudes with equanimity, expecting nothing – least of all an England victory on a ground where they never seem to win – accepting everything.

The arrival of a new type of member who has had the incalculable pleasures of membership dropped in his lap in return for filthy lucre does not bear thinking about. They simply will not understand.

The selling of honours, in one form or another, has a long and dishonourable tradition in this country, and not much good has ever come of it.

The MCC is one institution that must be protected from this practice at all costs. This is one set of family silver which, if sold, will never be reclaimed again. For better or worse, the club still does not admit women members.

The rules governing where one can eat, drink and smoke are quirky, to say the least, but they are always rigidly enforced. No matter how dishevelled a member's dress might become, he must take care to keep a tie round his neck.

Like any club worth its colours, the MCC is defined by its rules, and of these, none is more important than the rule that prospective members must wait an eternity before being allowed through the Pavilion doors.

These 250 new memberships are nothing less than a Trojan horse. Once inside the gates, who knows what may be spewed forth from its depths?

Be warned: when membership is up for sale, all standards are lost. It will not be long until streakers cavort freely in the Long Room.

London Evening Standard, 17 September 1996

David Acfield: reviving England's doldrums

Sandy Mitchell

England is trailing in yet another Test series and our greatest-ever match-winner, Ian Botham, has been to court over being called a cheat. Is it time to draw stumps on the national game in sheer embarrassment? 'Never,' David Acfield cries. If there is one man who can say for sure that behaviour on the pitch isn't cricket, and do something about it, it is he. He even believes he knows how to turn England into victors.

Today, we find him as far as it is possible to be in spirit from the shiny, green button of a Test-match ground. The City headquarters of the Save & Prosper insurance company are as pale and earnest as a letter from your bank manager. Mr Acfield works here as a departmental director, but it is not his real job as far as we are concerned. That is protecting the sacred spirit of the game as chairman of the Test and County Cricket Board's cricket committee, and leading the TCCB's working party into selecting, coaching and managing the England side. (We will find out in September whether his recommendations, announced this month, are accepted by the board.)

He has taken off his mustard-and-marmalade MCC blazer for now, wearing pinstripes instead. His ties carries the quiet stripes of the Essex county club, where he is chairman and where he played as amateur and professional for 22 years. Despite the subfusc, Mr Acfield manages to fill the office with clubroom *bonhomie*, tossing out matey greetings to a receptionist, and sagging comfortably into a boardroom chair.

'Cricket only mirrors the world we live in and we are in a rash, abrupt, aggressive age,' he says, qualifying his world-weary shrug with the comment that 'every year I lecture all the captains of the county sides, and I have said, "Hang on lads, there is a limit to what we will accept." The days of nice, gentlemanly play may have gone, but I still maintain that players must see themselves as role models. One captain said the other day, "How can you expect us to be competitive and then act the way we used to?" One fully feels for the players, but my answer is "Do it".'

An urgent buzzing cuts him off mid-stride. He pulls an electronic pager from his pocket, reads his message, wrinkles his tanned forehead cryptically – base rates are shooting up or down, one assumes – and moves on to diagnose the ills of the English team. 'We're not a million miles from being a very good side.' Talent is not the problem, Mr Acfield stresses. Nor is enthusiasm for the game: 'There is more cricket played in Yorkshire than in the whole of Australia. The biggest problem is county versus country.' Like out footballers, our best cricketers are required to play far too much, grinding out runs and wickets almost twice as often, in the case of a key player, such as Michael Atherton, as their foreign counterparts.

So Mr Acfield has proposed in his working party's report that the chairman of selectors should have a binding right to withdraw a player from a county match for a rest. More radical proposals, such as making the England team direct employees of the TCCB in order to extend control over their performances, he hit for six. 'I was accused the other day of being a traditionalist, as if there was something wrong with it. I think one should be careful of doing something radical – all the other countries do roughly the same as we do.' Except lose most of their matches.

'I enjoy sitting on committees,' he confided at one point, his Essex burr as flat as the county's marshes, although much more cheerful. One should not be too underwhelmed, then, to find that one of his big ideas is simply to form another committee, albeit a new one, of nine members to run all aspects of the England team. 'We have tried a supremo, we've tried a coach and a chairman of selectors, we had Ted Dexter's England committee . . .' The new, improved England Management Committee would include two former Test old-hands, perhaps Mike Gatting and David Gower, as well as the full house of TCCB executives responsible for youth development, overseas tours and the like. Whenever a committee suggests more bureaucracy, one fights an urge to throw open a window for some fresh air.

The beeper distracts us. We enquire, nosily, whether it is good news or bad? 'Good,' smiles Mr Acfield. 'A collared pratincole has been spotted on the Norfolk coast.' The pager, in fact, connects him to a messaging service for 'twitchers', and he delightedly admits that when it goes off in meetings he pretends it is delivering price-sensitive news. Some things never change. As an Essex slow bowler, whose success came from pegging away from a short run-up to drill the ball at the batsman's feet, Mr Acfield was famous for having once halted mid-stride on noticing a bird. Somehow, spotting a hobby flying overhead seemed more exciting than the taking of yet another wicket. 'I have to be able to say which family it is and which it is exactly, otherwise I go mad.' He explains his passion for fine wine, shared with many notable cricketers including Gatting and Gower, in the same terms. 'Where does it come from? What grape? What year? It is a bit like a detective problem.'

You might guess from Mr Acfield's affable manner that he is a *bon viveur*, but oddly there is no trace left of the schoolmaster after his years as an A-level teacher in Essex. In his cricketing days, county players were not paid enough to survive during the closed season without an alternative career. 'I don't think we were the same as today's players. It was a different society, a different life,' he recalls.

He had an even better reason for putting off the moment of turning professional until six years into his cricketing career. He was Britain's sabre champion four times, a gold medallist in the 1970 Commonwealth Games, and had he taken cash for playing cricket he would have been disqualified from taking part in the Mexico and Munich Olympics. 'I was the last amateur,' he says, and it is an ethos that he still exudes. When Test matches garner £1 million each from ticket receipts, and the rights to televise cricket are touted for some £60m, one should applaud this rare survival and his volunteer service on behalf of cricket.

As Mr Acfield's pager beeps one more time, drawing his attention to urgent matters, he passes a last remark: 'I can't promise to make England win. All I can do is help give the team an edge.' We take our leave, pondering how much longer we can strive both to win international matches consistently and play the game in the good old-fashioned way, and whether that day has not already passed.

Country Life, 22 August 1996

Odds and Ends

Introduction

Cricket is all about serendipity, the joy of discovery, at unusual places or in an unexpected context.

Who knows, come the new millennium and we are quite likely to find an article by Jessica Mitford revealing the identity of the over-the-cliff cricketer in St Helena. After all, he was in the Services and as he threw up his arms in terror while falling to his death, was he unwittingly germing an idea with a member of the opposing team, a forefather of one of her Nazi friends? I mean, nobody nowadays believes it was just the ghost of Napoleon . . .

Digging deep for the sweet taste of former glory

Tony Lewis

It was a bit of a shock, I can tell you, to see my name come up a few days ago in a sports agency news paragraph. It is true I have become a 'walking' person, daily up the lane towards the foothills of the Rhondda Valleys. As for speed, I am a touch short of Botham in his Hannibal mode – 4.3 mph for six hours a day – but why worry, even if I broke the world landspeed record the witnesses would only be sheep. Sheep do not file stories.

No, my name does not appear alongside those of current cricketers but then came last Thursday:

> Lee Germon of Canterbury next Wednesday in Bangalore will captain New Zealand at cricket in his first Test match. The last cricketer to lead his country on debut was A. R. Lewis of Glamorgan and England. Lewis's first match was also in India.

This was a bit of a shock. History, it is true, but I had never stopped to think that no one since 1972 had walked out to captain their country, as I did in New Delhi 23 years ago, without a single Test behind him.

I would enjoy a conversation with young Germon, though I would come clean from the start that 'young' was not an adjective attached to my name when I first played. I was 34 and, well, let me be fair to myself, a mature wine in need of decanting, of swilling energetically round the goblet so as to stir the sinking layers of potential.

I remember the phone call as Lee will. I was sitting, Test-less, in the kitchen with a wife, two tiny daughters and an electrician, when the telephone information came from Billy Griffith, secretary of the MCC, that I had been chosen to lead the MCC tour of India, Ceylon and Pakistan: a mere five months and eight Tests. My wife leapt up and kissed the electrician. This I have never been able to work out.

We drank champagne, the three of us, my wife explaining to the girls and to the electrician that 'Daddy's going to play for England. What a pity they didn't choose him before his legs started hurting.' Never mind, I was ready for action. It was early August, 1972.

Let me at 'em, I thought. When is the first Test? And then it hit me – late December. Four months away.

When did Lee Germon know that he was to play his first Test? A month? A few weeks?

D'you see? It is so easy for home Tests. You get the news on Sunday and you are with the team by Tuesday. For the man making his debut overseas it is different: you have months to wait. But remember this – the only novice chosen for a tour who knows for sure that he will play in the first Test or any Test is the debutant captain. Lee German writes his name down first next Wednesday, and then selects the other 10 players.

The long interim between selection and walking out for that first Test merits a book of its own. For me, four months passed. 'Good morning, skipper,' said the idiot greengrocer. At the local bring-and-buy: 'And we would like to make a special welcome for the captain of . . .' Don't say it, I used to pray. Don't say England. I haven't played yet. It's August. I could be dead and gone by Christmas.

I remember giant rugby forwards at Cambridge, having been selected for the Varsity match at Twickenham 10 days before the match, staying in bed almost every moment they were not training, so as not to be nudged by a passing push-bike under a Regent Street bus.

Lee Germon has gone through all that: he has tried on his blazer a few thousand times, even worn the sweater and cap and swung a bat in the mirror, but he is close now. Days away. Soon it will be Lee Germon, Canterbury and New Zealand.

I can imagine his flight to India when the captain's role is theoretical and victory in the series only a matter of putting plans into action. He can pop up the aisle of the aircraft and chat to a couple of key bowlers and discuss their field placings to left-handers.

He would have courted senior Test players who clearly thought they should have been captain before him. And the question nags away: 'Will I be good enough?'

And then comes India. The Kiwis are in Bombay at the moment. Thousands have acclaimed him. Not much changes in the land of cricket fever, garlands and 'best of luck, uncle'. Except that the raging swell of a Test match crowd is present only in one-day internationals. Hotel foyers are fairgrounds: the attention is flattering.

I remember walking along a chicken run of an approach from dressing rooms to field in New Delhi. One moment I was chatting quietly to the Indian captain Agit Wadekar, unable to see over the side walls into the stands.

Next moment a mighty roar erupted at the opposite side as the packed house caught sight of us. Then, out of the darkness into dazzling sunshine and an oven heat.

I wanted to get out there. I knew I was ready, but still my first Test match scoreboard had not clicked a single run. I was near the middle and I said to myself: 'I would say that I have a fair chance of playing for England in a Test match.'

The four months, the eternity, was nearly over. Now I could declare myself in the team to face Wadekar, call the toss, and then, even if blown up by a firecracker on the way back, I would have made the team-sheet and the record book. The worst that could happen – A. R. Lewis, absent ill.

Ah, well. Of such small happenings to such bit-part players on cricket's great stage are agency paragraphs made. In a short time now Lee Germon will learn a lesson for a lifetime. Possessing the uniform of a Field Marshal matters little if you fight a poor war. The days of standing around in a smart new blazer are gone. The greengrocer is history.

Now it is the dust and dirt of a bus ride back from the ground to the hotel in Bangalore, the million cyclists ringing the jubilee bells for Tendulkar's 300 or Kambli's 250 in the day and you are beginning to feel the heat.

Then it is time to listen to the wise old senior players, all to do with not dealing in blind hope but faith, in the talent and the method and the record which you have built up over the seasons.

Robert Louis Stevenson – Virginibus Puerisque:

Hope is the boy, a blind, headlong, pleasant fellow, good to chase swallows with salt.

Faith is the grave, experienced, yet smiling man. (Holiday reading.)

Lee Germon, captain in his first Test match, will be a wiser man on Wednesday.

Sweaty shirt – happy heart, if you know what I mean.

Sunday Telegraph, 15 October 1995

In the pantheon of the far pavilions

Suzanne Goldenberg

There were a couple of hundred spectators in a sea of empty seats, girls with plaits and wearing cricket whites shyly coming to pay their respects, and a cantankerous autograph-collector demanding signatures on the back of a book jacket for a collection already extending into thousands. 'Whatever comes in handy I take,' said E V Padmanabhan, aged 75.

But for the England women's team, the world champions, it was a moment to savour. At the Lal Bahadur stadium here, capacity 35,000, and at the other venues during their five-week tour of India, they were playing where the men play, at the stadiums they had seen on television, and they were getting the attention due to any visiting cricket side.

'Here we are seen in terms of English cricketers where at home we are just a very minor sport,' said Janette Brittin, England's opening bat and at 36 the veteran of the side.

There have been no reports of a mass exodus from government offices or people stumbling about the pavements with radios glued to their ears. The Indian sponsor, the New Delhi outlet for Kentucky Fried Chicken, which has been beset by legal problems because it has been the target of a political campaign to stop foreign investment, pulled out days before the start of the series, and there was no free-for-all for the broadcasting rights.

Purnima Rau, a native of Hyderabad who was replaced as captain on December 5, can only dream of the mobs that turn out for the male captain Mohammad Azharuddin when he steps out of his home in a local suburb. There is no offer for any of the Indian women to join Sunil Gavaskar on the Internet, and the country's heroes remain mainly male. 'When Kapil Dev was bowling, every one wanted to be a fast bowler; now everyone wants to bat like Sachin Tendulkar,' said India's new captain Pramila Bhat.

But although women players are eclipsed by their male counterparts, they still have it far better than in England. As well as the match fee of 2,000 rupees (£37) for each player, several members of the India side are employed full-time as cricketers by Indian Railways or Air India, leaving them free to practise.

Indian state-run television carried live coverage of the England matches until a regional athletics meeting intervened. The series has been reported in national newspapers, albeit with reference to the 'Eves' of cricket. And in small towns such as Lucknow and Patna the crowds have turned out in their thousands.

Some of the Indian fans have given their fanatical devotion violent expression. England's medium-pacer Clare Taylor got a taste of this when she was hit on the back of the head while fielding on the boundary in Patna. 'Every time I went near the fence, missiles rained down,' she said. 'Police baton-charged the crowd of 15,000 to restore order.'

Jo Chamberlain saw it differently. 'We are just treated like gods out here, everywhere we go,' said England's left-arm pace bowler. 'Probably when we go back we will wear our England tracksuits and people will say: "Well who are you, then?" '

But play yesterday, the second day of the third and final four-day Test at Hyderabad, showed up the tourists' fallibility. England were bowled out for 98 in reply to India's first-innings 184. Shyama Shaw, the middle-order bat who rescued India on Sunday with the top score of 66, took three wickets for 19 runs. Sue Metcalfe from Yorkshire was England's highest scorer with 23.

At stumps India were 36 for one in their second innings, giving them a lead of 122, and they are looking good to level the series after England won the second Test in Jamshedpur by two runs.

For both sides the series has been a chance to regroup after a slack period. After a decade in which Indian cricket was represented by a slow, ageing side, there was a clear-out this year and now the average age is 21.

On the field, whereas England's players can wear skirts, trousers are *de rigueur* for the Indians, a feature which attracted the 18-year-old left-arm spinner Neetu David, currently out with a hand injury, to take up the game. Most players come to it at college via other sports, but Rajni Venugopal started young. Her father was a keen player and from an early age she had to practise batting for three hours a day on a pitch at home.

It has been a voyage of discovery for England's players. Only Brittin had already played in India, during the previous tour in 1981, and for her team-mates the food, the crowds and the 17-hour train journeys have been revelatory.

Their tour, which ends with the final one-day international in Madras on December 15 with the sides level at 2–2 in that series, has also been a reconnaissance mission for the 1997 World Cup in India. And it has given the holders a chance to size up an emerging team. 'If we are going to retain the World Cup in 1997 then we are going to have to beat India,' said England's coach John Bown.

Guardian, 12 December 1995

Howzat!

Frank Keating

There is a view that village cricket is not what it was. Well, all down the centuries it never has been, has it? Such is the innate and timeless goodness of cricket's appeal that it has hung on for more than 300 years and over these years has always reflected the social background against which it is played.

A few summers ago – after revelling in the game, boy and man around England for upwards of 35 years – I was inclined to a jaundiced growl of middle-age when our team secretary stopped even telephoning of a Saturday morning if he was desperately looking for an old sweat to make up his numbers either that afternoon or on the morrow. See, I snorted, what did I tell you, they don't want us local stalwarts now, the game's been taken over by competitive outsiders and 'commuter-ringers' with their own buckskin pads and never-loaned choice of bats in the boot of their BMWs; men who set steely-eyed store by winning limited-over leagues and silver-plated knockout cups. No more the shared bat or box from the grotty bag on the floor of the pav, or clobber swapped by batsmen as they pass on their exits and entrances.

But this, of course, was just a passing generational thing. Moody male menopause and an ageing grouch sponsored by that storyline in *The Archers* a couple of summers ago had the late Mark Hebden and earnest Sid Perks conspiring to keep Eddie Grundy out of the Ambridge team. The earnest pair ruled that only those who turned up for net practice twice a week would get a weekend game, and that they were happy to field flashy outsiders (names unknown to scorer Marjorie Antrobus) if they could conjure up victory against Penny-hassott. Not to mention those two wets, Dr Richard and Nigel P, trying to rig a match.

Then, just like that, you come to terms with age and pride, and heartaches and arthritic limbs. And you stop yearning to be back in the joyous athletic springtime of your youth. Now on blue-bright, butterfly-bobbing days of summer, with a sweet susurrus tinkling through the trees against the lazy 'pock-pock' of bat on ball, I take my son to play on our village field up the lane from the pub. There, with pint in hand, the club's newest vice-president sits proudly, and with utter contentment, in his deckchair, pulls his Panama down against the glinting blaze of the sun, and stays to watch the very unities and verities of life itself being enacted out there on the soft green turf of England, just as Edmund Blunden wrote in 'Forefathers' 73 years ago:

'On the green they watched their sons
Playing till too dark to see,

As their fathers watched them once,
As my father watched me . . .'

The Little Chart cricket ground near Ashford in Kent illustrates the point. For it was on the serene, rolling downlands of Kent, and its neighbouring Sussex and Hampshire, that England's pastime of complex ethos and sweet simplicity first evolved and grew. Cricket's inheritance was handed down with relish by shepherds, cowmen and carters, farriers and foresters, who 'invented' their game on these sheep-cropped, short-grassed commons and pastures. During their 'lunch break' they would have played at defending their 'wicket' (the shepherd's three-pronged portable 'gate' that each one carried for use in pens or hedge-holes); or 'stumps', because the bowler's target might just as easily have been the base of a chopped-down tree in a wooded clearing.

Then the villages and towns marked out their white creases on the green, and the butchers, cobblers and tinkers became the countrymen's companions at the great game. The gentry, quite unabashed, took it up: noblemen, yeomen, and the clergy. And soon enough, down the centuries, first the British Empire and the Commonwealth was entranced by cricket. It still is.

The role of cricket is even remarked on by Professor G M Trevelyan in his timeless classic, *Social History of England*: 'Village cricket spread fast through the land. Squire, farmer, blacksmith, and labourer, with their women and children come to see the fun, were at ease together and happy all summer afternoon. If the French *noblesse* had been capable of playing cricket with their peasants, their châteaux would never have been burnt.'

And so – summer to summer, Saturday to Sunday, from over to over – the game goes on . . . Red-smudged bats, bright-striped blazers (and deckchairs), old codgers and callow schoolboy-fresh boys, chewing grass-stems and sprawling in front of the scoreboard . . . Sandwiches for tea, and the sun setting, golden-red, behind church spire or hayrick, pub or oasthouse.

Sir James Barrie wrote (and so he could have this century, last century, or next): 'A rural cricket match at buttercup time, seen and heard through the trees, is surely the loveliest scene in

England . . . for all Englishmen fall out for a moment to look over the gate of the cricket field and smile.' A wide, contented, and serene smile of timeless good days under the suns of summer. And civilisation.

Country Living, June 1995

Beaten 'Bury hold their heads high

Andrew French

The dream trip to Lord's did not have the fairytale ending – but Langleybury did not seem too disappointed.

There were tears from the Langleybury balcony at the end of an unforgettable day, which saw Caldy triumph by just six runs in the last over.

Yet the tears really did turn to cheers. Langleybury had experienced a weekend few others in Hertfordshire will ever enjoy and, although the result was not what they would have liked, they lapped up the atmosphere and will doubtless want seconds in years to come.

Memories came in bundles. Walking out from the England dressing room, watched by several hundred of their supporters. Sean Palmer rolling back the years with a classic spell of bowling. Paul Reynolds' magnificent display with the bat. Simon Palmer hitting the biggest six of the day. Jawid Khan milking the applause after an outstanding all-round performance.

There were many more moments that will be put away in the memory banks of those who were there, to be called upon time and time again in the future.

Doubtless the players will add many others, including their pre-final banquet, the pavilion and dressing rooms, and the very personal effect of walking out on to that hallowed surface.

Then each of the supporters will have their own story, most of them involving the scenes at the end as the crowd gathered at the front of the pavilion to hail the two groups of players that had produced such a cricketing spectacle.

It is hard to imagine that those involved could have enjoyed the occasion much more even if Langleybury had won.

They gave it their best shot, going so close to winning a game that will be remembered not only by those who saw it but also by the record books. Caldy's total was the third highest of all-time in the final; Bury's reply the second best by a team chasing.

The tension was amazing: sweaty palms and churning stomachs were numerous. It was an incredible game of cricket, the standard of play and pattern of game fully deserving the grand stage on which it was played.

Langleybury did not end the day as champions, but as Matt Fry so fittingly put it: 'We were winners today, we just didn't bring the trophy back.'

There will be plenty more chances to go back and ice the cake, but thankfully all those who have been so close over the years, the people who have guided Langleybury to their lofty position of today, were able to taste a slice on Sunday.

The day was blessed with sunshine and the Langleybury players were the first on to the field, having lost the toss.

Tim Beesley had the honour of the first ball of the day from the Pavilion End while club chairman Sean Palmer opened from the Nursery End and had loud lbw appeals to Caldy opener Phil Eymond turned down in his first over.

Eymond settled quickly and struck the day's first four in the third over and repeated the feat in the eighth.

Ian Rice took over at the Pavilion End in the 13th over but it was unlucky for him as Eymond took him for four second ball before effortlessly launching his fifth delivery for six over mid-wicket.

Matt Dunstone suffered a similar fate when he joined the attack at the Nursery End in the 20th over, Saunders clipping him for the four as the Caldy openers began to push the score along.

The only glimmer of a chance came in the 24th over as Beesley made good ground when Eymond hit Dunstone down the ground, but could not hold on to the ball.

Saunders began to dominate their partnership and Rice was again on the receiving end of another six over mid-wicket.

Eymond was the first to 50 though, benefiting from some good fortune as Asad Khan could not reach the ball as it came off the edge, allowing the Caldy man to run the two he needed. The cheers had barely died down when the next ball disappeared for six.

Langleybury badly needed a wicket and it finally arrived in the 29th over, Simon Baldwin having Eymond caught by Matt Fry on the mid-wicket boundary with only his second ball of the day.

However, Eymond and Saunders had a priceless 124 for the first wicket, allowing those who followed to enjoy slightly less pressure.

Saunders reached 50 in the next over and celebrated with a couple of fours before they added 20 off the next six deliveries from Baldwin, including a couple of sixes.

However, Baldwin fought back and had Saunders caught by Reid in the 33rd over, the opener having made a fine 76.

Asad almost ran out Craig Findlay after a fine full-length stop but then Jawid Khan picked up the first of his three wickets to send him back to the pavilion.

Caldy skipper Chris Ruddock hoisted Baldwin for another six at the end of the 35th over and he had just edged another four when Jawid had him caught by Beesley, leaving Caldy 184 for four in the 36th.

They reached 200 in the 38th over before Jawid had Keith Findlay caught behind in the last over, Caldy closing on 222 for five, five short of the second highest Final score in history.

Graham Reid and skipper Paul Reynolds began confidently and Reynolds found the boundary in the third over but the next, from Peter Urwin, was a maiden, as was the seventh from Keith Findlay.

Langleybury's patience was edging towards a run drought, and when Reynolds took a single in the 11th over, it was his first run for 22 balls.

So, when Reid was stumped the score was only 32 in the 13th over.

Yet Fry came in and showed his intentions with a four from his first ball faced.

Reynolds followed up with a pair of fours at the start of the 16th to bring up the 50 and Langleybury were 57 for one after 16 overs, compared with Caldy's 47 without loss at the same stage.

From then, Langleybury enjoyed a long spell when they were ahead of Caldy's score.

Reynolds began to open up, blasting a six over mid-wicket as the pace increased considerably, the skipper hitting 34 off 17 deliveries in a free-scoring period.

His 50 arrived with a single at the start of the 20th over and he picked up four more with the help of some poor fielding at long-on.

The 'Bury 100 arrived soon after but the pace had slowed slightly when Fry was out with the score on 113 in the 25th over.

Rice came in and hit a four just behind square before following up with a majestic drive through the covers for four more.

However, as he was threatening to do some damage he was caught by Keith Findlay off Urwin, bringing Asad to the crease.

His stay was almost very shortlived. He chanced a single first ball but almost collided with Reynolds as the pair crossed. Asad was forced to swerve and was glad to see the chance of a run-out go begging.

Going into the last 10 overs, 'Bury needed 81 with seven wickets left but they lost Reynolds next ball. He and Asad took a single on a misfield and the 'Bury keeper turned for a second. Amid all the noise, Reynolds did not hear his call, and when he did set off, that fraction of a second was fatal and he was run out.

However, his 73 was superb and a fitting tribute to his captaincy in the cup run.

The alarm bells were ringing next over as Asad made his way back to the pavilion and the run rate crept up to 9.25 with eight overs left and five wickets in hand.

Yet Jawid and Simon Palmer breathed new life into the reply, Palmer playing a four through square in the 34th over and Jawid beating the man at extra cover for another boundary.

Then Palmer unleashed the biggest six of the day, the ball just failing to clear the top tier of the stand next to the electronic scoreboard.

The Langleybury balcony sprang to life as the 35th over saw 14 runs added and there were signs that Lady Luck might be on 'Bury's side when first Jawid skied the ball but saw the chance dropped and then Palmer was given not out to some very animated appeals for caught behind.

The next over saw two turn into three as Keith Findlay's missed run-out attempt was then fumbled in the field and the Langleybury hoards were on their feet as Palmer found a gap at square-leg to add four more.

'Bury needed 32 off the last three with Jawid and Palmer in full flight, the latter taking four through point with the ball being palmed over the ropes by a fielder.

However, Palmer finally fell two balls later, holing out to Cooper at deep cover for a blistering 31.

Jawid was on the floor with cramp at the end of the 38th over as he and Baldwin chased 24 off 12 balls.

The pair ran a couple of twos but were called one short on the second occasion, and the next delivery saw them chance their arm too often as Baldwin was run out without facing.

However, Jawid and Matt Dunstone ran a couple more twos before Jawid stroked a magnificent four through mid-off to leave 'Bury needing 12 off the last over with three wickets standing.

Dunstone took a single first ball and Jawid added two more. Then his fine knock was over, stumped as he tried to make space for the big shot to the shorter boundary.

Beesley came in with nine needed off three balls. He ran two but was then bowled and the game was effectively lost.

Rather fittingly, Sean Palmer was to face the last ball. The best he could do was to tie the scores and he boldly went for the six but was caught at long on.

Like those of his teammates on the boundary, Palmer walked off with his head held high. Langleybury may have lost this war, but their battle to reach Lord's had been won.

It took then 20 years to travel the 18 miles to Lord's. They must be hopeful they will not need so long to cover the few yards they lost by in the final.

Watford Observer, 6 September 1996

Fields of dreams

John Major

If any cricket lover is in need of a spring tonic after the trials of the winter, Christopher Martin-Jenkins's *World Cricketers: A Biographical Dictionary* is surely it. The book is an astonishing feat of cricketing and social scholarship, containing a biographical and statistical record of every Test player since records began and numerous others besides. But what separates it from so many of its counterparts is that it is that most rare of beasts – a delightfully readable reference work.

I fell in love with cricket as a schoolboy, bewitched not just by the wonderful complexity and illogicality of the game, but by its romance. It seemed to me, above all other sports, to be essentially English in character, a game for heroes, with each match stamped by the personality and nature of the players and played and replayed again in the memory.

And it is this individuality that Martin-Jenkins captures so well, with charming insights into the players. Who can forget Alan Knott's devotion to fitness, yet how many of us knew that 'Prone to stiff muscles . . . off the field he was almost paranoically suspicious of breezes and draughts'? Mushtaq was fearless when facing 90mph short-pitched bowling, but was afraid of dogs, and Julius Caesar, who 'bore the burden of a great name, a nervous personality and a lack of inches', was a valued member of the Surrey side in the last century 'despite his own prevailing pessimism about his batting'.

As a youngster, I dreamt of playing for my country and would willingly have traded high office for just one appearance for England against Australia at the Oval. Many was the hour I would spend in my youth defending wickets drawn on a garage door or, alone, bowling at chalked wickets on a wall. Alas, my cricket did not profit from this commitment as much as Ray Lindwall's who in his youth, Martin-Jenkins recounts, 'bowled vigorously at paraffin tins in the street down which Bill O'Reilly made his way home, hoping to catch the great man's eye'. In the next life I shall bowl at paraffin tins and hope.

Even though my cricketing career did not take me on Lindwall's path to glory, my love for the game has never wavered, fostered by its never-ending ability to surprise and delight. And affection for the players he writes about shines out of Martin-Jenkins's sharp prose. Richard Hadlee would 'slice open the protective skin of an opening batsman like an expert surgeon'. Ouch. Curtly Ambrose is described as 'a country boy with a smile like a sliced melon', and Merv Hughes as having 'a canny brain lurking beneath the impression of brute force and ignorance'. And there was said to be only one greater appealer than the English wicketkeeper, George Duckworth, and that was Dr Barnado.

Perhaps what gives me most pleasure from this 800-page encyclopedia are the anecdotes and descriptions of players from the last century and the lesser-known Test cricketers. Walter Brearley, the fast bowler who played four Tests for England between 1905 and 1912, believed that no batsman could bat and dismissed them as 'probably a lot of ruddy teetotallers anyway'. Of Nobby Clark, who bowled for England in the 1930s, Martin-Jenkins writes, 'Should birds come flying overhead chirping merrily,' he 'would hurl oaths at them asking what they had to sing about'. Whether this was a tribute to the great Don, I don't know, but given what he did to English Test bowlers in the 1930s it certainly could have been.

This book is so well researched that the reader is almost tricked into believing that Martin-Jenkins has personally watched everyone he writes about. Take the Australian George Bonnor, who played for Australia in the late 19th century and was 6ft 6in, 16 stone and affectionately known as the Australian Hercules: 'Sporting a bushy beard, he was no mere slogger, but able to play quite an orthodox game at times, much to the disgust of some of his colleagues, who argued that his business was to hit hard and often.' During a Test at the Oval he is said to have hit the ball so high that the batsmen were on their third run before he was caught.

If this book toasts success, it is also rich in pathos. Dr Roy Park played once for Australia in 1921. He was bowled first ball and his wife is reputed to have bent down to pick up her knitting and missed her husband's entire Test career. Chris Cowdrey, the day before his one game as England captain at Headingley, was barred from the ground by an over-assiduous gateman who failed to recognise him. And Frederick, Prince of Wales, tragically died from an abcess caused by a blow from a cricket ball in the 18th century.

Martin-Jenkins also reveals how intertwined cricket has been with public life, perhaps, for some, an antidote to it. Sir Spencer Ponsonby Fane, Palmerston's private secretary and bearer of the Treaty of Paris to England after the Crimean war, had a reputation for running out himself and his partners when he played for Surrey. King George VI apparently performed a royal hat trick at Windsor when he bowled out Edward VII, the future George V and the future Edward VIII in consecutive balls. And the much-loved Alec Home was reprimanded on an MCC tour for the cardinal sin of cleaning his bat with a razor blade, which his captain apparently described as being 'as bad as pouring water into port'.

In short, this is a book to grace any cricket-lover's bookshelf and to brighten the dreariest day when rain stops play. Although it is crammed full of cricketing gods and their heroic deeds, pride of place should perhaps go to Sir Arthur Conan Doyle. To take only one first-class wicket, as he did, would be cause enough for untold celebration in my book, but to have bowled W. G. Grace . . . joy of joys. Was it sheer luck, my dear Holmes? Who can tell? But I can tell that this is a book worth reading. It is an invaluable addition to the glorious literature of the greatest game of all.

Sunday Times, 21 April 1996

Allure of the timeless Test

Nick Coleman

There is a small ellipse of rich green grass behind the Warner Stand at Lord's. It is about the size of a tennis court and is girdled by a low wall. A path bisects the lawn allowing foot-traffic to approach a tastefully appointed stand at which Pimm's is served by the jug. At 10.25am on a Test match Sunday the green is alive with activity.

Vigorously, yet decorously, members stake out their patch, unfolding, clipping, stacking, spreading, entrenching their picnic gear – their rugs, their hampers, their portable tables – until the green is a quilt of tiny fiefdoms, each one moated with nine inches of grass, rising at each centre to a mighty castellation of the latest in ice-box technology. Having established themselves, the members then go away and watch the cricket. By 11.02am the green is empty of people. Only the ice-boxes and hampers remain, monumental on their rugs. There is an atmosphere of sumptuous desolation. It is as if some boffin has invented a neutron bomb which, on detonation, vaporises MCC members yet leaves their picnic equipment standing.

The cricket on Sunday was not exciting. It was a day of drift and counter-drift, in which the initiative was offered but declined by both sides for fear of disturbing the nervous equilibrium established over a Test match and a half of fretful striving. The image that filled the mind was of two underweight sumo wrestlers lacking the strength to hump one another out of the ring, instead tacitly agreeing to mooch about in the middle and clash bellies for formality's sake. There were side-issues of course – Rahul Dravid's approaching century, for one, Alec Stewart's approaching superannuation, for another – but by and large torpor reigned. In the stands the usual things were going on: people lining up snacks for the first session, testing the rigidity of the seat-backs in front, settling under their hats.

Lord's is beautiful on days like these when the sun plays peekaboo from eleven until the close, dividing the ground into dissolving sections of light and shadow. It is possible on these days to stare without blinking for minutes at a time and see everything happening at once in synchronous fragments. I like to sit near the top of the roofless Edrich Stand, out of the breeze but high enough to include within a single field of vision the action in the middle and all the peripheral stuff, which is essential if you want to do Lord's properly. The peripheral stuff at Lord's is always central stuff. The tone, the order, the *meaning* of the place is governed by its architecture and the way it disposes of space, which is another way of saying that wherever you are at Lord's you get the feeling that you are being watched.

To the left of the Edrich the high modernist-colonial rigging of the new Mound Stand rises like sculpture above the boxes of the corporately sponsored. Ahead range the Members' Stand, the Pavilion, the press box, the Warner. To the right, you follow the declining curve of the Edrich's twin, the Compton, which rakes down to the four-square emulsioned Grandstand and its all-seeing eye, Father Time, who can, on good days, look benign.

It is a pie chart, Lord's; a diagram of a vision of society expressing not a single indivisible whole but a construction of discreet but interlocking parts, each of which stands as an essential constituent in the self-regard of the others. Some parts you are entitled to enter, others not. At all times you're aware of your place, and of being patronised. Lord's is Victorian democracy realised in bricks, mortar and the abstract principle of enclosure.

I have a feeling I like the top tier of the Edrich Stand because it appears to be neutral in this respect. It is featureless. It has no emblematic status. Underneath, on the lower tier, is the place for getting pissed and shouting. Above and to the left, separated by an eight-foot void and a couple of sets of railing, are the enclosures of those privileged by money, who get drunk and chit-chat. Opposite, across the grass, up the slope, behind a picket fence in the lap of their giant red pavilion, sit the men in orange and yellow ties, the proprietors. They seem to be miles away in several senses, immobilised certainly by distance, possibly by fatigue, disappointment and pink gin. They were all fighter pilots and submarine commanders once. And when they do move, they walk slowly around their cloisters in twos and threes under panama hats looking pained, their eyes travelling ahead reluctantly, freighted with dread.

'Accountable,' gloomed one, without looking at his partner as they passed slowly through the Mound Stand ambulatory, mid-morning. 'Someone must be *accountable* . . .' His partner made a dark sound in his throat but did not reply.

So I like it up there on the Edrich top tier because in my mind it sets me above snobbery (which is, let's face it, in itself an act of snobbery by internal memo rather than by exhibition). Here, you can participate without actually participating. You can watch dads and their sons doing their stuff.

For instance: a middle-class son is restrained by his father from leaping up in the middle of an over to visit the gents. 'You know why, don't you?' dad says reprovingly. He is kitted out in the warm-weather togs favoured by middle-aged Englishmen in the pomp of fatherhood: big khaki shorts, socks, sandals, pink polo shirt, a sucked-looking floppy cricket hat – baby clothes in all but size and context. His son wears a baseball cap and a frown. 'Yeah. Sorry.'

In the row behind, another tussle. The voices are public school, one ex, one current; one past its youth, the other full of it.

'So . . .' It is the younger voice, filling a pause that has endured since the last pass of the vacuum flask. 'So, what were your moments of personal cricketing glory?'

There is a good 10 seconds of silence during which it is impossible not to think of an empty bucket plummeting down the shaft of a deep, dry well.

'Oh, I don't know, really,' replies Older Voice, evasively.

'There must have been some?'

'Well . . .' Older Voice sighs. 'Well, I did most of my cricketing for my house at school. Didn't play very often. Hardly at all in fact. I don't think I was a key member of the team.'

'But you must have had a moment of glory. A brilliant catch? A big six? You know . . . a *run out*?'

'I didn't have any glory at all, I suppose.' He sighs again. 'Didn't get picked very often. Never seemed to score more than about 20. Don't know why, really . . .'

'Oh.'

There is another pause. Alan Mullally pitches short and the ball balloons off Dravid's head. There is a gentle expulsion of air from the nostrils of Older Voice.

'Um . . . and you? *Your* moments of cricketing glory?'

'Well, I haven't scored a century yet . . .'

A West Indian gent, carrying his MCC's steward's moss green jacket and a bag, settles himself in the seat in front. It is 12.30; half an hour to lunch. He unpacks a huge baguette and begins to work his way through it as Peter Martin chunters in from the Nursery End to Srinath. The steward's ears go up and down as he chews. The Lancashire swing bowler's knees pump as he runs, and as he lengthens his stride before delivery, the steward's ears and the bowler's knees for a moment become synchronised in motion. Then the ball is released, the mouthful swallowed and the overspill of wobbling flesh at the steward's neck retreats back within the rim of his collar. The ball beats the bat. 'He's bowlin' well, that boy,' says the steward, rotating his head benevolently to address his nearest neighbour, which is me. 'Y'know, I like the look of that boy. D'you mind if I smoke?'

He is a charming man. He works the lift to the private boxes in the Mound Stand. This year he has had Mick Jagger and J Paul Getty in. He drinks from two bottles, one containing colourless fluid, the other something pink as geraniums. He tells me an innocuous anecdote about one of his regular customers in the lift, which I would like to recount but dare not for fear that Lord's would visit itself terribly upon its steward. Lord's is a genteel place but one fairly seething with oedipal rage.

It is one o'clock. The players troop off and spectators swarm down staircases, over concourses, into action. In the Compton Bar a weary man pours UHT milk into the black plastic dustbin provided and drops the empty plastic UHT container into his cup of coffee. He curses mildly, shakes his head and walks back out into the sunlight.

Meanwhile, behind the Warner Stand the grassy picnic area is alive again. It is taking on the look of a garden party. Glasses chink and people hitch their legs up underneath their bodies to ride sidesaddle into lunch. And all the ice-boxes are exactly where their owners left them, because at Lord's they are safe. Safer here by far than in their own homes.

Independent, 26 June 1996

Commentary cues

Richie Benaud

One of the problems which was around when I still played cricket was the matter of common ground between media and players on the question of how much each knows about the other's job. The media know that some players flounder when asked questions; they know that some players, even captains, can be like time bombs if you allow enough silence after an answer. The media is also well aware that, given the task of writing an account of a day's play, a player might hardly be able to put thirty words together for the intro and, if he did, it would take him an hour and the edition would be gone. Some players, astonishingly, are too lazy even to write their own copy, but they are certainly agile enough to pick up the cheque.

Alongside that is the question of what cricket the media man has played, if he has played any at all, if he just likes the game and has always had an ambition to write about it, or if his father owns the newspaper. If a newspaperman, or a television commentator, is writing or talking about the game at Test level, and he has never risen above a village or an outback match, then a player might have some difficulty with the reports about his perceived lack of technique in a Test match against the ball which swings out and then cuts back between bat and pad before taking the leg bail. This is the most contentious cricket media question, without answer, that I have found over the past forty years.

These days millions of viewers of the TV screen have a first-hand sighting of what goes on, and consider they have every right to be experts on all aspects of cricket and to offer their opinions – and do so. They all have good memories for everything that happens on the field, though that has been a trait of cricket followers the world over in the past fifty years. Some cricket spectators in fact have *very* long memories. A few are brilliant with their repartee, and when they marry that with their memory, the effect can be devastating.

Forty years ago, I toured the West Indies and played in all five Tests. Led by Ian Johnson, Australia won the First Test by nine wickets, drew the Second and won the Third in Georgetown by eight wickets in only four days. When we played the Fourth, in Barbados, we made 668 and had them in all kinds of trouble at 147/6 on the third evening. The next day, the overnight not-out batsmen, Denis Atkinson and Clairmonte Depeiza, batted throughout the five hours' play. The following morning, I bowled Depeiza straight away with one that ran along the ground.

In 1991, I was in Barbados and just about to host the Channel Nine 'intro' to the one-day game eventually won by the Australians. The crowd was in high good humour at Kensington Oval and some, pre-match, were even celebrating their anticipated victory. Loudly! In my earpiece the voice of director Geoff Morris said, 'Fifteen seconds to on-air' and, at the same time, the ground went quiet.

Then, 'Hey, Sir Richard Benaud. You the son of that guy who couldn't get out Atkinson and Depeiza all the fourth day in 1955?'

Right match, wrong family connection.

'If you couldn't bowl them out, you do right to take up television, man,' he continued, just as I began my intro.

'Good morning and welcome to this delightful island of the Caribbean.' I said it through my own laughter and that of hundreds of spectators in the Kensington Stand right behind me.

You need to keep your sense of humour on television and to bear in mind a few little things to help you through commentaries. I'm often asked for advice on how to commentate, but simply copying someone else never works. You must be an individual and there are a few little notes I keep which are of some benefit in my own commentaries and general organisation. They would not suit other commentators but might or might not be of some assistance, in a general sense, to any younger people who are thinking of moving into the commentary position. In my general organisation, working in the office and in business, the approach to a day, a week and a year of work, I try to bear in mind:

Do your best, never give up.
Golf course behaviour mirrors business behaviour.
The same error twice is only one mistake, but a very big one.
Make your own luck, keep two overs ahead of the play.
Mediocrity is contagious.
Silence can be your greatest weapon.

Then, in the television commentary box, there are many aspects of discipline to be observed; it is necessary to be organised, particularly if you also have other media work to do, as happens with me. My freelance work includes television commentaries, writing for newspapers, working for radio, writing feature and special articles and doing interviews.

There are literally hundreds of things which might be said by a commentator which should not be said. Some of them find their way into journals like *Private Eye* with 'Colemanballs', some have been spotted more recently in Desmond Lynam's excellent book, and some are imprinted on the minds of those who have heard and now cherish them. Some will never be forgotten by the commentator who uttered them. They are inscribed on his or her mind for ever.

These are the ones I try to avoid. Even so they will slip through occasionally although it is a matter of lack of concentration if they do. It doesn't make me feel any better when it happens and it's then a matter of concentrating harder and trying to make certain it doesn't occur again:

Put your brain into gear before opening your mouth. Try not to allow past your lips:

He is a doyen, a guru or an icon . . .
He gives 120 per cent, or 150 per cent, or even 200 per cent . . .
At this point in time . . .
Of course . . .
You know . . .
Well, yes, you know, I mean . . .
To be perfectly honest . . .
Really and truly . . .
I really must say . . .
I must ask you . . .
As you can see on the screen . . .
Have a look at *this* . . .
The corridor of uncertainty . . .
That's a tragedy . . . or a disaster . . . (The *Titanic* was a tragedy, the Ethiopian drought a disaster, but not the fall of a wicket or a dropped catch.)

Don't take yourself too seriously!

This very short list needs to be read in conjunction with the amount of concentration needed to be a commentator: it is fierce, the same as applies to successful players and captains. One or two people I know say working on television is a 'doddle'. Not for me it isn't. If you're not prepared to concentrate and to work as hard as is required, then you are better off in another job.

But, above all, remember a job as a cricketer or a TV commentator might need fierce concentration but, just as important, you also must have a bit of fun, otherwise it just turns into an ulcer-making dirge!

One thing of which you can be certain about television commentary is the advice noted earlier, that silence is your greatest weapon. Timing is another. It is no use talking about something, making comment on a happening if there is nothing to do with that on the screen.

We were covering a Test match at Lord's five or six years ago when there was a commotion of sorts on top of a building on the eastern side of the ground. There was a small group of people having a barbecue on top of one of the rooftops and along just a little further was a lady who, even without the benefit of binoculars, I could see was dressed in slightly eccentric fashion. What there was of her garb seemed to be black. Closer examination showed it to be filmy black, possibly lace. She was standing in front of some lettering but I didn't have time to pay attention to that because the bowler was coming in at the Nursery end.

In between balls there were murmurs from the crowd who by now were paying as much attention to the lady on the roof as they were to the game. Keith Mackenzie, our producer/director, said into my earpiece, 'I'm going to have to show what's happening if nothing comes from the next ball.' I said, 'Okay' and then made a comment about the quick single that had been taken. Keith cut to the roof across the road and there she was, looking different now she was much closer on the screen from the way she did to the very naked eye. The lady, clad in black fishnet stockings and with a thick piece of string across her frontage, was draped over a well-lettered, well-planned and painted sign advertising vodka. It proclaimed, 'Fiona Vladivar loves Richie Benaud.' I said, 'And just think, that's only her mother.'

The Appeal of Cricket, Richie Benaud
(Hodder & Stoughton, 1996)

Age of despair

Marcus Berkmann

Age, they say, is in the mind, but for the Captain Scott Invitation XI this season it has also proved to be in the knees, the eyes, the ankles, the shoulders and the heart. Last year, when we were just thirtysomething, we creaked and groaned in the field and moved more slowly than ever before. This year we are thirtysomething plus one, and we are barely capable of any movement at all. A couple of weeks ago I watched Charlie Dinnerparty, who is famed for leaving matches early because he has to go to a dinner party (having arrived late after a lunch party), running for a ball through what appeared at first glance to be treacle, but may just have been a heavy crude-oil spill. You know those dreams in which you are running as fast as possible but can't move an inch? That was Charlie as he valiantly tried to catch up with the speeding ball. His limbs were whirling with effort, his teeth were clenched, his despairing grunts could be heard half a mile away – but the actual distance he covered was negligible 'Too many dinner parties,' we all crowed. He's only 33.

Not that the rest of us were much better. During the same game I finally gave up trying to hide certain people in the field, because there's nowhere you can hide all nine fielders. Arvind, the lubricious solicitor from Delhi, has long been a prime candidate for outfield concealment, for although he fields like a terrier to his own bowling, he fields like a fat, asthmatic terrier which has had all its legs amputated to everyone else's. But even Arvind didn't look that bad in this game. We were all in a terrible state. Harry: dodgy knee (can't bend over). Ian: throwing arm gone.

Francis: never had one in the first place. Terence: blind as a bat. Neal: fat. Martin: fatter. Bill: fattest. As we approach our cricketing dotage, we are each acquiring our own specific frailties. As captain I try to be sensitive, but sometimes it's a struggle. According to one player, the worst thing now is to be asked to save the single. The batsman hits the ball straight at you, you pick it up, throw it in, but he's taken the single anyway. So you come in a few yards. He does the same thing. You come in further. Sooner or later, feeling humiliated, you try to buzz in a ball at full speed, but you throw it so high and wide that no one can cut off the four overthrows. A quick single has thus become a throat-slashing five. The player suggested we stopped trying to save the single and just concentrated on keeping it down to four.

I'm sure we never expected it to happen this way. We knew that cricketers in their thirties tend to pick up more and more injuries, so we probably thought that we would spend vast amounts of time on the treatment table, tending pulled ligaments, groin strains and the like. Not that any of us has a treatment table as such, but you know what I mean. What we didn't realise is that it's usually fit people who suffer injuries. As John Emburey has wisely observed, if you're going to pull muscles, you need to have them in the first place. Tim, the perennially angry fast bowler, is consistently exercising and keeping fit, and so crocks himself on an almost weekly basis. Arvind's idea of exercise is to saunter down a flight of stairs on his way to another enormous lunch, and he never misses a game.

For most of us the manifestations of middle age are altogether more humiliating. Harry turned up last week with a huge comedy bandage on his toe, having endured his second ingrowing toenail operation in a fortnight. At least one player on the team has gout. And not long ago we had a wicketkeeper who had a severe case of the Viv Richards. Once he was in such discomfort that he was forced to insert one of his wife's Always Ultras in his jockstrap to stem the dismal flow. Unfortunately, while he was batting, this now sodden item somehow came loose and fell down his trousers on to the pitch, slightly short of a good length. Soon afterward he gave up cricket forever, expressing the vague but no doubt heartfelt intention to become a Buddhist monk. Such are the cruel effects of age. The rest of us await our own ends with no little trepidation.

Wisden Cricket Monthly, August 1996

Honourable draw an important part of civilised sport

Tim Rice

The Test match just gone was a confusing one, full of contradictions, graced by the presence of Keith Miller and saddened by the announcement of the death of Ray Lindwall.

The sensational revival of New England that had been on display at Edgbaston seemed to have disappeared somewhere on the M40; the two Indian batsmen who took the game beyond England's reach were not the two who should have done; the English batsman only brought in at the last minute because of injury to another gave the selectors a headache by top-scoring in the second innings.

The crowd's two most lively moments over the entire five days were: (a) before a ball had been bowled, paying tribute to an umpire, and (b) while balls were not being bowled but being fired (or not) into a net 10 miles away. Was the football crowd similarly tuned into events elsewhere? Did wild cheers reverberate around Wembley with the news that Mullally had bowled a maiden?

And in the end, after five days of honest endeavour, it was only a draw. Only a draw – not a phrase that the wise spectator would use. The *cognoscenti* love draws, even ones doomed to be so long before the final hour. They regularly mirror life with far more accuracy than thumping great wins or depressing defeats.

Most of our three score years and 10 are dedicated to getting away with a draw and as the Dickie Bird of destiny removes the bails for the last time, most of us would happily settle for a split decision.

No other sport accepts draws with such readiness, with the possible exception of another primarily intellectual occupation, chess. Football is doing all it can to disabuse its followers of the notion that two teams could be equal by making the mathematical sharing of points impossible and by allowing many of its most important fixtures that inconveniently end all-square to be decided by another sport altogether. Why not synchronised swimming instead of a penalty shoot-out? Virtually as relevant to all that has gone before.

Tennis lost much of its appeal for me when officials anxious to get back to the hospitality tent brought in the tie-break. The most entertaining Grand National of all time was the year it was declared null and void. Strange that in a politically correct egalitarian age so many sports are more determined than ever to show that winning is more important than taking part.

In 1953, England drew with Australia four times before their famous win at the Oval that brought the Ashes home for the first time since the end of the Second World War. Two of the draws, at Nottingham and Old Trafford, were brought about by bad weather, but the other two were by far the most entertaining games of the series. At both Lord's and Leeds that year, England were going down with all hands until the very last moments. Had either match been a timeless Test, both would have been long forgotten.

At Lord's, Willie Watson and Trevor Bailey dug in with flawless resolution for nearly an entire day to turn the boring formality of Australian triumph into riveting inconclusiveness. At Leeds, Bailey was in the thick of it again, this time as a bowler, in halting Australia's last-afternoon gallop across the finishing line. To the disinterested observer, these draws were vastly superior to England's comfortable win when Surrey's immortal Laker and Lock found their home pitch not untailored to their needs.

Who can forget Lord's 1963 or Johannesburg 1996? Name me a boring tied match. No result is often the best result but, sad to say, this is a view held with less and less enthusiasm lower down the ladder, with too many games being limited-overs fixtures, ground out for league points.

We at Heartaches CC, however, are doing our best to keep the flag of inconclusion flying. We spurn limited-overs contests. We began 1996 with four straight draws and all four went to the wire.

Few innings have given me the satisfaction that I derived from my sterling nought not out from the No 11 berth that made it honours even against Harold Pinter's bruisers.

The mark of a civilised sport is one in which a game can be completed with no side victorious. Long live the draw.

Daily Telegraph, 26 June 1996

School's out as developers take control

Mark Nicholas

By chance I was in Wandsworth in south-west London on Saturday afternoon. It would be nice to say I was betwixt a morning's cricket at Lord's and an afternoon's tennis at Wimbledon. But alas, no, I was making for Sainsbury's Homebase, which is just off the Wandsworth Bridge roundabout, next to B&Q and the drive-in McDonald's.

Up on the busy East Hill beyond these monuments to modern retailing is the Surrey Cricket Centre, formerly the Alf Gover Cricket School.

I parked at the front of the dilapidated buildings and edged nervously around the corner to the little side entrance. I say nervously because I went to Gover's as a boy and was concerned that an old friend may have withered. It had indeed withered, though worse was to come with the news that this week an extraordinary, if small, piece of English cricket will die.

As from Friday there will be no more nets or coaching, as from a week or two there will not even be a shop. The redevelopers are to rebuild.

The school opened in 1928 under the beady eyes of Herbert Strudwick and Andy Sandham and though it was closed down and used for storage during the Second World War it was opened again soon after by the now legendary Surrey and England fast bowler Alf Gover.

Alf *was* the place really, wheeling away, over after over in England sweater after England sweater and telling you yarn after yarn until in 1989 and at a remarkably sharp-looking 81 years of age, he could wheel no more. They all came to see Alf, lords and knights, prime ministers and princes of the game: Lord Rix, Sir Garfield Sobers, John Major, Vivian Richards and many, many more.

I found the side entrance and climbed the steep stairs before tiptoeing alongside the shop and turning right into the rows of ancient wooden lockers, painted cream, of course, the colour of Alf's turned up flannels and the colour too of his trademark cravat, and made my way into the tired-looking nets.

Not a thing had changed. The ancient dark room had kept its character. It smelt of cricket.

For a time the school was lit by gaslight and Alf justified this saving by saying that it made the ball swing. Alf Gover could make a ball believe anything.

After he retired and sold it on, it was leased from developers by John Fordham, who got it up and running after months of rotting and whose sports shop will suffer imminently. Fordham has done a remarkable job to keep the tradition alive when one considers the competition from the Lord's Indoor School and from the Ken Barrington Centre at the Oval. If anyone is looking for cricket gear they should go and shop with him; the sale is on and the history, and the smell, make the visit worthwhile.

Daily Telegraph, 1 July 1996

The cricketing cliff-hanger of St Helena

Fraser Simm

The heady mixture of a long-cherished sport and the unusual byways of historical research may be something that would thrill many who follow the game of cricket. It was my opportunity to indulge in these when I took up a four-year posting on the island of St Helena. Although small and insignificant in terms of modern history, the colony still retains a special place in the annals of romantic history as the last refuge of Napoleon. His sudden appearance on this remote rocky outcrop gave it the instant glare of world renown; and after his passing its name has kept hold of a certain mysterious lustre.

It may be held to be entirely in keeping that St Helena also holds a place in the annals of cricket history; not a major part on the stage of international cricket but its own footnote amongst the anecdotes of unusual events in the game's lineage.

I cannot recall when I first heard of the entry titled 'Death of a fielder from falling over a cliff', but it was certainly before I set foot on the island. It featured in all the history books of the colony, and three years ago, there was a reference to it in the pages of *Wisden Cricket Monthly*. Although I was familiar with the tale, this made me curious. On the island, the incident of the cricketer who fell to his death while playing on Francis Plain is recounted by word and in a 1980 history, there is a photograph of two cricketers on Francis Plain and a caption which tells that a player once was killed falling over a cliff on the island. A later book added pictures depicting the incident from the *Graphic* newspaper. But when the incident is mentioned on the island the details seem uncertain: questions such as What happened? And When did it happen? remain unanswered as the accident recedes back into history.

The *Wisden* article lead me to a rare book, published in 1897, called *Curiosities of Cricket*, which listed unusual incidents in the game's past. I obtained a copy of the book which listed matches such as 'Heavy with Sin v Light with Honesty', 'Man and dog v. one-armed man and son' and events such as 'Paralysis of batsman from collision with bowler' and 'Death of fielder from falling over a cliff when following ball'.

The last incident is described as having happened at Salisbury Plain, St Helena in 1886 and the source was the *Graphic*, 20th February 1886. Here we have some hard facts, but the reference to Salisbury Plain raises a question at once. There is no such place on St Helena as Salisbury Plain! All recent cricket matches are played on the only area of ground on the island flat enough for this activity, which is at Francis Plain. Francis Plain does lie at the top of a high cliff, although nowadays, the nearest cliff is well beyond any possible outfield. A quick perusal of the records in the Archives showed that in the 1880s many cricket matches were played at Francis Plain, so why Salisbury Plain?

The next step in the trail had to be the *Graphic* newspaper itself. Although the newspaper no longer exists, with the help of my sister, who is a librarian, and a local enthusiast, Trevor Hearl, the narrative of the visit plus a page of the engravings were uncovered. Both are dated 20th February 1886. The narrative tells of 'a visit being made in July' and 'The cricket-ground called Salisbury Plain is very dangerous for out-fielding, and the pitch is very bumpy. One poor Jack Tar lost his life while playing. He got up too much steam in running after a ball to long-leg, could not stop, and went over a precipice, a sheer drop of sixty feet.' The reference to July would presuppose that this took place in July 1885.

Turning to the nine engravings by Captain E. A. Smith, it is clear that he had a detailed knowledge of St Helena. The first depicts a boat heading for the steps with the caption 'We go ashore'. The zig-zag road that is 'Side Path' is clearly visible (this is the main road out of Jamestown into the hinterland of the island). An accurate picture of Napoleon's tomb follows and engraving No 7 is of a cricket match, captioned 'We play Cricket on Salisbury Plain'. In the background is a fort overlooking the Plain – this can be easily identified as High Knoll Fort – and the players can be seen playing on a dark strip which may be a matting wicket. Despite the caption, the view would appear to be of Francis Plain. That would seem to solve part of the mystery – the venue of the match was indeed Francis Plain but, in a slip of memory, the author inserted that most famed of Plains – Salisbury!

The last two engravings show a sailor 'Jack' in uniform falling over a cliff, and four sailors carrying a stretcher with a body on it down a path – which resembles a rocky road leading from Francis Plain, now known as the Barnes Road. The caption is 'And our festivity comes to an end'. The interesting word here is 'our', just as 'We' is used in 'We play Cricket on Salisbury Plain'. The subjective references suggest that the incidents took place at the same time as the visit – and were not hearsay. The visit in July and the action in the engravings are linked.

The only difficulty with this is that there is no mention at all of the tragic accident in the weekly *St Helena Guardian*. The paper is a good source of comment and news and regularly gave scores and details of cricket matches, but looking through every edition from 1868 to 1886, I found no reference to the unique and sad incident of the death of a fielder. This is a strange omission. Neither is there a reference to it in the death records in the archives nor in Jackson's *History of St Helena* published in 1903 – although a major rockfall of 1890 when nine were killed is mentioned.

One cricket match in July 1885 features in the *Guardian*: Royal Artillery v United XI on 9th July at Francis Plain. The scores were 29 & 29 against 36 & 24/4, the United XI winning. On 15th August 1885, HMS Rapid & Forward played the United Island. In a full report of the game there is no mention of the incident.

At the last moment, the trail has gone cold. The strength of local hearsay plus the strong secondary evidence from the *Graphic* support the view that the fielder did actually fall to his death, and that it probably happened in July 1885. But after two years of digging, the exact details are still hidden and must still await discovery.

Cricket Lore, Vol 2, Issue 8, 1996

Stumped and bowled in Tipperary

Terence Prittie

Terence Prittie is the son of Lord Dunalley of Kilboy, Co Tipperary. Returning from a prisoner-of-war camp in Germany, he became sports journalist with the Manchester Guardian *in 1946. He wrote several books on cricket, for example* Lancashire Hotpot, A History of Middlesex Cricket Club, *and an autobiography,* Through Irish Eyes. *In this piece of writing he describes a game in Tipperary.*

The quality of the Nenagh side had improved beyond measure, and old Paddy Flannery had been forced to retire for the second time, but travelled with the team to watch them play and to chuckle and chirp like a grasshopper from the tall grasses beyond the outfield. A formidable batsman had been enlisted in the shape of Dr Tony Courtney, a legendary figure in the neighbourhood. A mountain of a man, he had been capped for Ireland several times at rugger and there were many tales of his feats on the field of battle, usually concerned with French or Welsh who were unwise enough to 'play dirty' with him and his friends. He had more than once driven over a 295-yard hole of the local golf course. Later in life he was to become a recruiting agent for the IRA, picking likely lads from a street corner which gave him a clear view of the doors of four public houses.

Dr Tony, on this occasion, was well-set when my father put himself on to bowl. Thirty years earlier he had bowled well for his regiment. Now, his arm was a trifle stiff, but he still had plenty of ideas. His first three balls were models of the defensive slow-medium off-break bowler's art, pitching just short of a length eighteen inches outside the off stump. Dr Tony watched them go by with an impassive face.

The fourth ball was a dream for the hitter off the front foot, a half-volley just clear of the off stump. Dr Tony's left leg went out, down came his bat like a flail, and there was the clean smack of the really full-blooded drive. Left to its own, it would have been a six, but it was hit with the flat trajectory of the perfect golf-drive, and rose slowly. Reaching my father in a split second, it must have been eight feet up.

For a man of nearly sixty, my father did well to pick out the line of the ball when off-balance. He leapt acrobatically and slightly to one side, and took the ball full on the palm of his left hand. It dropped like a cleanly-shot jack snipe, stone dead, at his feet. He stood, rubbing the injured hand, with a meditative but most unpleasant look in his eye. Dr Tony, with a solicitous look on his face – after all, my father was host, ground-owner, organiser, the lot – took several tentative steps down the wicket. He could have had no possible idea of going for a run. My own thought was that he was going to apologise.

Suddenly my father stooped, picked up the ball and threw it at him. I say 'at' without any doubt, for I could follow the line of the ball, and could see the look in my father's eye change to a glint of triumph as he saw that he had aimed straight and true. The ball hit Dr Tony above a flapping pad on the right knee-cap, the one with which he had been having trouble ever since a Welsh wing three-quarter had come half-way across the field to put his boot into it. He staggered, and fell. From his knee, the ball rolled slowly on towards the stumps, tapped on one like a tentative beggar at the door, and a bail dropped almost unwillingly to the ground.

We won the match by ten runs. The *Nenagh Guardian*, reverting to earlier, erratic habit, entered the incident into the score-sheet as 'Dr A Courtney, stumped *and* bowled by Lord Dunalley, 28'.

Terence Prittie, from *A Short History of Irish Cricket with Literary Connections*, Roy Clements (Dari Press, 1996)

Commies, Nazis . . . and cricketers

Miles Kington

From Lord Draynsham
Sir,
I have seen many tributes to my childhood friend, the late Jessica Mitford, but I have seen no mention of the one thing that struck immediately all who knew her at all well – her deep and passionate love of cricket. The one great sadness of her early life was that, however fertile her parents were, they had not produced enough children to form a whole cricket XI, so they often had to call upon servants and retainers from around the country estate to form a whole Redesdale XI.

This, of course, presented no difficulty to Jessica, who was tremendously egalitarian (before she became a Communist and therefore a bit more of a snob), and she had no objection to servants playing on the same side as aristocrats – indeed, as in the case of J M Barrie's *The Admirable Crichton*, she tended to think that servants made better cricket captains than her peers did.

Incidentally, she always used to accuse the English of hypocrisy over class, and when challenged to back it up she would say: 'Only the English would have no difficulty in using the same word to mean "absolutely equal" AND "innately superior".' When challenged to say what this word was, she would say 'The word "peer".' And she had a point, by Jove!

Yours etc

From Lady Draynsham

Sir,

What my husband set out to say in the above letter, and quite forgot to mention, was that Jessica's love of cricket may have been unwittingly responsible for the rise of Nazism. In the early 1930s, at those unforgettable country cricket weekends which Jessica used to organise, she used to encourage her sisters to bring friends along to help bolster the team. One weekend Unity brought along one of her dreary German political friends, a Herr Goebbels, who kept talking about what the Nazis were going to do when they were in power. 'Get the right uniform, the right songs, the right march and the right leader and nothing is impossible!' he would shout. Well, he was not much good at cricket as it turned out – he was always shouting at someone else to stop the ball – but he was fascinated by the role of the umpire, and especially by the gesture of giving a batsman out. 'Have you noticed,' he said to me, 'how wonderful it is when the fielders appeal, all raising their arms, and then the umpire slowly raises his aloft too to show solidarity?! I must remember this . . .'

Six months later Hitler was doing exactly the same. Need I say more? Every time I saw Herr Hitler on the newsreel doing the Nazi salute, I would rise to my feet and shout 'Out!', which caused some hilarity in our local cinema, I can tell you!

From Gennadi Ivanovich Orlov

Sir,

In all the tributes to the late Jessica Mitford, I have seen no mention of her abiding love of cricket and her long-standing ambition to reshape it along Marxist-Leninist lines. She used to come to Moscow to have long talks with Stalin about this, and he showed every sign of agreeing with her, though we know now that he secretly did not consider a reform of cricket to be a high priority. Her theory was that cricket should be egalitarian to the extent of all the fielders being equidistant from the pitch. Stalin would chuckle and say: 'Good idea, if they are all equally good and the batsmen always hit the ball the same distance!'

Many Communist sympathisers lost their faith when Stalin and Hitler signed the Nazi-Soviet pact, but Jessica never did. I happen to know that this was because she got a telegram from Stalin himself saying: 'DON'T THINK OF THE NAZI-SOVIET PACT AS A BETRAYAL – THINK OF IT AS A SPORTING DECLARATION! NOW LET US SEE WHAT HERR HITLER CAN DO ON A CRUMBLING WICKET IN THE FOURTH INNINGS!' This, to Jessica, excused everything.

Yours etc.

From the Rt Hon William Gentry
Sir,
I am surprised that none of the tributes to the late Jessica Mitford mentioned that cricket was the reason she moved to the USA. 'Oh, Willikins!' she would occasionally whimper to me down the phone, 'I know that the revolution will come one day, but I also know that it will sweep cricket away with it! What shall I do?'

'Go somewhere where they don't play cricket,' I would advise her, 'and forget all about it.'

And so she did, and went to California.

Yours etc.

Independent, 29 July 1996

Retired hurt

Simon Barnes

I failed to score 1,000 runs in May this year. In fact, the closest I have ever come was a shortfall of a mere 993. Ah!, but I batted like a god that year: Bacchus, perhaps. This year, I did not score a single run in

May, or June, or July, and the chances of scoring a run in August are diminishing fast.

There is a moment of truth that confronts all cricketers of similar merit. It occurs on the morning of the first match of the season, when you open your kit-bag for the first time since the previous September and are once again amazed at the failure of socks and flannels to clean themselves in the course of an endless winter.

Somewhere in my house lurks a kit-bag that has been unopened since the last match I played – in September 1994 – when we, the mighty Tewin Irregulars, played the Vatican XI, a side mainly comprising Roman Catholic priests and led by Barnaby Dowling, the Jardinesque incumbent of the parish of Ely. They beat us by a considerable distance, and my only useful contribution was a slash through the slips that came quite close to putting Father Barnaby's eye out.

Happy moment! But really, I have not lifted a bat in anger, nor bowled my wily non-turning offbreaks, nor yet my occasionally-actually-turning leg-break variation (off which I once had a member of the Barbados second XI stumped off his third ball for 12), for all but two seasons. Perhaps I must admit that I have Retired.

There is something terribly aging about the word. It is not that I can no longer run about, it is not that I am concerned that I can no longer bat and bowl with distinction, for you never miss what you never had. But the chances of playing again before the kit in my bag disintegrates look remote.

Why is this? Partly, because of the Great Tewin Diaspora. People move: we have former Irregulars in places like Uganda and the Forest of Dean. Also, at a certain age, the most unlikely people suffer from fits of ambition and want to work on Sundays. Others merely divorce: both members of our once fearsome opening attack fell victim to the younger woman and daren't play for the Irregulars again in case their wives turn up.

And so Friday nights and Saturday mornings brought in more and more of those terrible calls: hate to let you down, but I've got to go to the office/paint the lavatory/go and see the kids. The Saturday night ring-rounds became simple desperation: still only six players and down to the letter T in the phone book.

More and more people seem to realise that they have Retired. And perhaps I have as well. I feel a little old at this realisation. It is not that I have lost my taste for folly and danger; no one with two horses (let alone the two I've got) can say such a thing.

One loses many things: fitness, such ability as one had, time. But perhaps one loses the most important thing of all, the taste for being part of a gang of men. Oh, I have wonderful memories of many a team-mate, great and continuing affection for them all: Steady Eddy, Murray, Salty, the Fish, Edge, the Finches, Ruby, and on and on, vast legions of irregular Irregulars that stretch across the decade-long history of our fabled and glorious institution.

It is not the eye that goes, it is, as it were, the muscle of camaraderie. The pleasures of a sweaty embrace when you lunge for a catch and for once emerge triumphantly ball-full; the joys of massed, bibulous hilarity and din at the Plume of Feathers afterwards; and also what Albert Camus called 'the stupid desire to cry when we lost'. Do I no longer relish the lagery hug of consolation at the end of a long hot day of defeat? I grow old . . . I grow old . . . I shall wear the bottoms of my flannels rolled.

The Spectator, 24 August 1996